THE FORUM AND
THE TOWER

The Forum and the Tower

HOW SCHOLARS AND POLITICIANS HAVE IMAGINED THE WORLD, FROM PLATO TO ELEANOR ROOSEVELT

MARY ANN GLENDON

OXFORD
UNIVERSITY PRESS

OXFORD
UNIVERSITY PRESS

Oxford University Press, Inc., publishes works that further
Oxford University's objective of excellence
in research, scholarship, and education.

Oxford   New York
Auckland   Cape Town   Dar es Salaam   Hong Kong   Karachi
Kuala Lumpur   Madrid   Melbourne   Mexico City   Nairobi
New Delhi   Shanghai   Taipei   Toronto

With offices in
Argentina   Austria   Brazil   Chile   Czech Republic   France   Greece
Guatemala   Hungary   Italy   Japan   Poland   Portugal   Singapore
South Korea   Switzerland   Thailand   Turkey   Ukraine   Vietnam

Published by Oxford University Press, Inc.
198 Madison Avenue, New York, New York 10016

www.oup.com

Oxford is a registered trademark of Oxford University Press

Library of Congress Cataloging-in-Publication Data
Glendon, Mary Ann, 1938–
The forum and the tower : how scholars and politicians have imagined the world, from
Plato to Eleanor Roosevelt / Mary Ann Glendon.
p.   cm.
Includes bibliographical references and index.
ISBN-13: 978-0-19-978245-1 (hardcover)
ISBN-10: 0-19-978245-8
1. Political science—History. 2. Scholars—Political activity—History. 3. Learning and scholarship—
Political aspects—History. I. Title.
JA81.G56   2011
320.9—dc22   2011006021

3 5 7 9 8 6 4

Printed in the United States of America
on acid-free paper

FOR MARTHA AND DAVID MARTINI

CONTENTS

PREFACE

[T]here is a dispute among those who agree that the most choiceworthy life is that accompanied by virtue as to whether the political and active way of life is choiceworthy, or rather that which is divorced from all external things—that involving some sort of study, for example—which some assert is the only philosophic way of life. For it is evident that these two ways of life are the ones intentionally chosen by those human beings who are most ambitious with a view to virtue, both in former times and at the present; the two I mean are the political and the philosophic.

Aristotle, Politics *Book 7, Ch. 2*[1]

For as long as there have been governments and people to study them, statespersons and scholars have pondered the relative merits of life in the public forum and life in the ivory tower—the different skills required, the temperaments suited for one or the other way of life, and the relationship of the study of politics to its practice. As a law professor, I have known many gifted young men and women who went into politics, and many more who were drawn in that direction, but who turned away for fear of losing their moral compass, or their families, or both. I have also had many students who became academics, but kept searching for ways to "make a difference" in the world around them. It was primarily for my students—young men and women seeking to hold theory and practice together with integrity—that I initially assembled these accounts of how remarkable individuals in the past have struggled with choices similar to those we face today.

I believe, however, that these stories of success, failure, collaboration, conflict, and compromise—punctuated with moments of heroism—have much to say to all of us. For nearly everyone today engages in political activity, if only as an informed voter, and never before have so many men and women come to regard lifelong learning as essential to a full and happy existence.

Whatever one concludes about whether the pursuit of knowledge is more choiceworthy than politics for those who are capable of it, there is no doubt about one difference between the two ways of life. Scholars can debate endlessly about the wisdom, justice, advantages, and disadvantages of a course of action, but statespersons must make decisions and take responsibility for them. A modern day scholar-statesman, Henry Kissinger, once put it this way to a gathering of academics and public officials: "As a professor, I was responsible primarily for coming up with the best answer I could divine. As a policymaker, I was also responsible for the worst that could happen. As a professor, the risk was that the important would drive out the urgent. As a policymaker, the risk was that the urgent would drive out the important." [2] The political actor, he went on to say, "lives in the world of the contingent; he or she must deal with partial answers that hopefully are on the road to truth. In fact, the attempt to achieve the ultimate in a finite period of time can produce extraordinary disasters."

Max Weber would have agreed. In his famous lecture on "Politics as a Vocation," he said that if a statesman focuses too narrowly on the ultimate good, "the goals may be damaged and discredited for generations, because responsibility for consequences is lacking."[3] Weber's ideal politician was the one in whom the ethic of ultimate ends and the ethic of responsibility complement each other. Such a person, he wrote, "is aware of a responsibility for the consequences of his conduct and really feels such responsibility with heart and soul." Inevitably, such a person is burdened with "the knowledge of tragedy with which all action, but especially political action, is truly interwoven."

The knowledge of tragedy can never be far from a statesperson's mind in the age of weapons of mass destruction. During the years he served as a presidential advisor, Kissinger said that what haunted him most was the possibility of being faced with a responsibility more terrible than any confronted by any political leaders until the twentieth century.

> If I were to define what issue concerned me most when I was in government, it was the issue of what I would do if the President ever said he had no other recourse except nuclear weapons. The reason it preoccupied me is because, in the nature of the job, I knew better than most people what the consequences would be. On one level, I thought nobody has a moral right to make a decision involving the death of tens of millions. But on another level, I knew that if this is proclaimed as our attitude, we will turn the world over to the people who have no hesitation to commit genocide. I never had to resolve that issue because there was only one other nuclear country, the Soviet Union, which, however much it was a rival, calculated the costs of a nuclear war in a comparable way.[4]

The 1973 Nobel Peace Prize winner offered those observations at a meeting in Rome, the city where, two thousand years earlier, Marcus Tullius Cicero, had preached—and to a great extent personified—an ideal of the statesman as a man who combines experience in the management of great affairs with the mastery of philosophy, which he termed "the richest, the most bounteous, the most exalted gift of the immortal gods to humanity."[5] Philosophers, Cicero said, should not stand aloof from the fate of their cities. But he cautioned them that if they put their talents at the service of the polity, they must learn what the wise statesman knows: how to operate within the limits of the possible.[6]

History provides few examples of prominent political actors who, like Cicero or Edmund Burke, are remembered for important contributions to political thought as well as for distinguished public service. As for political theorists who have ventured into politics, some of the most eminent—Plato, Tocqueville, and Weber, for example—were strikingly ineffective in the public arena. In some cases, the circumstances were unfavorable; in the case of others, the fault was not only in their stars but in themselves. The qualities that make an excellent scholar or teacher, as Weber admitted, do not always coincide with the qualities that make one an effective public actor.[7] The optimal confluence of gifts, favorable conditions, and plain luck will always be elusive.

Scholars have often exerted considerable influence on politics as advisers to rulers, or, indirectly, through their writings. But the "influence" of scholarship can be a tricky business. Some of the most influential thinkers—Hobbes, Rousseau, Marx—had little or no experience in the world of practical politics. Moreover, ideas taken out of their original contexts can morph into surprising forms. Concepts lifted from the works of Machiavelli, Rousseau, Montesquieu, Locke, and Marx have had far-reaching effects on political discourse and movements, but not always the effects that those authors hoped for or expected. In fact, as many of the stories collected here illustrate, the ideas that migrate from political theory into political practice are often mere fragments, yanked out of the settings that gave them nuance and balance. Sometimes the political ideas that travel furthest have been the least well-thought-out notions of the author in question.

Of particular interest in today's complex societies are the occasions when teamwork between scholars and statespersons produced lasting achievements. The Emperor Justinian and his chief legal advisor Tribonian gave us the *Corpus Juris Civilis*, a work that remains the foundation of the world's most widely distributed legal systems. Centuries later, Napoleon and Portalis deliberately emulated them, producing the Civil Code that Napoleon regarded as his most enduring legacy. In the young United States, a remarkable group of statesmen, steeped in the works of Locke, Montesquieu, and Blackstone, designed a framework for the world's most successful democratic experiment. In the aftermath of World War II, Eleanor Roosevelt and Charles Malik worked closely with a multinational committee of philosophers and diplomats to produce the document that still serves as the polestar of the modern human rights movement, the 1948 Universal Declaration of Human Rights.

The biographical essays in this book explore a variety of interactions between philosophers and politicians, some torn between the forum and the tower, all grappling with tensions between political ideals and practical realities. The essays are loosely linked through their portrayals of people engaged in perennial political arguments—arguments about human nature, reason and passion, tradition and innovation, liberty and law. Their stories also provide windows through which one can observe how ideas are interpreted, reinterpreted, and often misinterpreted as they move from the works of philosophers and social theorists into political rhetoric and action. Keeping countless conversations with students in mind, I have paid special attention to letters, diaries, and memoirs that provide glimpses of the satisfactions and disappointments, opportunities and pitfalls, sacrifices and rewards, of lives devoted to action, contemplation, or some combination of the two. As the protagonists of these essays I have chosen figures whose stories have always seemed to capture the imaginations of the young people in my classes.

In the cases of political actors, I have interrogated their biographies with the questions that so many of my students have wrestled with over the years: Is politics such a dirty business, or are conditions so unfavorable, that I couldn't make a difference? What kinds of compromises can one make for the sake of getting and keeping a position from which one might be able to have influence on the course of events? What kinds of compromises can one make for the sake of achieving a higher political goal? When does prudent accommodation become pandering? When should one speak truth to power no matter what the risk, and when is it acceptable, as Burke put it, to speak the truth with measure that one may speak it the longer? When does one reach the point at which one concludes, as Plato finally did, that circumstances are so unfavorable that the only reasonable course of action is to "keep quiet and offer up prayers for one's own welfare and for that of one's country"?[8]

The answers to such questions will always vary with persons and circumstances, but the questions are as pertinent to us today as they were to Cicero two thousand years ago.

The Forum and the Tower

INTRODUCTION

The statespersons and scholars in this collection of essays possessed an abundance of the quality that the ancient Greeks called *thymos* (spiritedness) and that the authors of *The Federalist* prized as "the love of fame, the ruling passion of the noblest minds."[1] They were also powerfully drawn—in different ways—by the *eros* of the mind. The desire for recognition led some to pursue a life in the public forum. For others, the quest for knowledge became their central preoccupation.

Many of these individuals were surprisingly slow to discern where their talents would lead them. Plato's sole ambition as a young man was to follow in the footsteps of family members who were prominent in the public life of Athens. It was only in profound disillusion after the death of Socrates that he turned to philosophy. But his desire to have an influence on the course of events remained so strong that it drew him later into two dangerous trips to Syracuse, where he imagined he could enlighten that city's intellectually curious but tyrannical rulers. In his "Seventh Letter," he explained that he went to Sicily at age forty, against his better instincts, impelled by "a feeling of shame with regard to myself, lest I might someday appear to be a mere man of words, one who would never of his own will lay his hand to any act."[2] That expedition—and a similar one twenty years later—were spectacular failures. Yet without those experiences it is doubtful whether the author of the ideal *Republic* could have written his most political, practical, and personal dialogue, *The Laws*.

John Locke as a bookish youth set his sights on an academic career and was quite content with the prospect of spending his entire life as an Oxford don. It was not until he was in his mid-thirties that a chance incident brought him into the company of prominent politicians. After he began to enjoy the kind of influence to which Plato had aspired in vain, he gave up his academic post, though he continued writing. By the time of his death in 1704, he had played a leading role in the great public events of his time, including the "Glorious Revolution" that initiated England's transition to constitutional monarchy.

Though Alexis de Tocqueville was poorly suited by talent and temperament for a political vocation, he insisted throughout his life that politics was his destiny and that his writings were merely a sideline. As soon as he completed his legal studies, he focused all his energies on positioning himself for a role in government, confiding to his future wife that, "With limited abilities, I yet feel vast desires; with delicate health, an inexpressible need for action and emotion."[3] Even his famous trip to the United States was undertaken in part to build up his credentials. After the first edition of *Democracy in America* became a runaway best seller, he told a close friend: "I have always placed the life of action above everything else." His political ambition was not strong enough, however, to overcome the personal quirks and the fiercely independent streak that doomed him to a relatively marginal role during his service as a member of the Chamber of Deputies and his brief stint as Foreign Minister under Louis Napoleon. It was only as he approached his death at age fifty-three that he came to see his writings as his most important legacy, and to realize that his major contribution to politics would be in the realm of theory rather than practice.

Max Weber, too, longed for a leading role in the public arena, even after his writings had made him a towering figure in social thought. In his 1918 lecture on "Science as a Vocation," he had emphasized that "the qualities that make a man an excellent scholar and academic teacher are not the qualities that make him a leader to give directions in practical life, or, more specifically, in politics."[4] Yet he could not recognize in himself what was obvious even to admirers like Karl Jaspers: that his self-critical faculties were so highly developed as to disable him from decisive action.

Lebanese philosopher Charles Malik, by contrast, yearned more than anything to devote himself to teaching and writing, yet was astonishingly good at diplomacy. As a young professor in Beirut, he reluctantly agreed to represent his newly independent nation at the UN's Founding Conference in 1945, but he wrote to his Harvard mentor Alfred North Whitehead that, "My interest in politics and diplomacy is only temporary. My heart lies definitely in teaching and speculation to which I shall return as soon as I find my mission reasonably fulfilled."[5] It would be many years, however, before Malik returned to the classroom. During the 1950s, he became one of the most important, and most respected, diplomats on the world stage, elected by secret ballot to nearly every major post in the UN, including President of the General Assembly. Working in tandem with Eleanor Roosevelt, he played a key role in shepherding the Universal Declaration of Human Rights through the tortuous process that led to its approval in December 1948. He finally came to accept that "if decent people do not go into politics, leadership must pass to others, no matter how perverted and false those others may be." But he never overcame his distaste for what he regarded as a world of "untruth."

Not only did several of the protagonists of these essays find themselves following a different vocation from the one for which they originally thought themselves suited, but many were wide of the mark in judging what would be their principal legacy. If that knowledge dawned on them at all, it generally arrived when they were too old for it to have made a difference in their career choices.

Cicero, Roman to the core, thought of himself as first and foremost a statesman, and rarely faltered in his conviction that a life of public service was "the course that has always been followed by the best men."[6] When his friends tried to talk him out of going into politics by pointing out that the Roman Forum was full of corrupt characters, he shot back: "What stronger reason could brave and high-minded men have for entering politics than the determination not to give in to the wicked, and not to allow the state to be torn apart by such people?"[7] Yet his efforts to preserve the form of government he called republican were doomed to failure. Later generations would remember Julius Caesar as the towering political actor of the age, and would honor Cicero for writings that helped to forge the great synthesis of Greco-Roman traditions that has nourished Western philosophy, politics, and law. The magnitude of those accomplishments was acknowledged by Caesar himself, who once said that it was a greater achievement to have extended the frontiers of the Roman genius as Cicero had done than to have extended the boundaries of the Roman Empire.[8]

Edmund Burke, at the end of his life, insisted on more than one occasion that he wished to be remembered for his efforts on behalf of the oppressed peoples of India. He had been bitterly disappointed by his failure to secure the conviction of Warren Hastings on a bill of impeachment for presiding over a vast system of abuses as Governor-General of Bengal. During the trial, Burke had portrayed in graphic detail the atrocities—including bribery, extortion, and torture—that were committed in India under the British Raj. The acquittal of Hastings, he felt, had brought shame and disgrace to the entire nation. Unable to bear the thought that future generations of Englishmen might never learn of the cruelty and corruption that their country had tolerated, he told the friend charged with looking after his estate: "Let my endeavors to save the nation from that shame and guilt be my monument; the only one I ever will have. Let everything I have done, said, or written be forgotten but this."[9] Today, with hindsight, we know that Burke's efforts were not in vain: he was instrumental in setting in motion the forces that eventually put an end to the oppressive system that had prevailed under Hastings. But it was Burke's impassioned *Reflections on the French Revolution* that captivated the next generation of English writers—Scott, Wordsworth, Coleridge, and Southey—and that became a classic of political theory.

It is only rarely that *thymos* and the *eros* of the mind are as felicitously combined as they were in Cicero and Burke. Some of the protagonists in the essays that follow opted early for philosophy or statesmanship and seldom looked back. Others, like the students whose questions prompted me to write this book, were tugged in many directions. All of them "made a difference," but often, as we shall see, in ways that they never imagined.

ONE

PLATO IN THE REAL CITY

Plato's far from brilliant career in politics should give heart to career-changers and late-bloomers, for his sole ambition as a young man was to follow in the footsteps of other family members who were prominent in the public life of Athens. But, as Max Weber observed in his lectures "Politics as a Vocation" and "Science as a Vocation"—and as borne out by Weber's own unsuccessful forays into political life—the qualities that make a first-rate thinker are not the same as those required for success in statesmanship. Either path, moreover, can be blocked by circumstances outside the control of the aspiring scholar or statesman.

Plato was exceptionally unlucky in his attempts to play a leading role in public affairs. Yet it is easy to see why he long felt sure that he was destined for the active rather than the contemplative life. Born around 428 BC to a wealthy and influential aristocratic family, he served with the Athenian forces in the Peloponnesian War and was decorated for bravery.[1] In the turmoil that followed Athenian defeat in 404, a coup d'état brought to power an oligarchy led by Plato's distant cousin Critias. That group—known as the Thirty Tyrants—included many of his relatives and acquaintances. Later, he recalled that when they took him into their inner circle, he accepted the invitation "as something to which I had a claim."[2] The effect on him, he said, "was not surprising in the case of a young man; I considered that they would, of course, so manage the State as to bring men out of a bad way of life into a good one." Indeed, he may have had his own youthful self in mind when, in the *Gorgias*, he had the Sophist Callicles taunt Socrates, saying that an older man who still studies philosophy "is doomed to prove less than a man, shunning the city center and market place, in which the poet said that men win distinction."[3]

The word "tyrant" in ancient usage merely described a ruler who had gained his position by usurping legal authority, and several tyrants in fact had been thought to rule rather well. The youthful Plato thus had reason to hope that his city's government would be in good hands. But the Thirty Tyrants of Athens did more than their share to endow the term with its present negative connotation. "In quite a short time," Plato tells us, "they made the former government seem by comparison something precious as gold."[4] Disillusioned, he severed his connection with their administration.

But his hopes were revived when the Thirty were overthrown and replaced by a government that restored the city's democratic constitution: "Once more, though with more hesitation, I began to be moved by the desire to take part in public and political affairs."[5] The new democratic regime, however, proved even more disappointing to Plato than the oligarchy had been. The last straw was the trial and execution in 399 of his friend and teacher Socrates, whom he revered as "the justest man alive."[6]

Relinquishing all hope of influencing the course of Athenian democracy, Plato embarked on a series of travels through Greece, Egypt, Sicily, and the Italian peninsula. Though little is known about his activities in this period, it is thought that he studied for a time in the school of Eucleides of Megara, a Socratic philosopher famed for his skill in dialectics. What is certain is that, somewhere along the way, Plato was drawn to the way of life that had not been his first choice. By the time he returned to Athens, twelve years later, he had already completed some early dialogues reflecting on the life and teaching of Socrates.

Toward the end of his voyages, he had a fateful encounter in Syracuse, then the capital of an extensive Sicilian empire. There, he met and befriended a young man, Dion, whose intellectual and political preoccupations, he felt, were close to his own. Plato was deeply impressed by Dion, "who rapidly assimilated my teaching as he did all forms of knowledge, and listened to me with an eagerness which I had never seen equalled in any young man."[7] Dion for his part was so awed by Plato's brilliance that he persuaded his brother-in-law, Dionysius I, the tyrant of Syracuse, to invite the interesting Athenian for an audience at court.[8] Dionysius was a man with some intellectual pretensions, a patron of the arts, and a poet who is said to have been as proud of his literary works as of the military prowess that had enabled him to extend the Syracusan domain. He is described by Plutarch as a man with "wit enough, but troubled with many vices." Among those defects, unfortunately for Plato, were a craving for flattery and zero tolerance for criticism.

The interview went badly. Dionysius became increasingly irate as he noticed his courtiers smiling while Plato discoursed on the life of the just man as compared to the unjust man. Interrupting to change the subject, he asked Plato what business had brought him to Sicily. Plato's reply, "To seek a good man," was not the most politic thing to say under the circumstances. Taking it personally, the thin-skinned tyrant flew into a rage, saying, "By the gods, to hear thee speak, it seems thou hast yet found none!"

Dion, alarmed and fearing the worst, hustled his friend onto a ship headed back to Greece. But Dionysius was unwilling to let the insult pass. He sent orders to the ship's captain to either kill Plato or sell him as a slave. The captain chose the latter course, and Plato had to be rescued by another friend, who repurchased him and brought him home.

Upon returning to Athens, Plato—then in his forties—founded the center for research and study known as the Academy. The institution quickly became a magnet for young men who wished to study philosophy, science, and mathematics. Under Plato's direction, the

Academy was the center of Greek intellectual life, and it flourished for many years after his death. Its most illustrious alumnus, Aristotle, is said to have spent twenty years in residence there.[9]

Although Plato is commonly thought of today as a speculative thinker with his head in the stratosphere, the fact is that he repeatedly immersed himself in the affairs of the "real world," sometimes at great personal risk. Even after he was a famous philosopher, and advanced in years, he could not resist the temptation to be drawn back into politics. Twenty years after the death of Dionysius I, Dion wrote to Plato, entreating his old friend to return to Syracuse where the new ruler, Dionysius II, professed to be interested in philosophy. According to Plutarch, Dion "hoped, by Plato's coming, to bridle and lessen a little the over-licentious and imperious tyranny of Dionysius, and thereby to frame Dionysius a wise and righteous governor."[10] What Dion did not disclose to Plato was his own determination, if that plan failed, to overthrow the regime.

Although Plato was then sixty years old, he convinced himself that "if ever anyone was to try to carry out in practice my ideas about laws and constitutions, now was the time for making the attempt."[11] He undertook the trip, he wrote, not only out of his friendship for Dion, but also out of "a feeling of shame with regard to myself, lest I might someday appear to be a mere man of words, one who would never of his own will lay his hand to any act."[12]

This time the visit began well. Plato was given a royal welcome and an honored place in Dionysius's court. Dionysius the Younger, like his father, wished to be seen as a man of culture and learning. He took pride in the fact that a renowned philosopher had come to converse with him. For a time, Plutarch tells us, the atmosphere in the court seemed to change dramatically. The Syracusans were astonished by "the wonderful modesty and temperance that was begun to be observed in feasts and banquets, and the great goodness and clemency of the tyrant in all things, in ministering justice to every man."[13] Imitating their leader in his latest enthusiasm, "every man in the court was desirous to give himself to learning and philosophy." For a few months, the royal palace was "full of sand and dust with the number of students that drew plats and figures of geometry."

But the fad did not last. First, Plato's friend fell victim to palace intrigues accusing him (not altogether without reason) of conspiracy to seize the throne. Dionysius exiled Dion to Italy, from whence he made his way to Greece, where he took refuge in the Academy. Dionysius, still eager to continue his conversations with Plato, convinced the philosopher to stay for a while. But courtiers began to whisper that Plato was not the disinterested thinker that he seemed to be. They said that the Athenians, having failed to conquer Syracuse with military might, had sent their cleverest sophister to undermine the regime from within—all to the eventual benefit of Dion. Dionysius, increasingly wary, placed Plato under a kind of house arrest in the royal palace. There, he paid frequent visits to his "honored guest." The tyrant "had a marvelous desire," says Plutarch, "to hear Plato's philosophy, but on the other hand, he reverenced them that did dissuade him from it, and told him that he would spoil himself, if he entered over-deeply in it."

As Plato himself later described those conversations, they became ever more frustrating for both men. Dionysius was extremely eager to win Plato's approval, "but when confronted with the one way in which this might have been done, if it was to be done at all, he shrank from coming into close and intimate relations with me as a pupil and listener to my discourses on philosophy, fearing the danger suggested by mischief makers, that he might be ensnared, and so Dion would prove to have accomplished all his object. I endured all this patiently, retaining the purpose with which I had come and the hope that he might come to desire the philosophic life. But his resistance prevailed against me."[14] Eventually, Dionysius gave up on philosophy, and permitted Plato to return to Athens.

After a time, as Plutarch takes up the story, Dionysius "began again to wish for Plato, and to condemn himself for that he had no wit to use him well when he had him at his commandment, and that he had not heard so much as he should have done of him; and, like a tyrant as he was, madly carried away with light desires and easily changing mind from time to time, a sudden vehement desire took him in the head to have Plato again."[15] All of Plato's instincts told him to decline the tyrant's invitation. But Dionysius, searching for ways to persuade him, found a weak point. He promised that if Plato would return, he would follow the philosopher's advice in dealing with the exiled Dion, including Dion's vast property holdings. When that offer became known to Dion and his family, they deluged Plato with letters pleading with him to intervene.

Reluctantly, Plato made the arduous sea voyage to Sicily again. Once again, he was welcomed with a great show of friendship. But Dionysius immediately went back on his word and began offering Plato large sums of money if he would denounce Dion. Moreover, the tyrant was as deaf as ever to Plato's exhortations to establish "the rule of laws" in a regime where "philosophy and power really met together."[16]Meanwhile, evidence mounted of Dion's plans to overthrow the regime. When Plato refused to turn against his friend, the full force of the tyrant's wrath descended upon him. Barely escaping from Syracuse with his life, Plato finally accepted that his efforts to make the king into a philosopher had been futile.

As soon as he reached Greece, he sought out Dion, whom he found at the Olympic Games, seeking to round up supporters for an expedition against the tyrant. After hearing Plato's account of what had transpired in Syracuse, Dion asked Plato to encourage his friends to join the force he was assembling. Several of Plato's friends did, in fact, join Dion in his successful overthrow of Dionysius, but Plato refused to have anything to do with the venture. He declined, he later explained, "because I was disgusted with my misguided journeyings to Sicily and my ill-fortune there."[17]

Equally disgusted with the state of affairs in Athens, Plato never again attempted to enter the sphere of politics. Although Socrates had maintained that good men should accept public responsibilities so as to avoid being ruled by those who are evil,[18] Plato finally concluded that there are times when circumstances are so unfavorable that the only reasonable course for a wise man is to "keep quiet and offer up prayers for his own welfare and for that of his country."[19]

Were it not for his disheartening experiences in politics, however, it is unlikely that Plato could have written *The Laws*, his last, most personal, and most political dialogue. It is a pity that *The Laws* is so little known today. Of all the dialogues, it is the one that speaks most pointedly to the social sciences, and it still has important things to say about the great perennial questions of the scope and limits of law, the rule of law, the relation between law and custom, and the cultural underpinnings of good government.

No doubt Alfred North Whitehead exaggerated when he claimed that "the safest general characterization of the European philosophical tradition is that it consists of a series of footnotes to Plato."[20] Yet it is striking that many of the thinkers who made their names by challenging classical political thought borrowed some of their most memorable images and ideas from the philosopher who was one of the chief objects of their attacks. In *The Laws*, especially, one discovers much that was re-invented, or appropriated, by early modern philosophers—Machiavelli's distinction between legislating for imaginary kingdoms and making laws for a real city; Hobbes's war of all against all; Montesquieu's insistence that lawmakers must keep in mind the geographical situation and the cultural condition of those for whom they legislate; and the distinction between citizens and subjects that was so central for Rousseau and, in a different way, for Tocqueville.

The dialogue in *The Laws* takes place among three elderly pilgrims who meet on the road from Knossos to the temple of Zeus on the island of Crete. Since the trek ahead is a long one, the protagonist, known only as the Athenian Stranger, proposes to Kleinias, a Cretan, and Megillos, a Spartan, that they beguile the time with conversation about the government and laws of Crete and Sparta. Both Crete and Sparta were renowned for their good laws.[21] In fact, the shrine that is the travelers' destination commemorates the supposedly divine origin of the laws of Crete. Athens, according to the Stranger, was less blessed: it suffered from numerous civic ills that he attributed to misuse of liberty and lack of restraint on the part of rulers and ruled.

In some ways, the nameless Athenian resembles the Socrates of Plato's earlier dialogues, but he is less charming and more pious, his speech is less elusive and more pedantic. In fact, the regime outlined in *The Laws*—with its checks and balances, private property, child-raising families, rights for women, and condemnation of homosexuality—is so different from the ideal polity of *The Republic* that some scholars have doubted the authenticity of the later work. But most, more plausibly, conclude that the Stranger is as close as we get to the voice of Plato himself,[22] a Plato nearing the end of his own journey through life, an old philosopher making one last attempt to advise princes, this time through the written word.

When the Athenian asks the Cretan and the Spartan how their polities came to have such excellent laws, Kleinias and Megillos both respond readily that their laws originally were given to them by a god.[23] But they do not sound very confident. In Crete, the lawgiver "is said" to have been Zeus ("at least that is our tradition"), and in Sparta, "I believe they say it is Apollo." Later, as they begin to conjecture about the historical development of political systems, the travelers agree that in simple early societies, custom must have preceded law. The key to good laws, they speculate, has something to do with good habits developed over time—self-restraint on the part of citizens, and some form of checks on the power of rulers, whether the regime be a monarchy, aristocracy, or democracy. One thing is clear: good government cannot be taken for granted, for anyone can see that many cities have not developed the kinds of customs and laws that are conducive to dignified living. The Athenian, reflecting on his own troubled city, remarks ruefully that, after all, "It looks as though some god was concerned on Sparta's behalf."[24]

Later, we learn that the Stranger really does seem to have a view about the sense in which a god might aid lawmakers. But his notion has nothing to do with the legendary inhabitants of Mount Olympus. He says, "It may be, as the story goes nowadays, that ancient legislators were descended from or instructed by gods."[25] But today's legislators "are human beings legislating for the children of humankind." What interests the Stranger is that human beings are endowed with a divine spark of *reason* that makes it possible for them, individually and collectively, to gain control over their most primitive impulses. "We should run our public and our private life, our homes and our cities," he says, "in obedience to what little spark of immortality lies in us, and dignify this distribution of reason with the name of law."[26] "It cannot be an accident that the name of this god-given and wonderful institution, law (*nomos*), is so suggestive of reason (*nous*)."[27]

In a memorable series of lectures at Boston College on the late Platonic dialogues, Hans-Georg Gadamer postulated that in passages like these the author was quietly promoting monotheism at a time when Greek folk religion was fading. Kleinias and Megillos, with their hemming and hawing about the origins of their laws, plainly have doubts about the tradition that ascribes their laws to anthropomorphic deities. But at the same time, they are reluctant to embrace the opinions of "some people" that law is only the will of the stronger, and that laws merely serve the will of the lawmaker.[28] They are relieved to be invited to think about good laws and customs in another way—as the creation of fallible beings endowed with a faculty that enables them to reflect on experience, to give themselves rules, to orient their conduct toward the norms they establish, and to review those norms in the light of experience, correcting them where necessary.

But reason, alas, is fallible, subject to all kinds of distortions, personal and cultural, conscious and unconscious. And human beings are constantly torn between reason and passions "like puppets on strings."[29] So how to assure that this fragile faculty will be used well? The interlocutors soon find themselves caught in a strange loop: wise laws can play an important role in promoting good government, good character, and good habits. But wise laws can only be produced by wise lawmakers, and good government requires the kind of statesmen and citizens who are disposed to understand wise laws and abide by them. It sounds as though the best laws will emerge only where they are least needed.

At this point, Kleinias reveals that his interest in the conversation is not mere intellectual curiosity. He announces that he has just been appointed to a commission charged with the duty of establishing a new Cretan colony, and providing it with a constitution and statutes. It would be very helpful to him, he says, if the three travelers could spend the rest of the day "founding a city in speech" as they stroll along, taking frequent stops for rest under the cypress trees.[30]

The task is one that would have been familiar to Plato. The foundation of a colony in his day was always accompanied by the preparation of a specially designed set of laws, and the mother city commonly called upon expert advisors to assist in the process.[31] One purpose of the Academy, in fact, was to train statesmen and equip them with a philosophical background.

Megillos and the Stranger gladly accept the proposal. All agree at the outset that there is no question of aiming for an ideal state; the new colony will be inhabited by real men and women, not by gods, or "people of wax."[32] Even to attain a "second-best" polity would be a considerable achievement.[33] They recognize that what the legislator can accomplish will be greatly affected by the physical situation and economic circumstances of the city.[34] How many people will live there? Will it be inland or on the coast? What kind of neighbors will it have, and how close will it be to other cities? Will the colonists be primarily engaged in agriculture or commerce? Will they be of similar or diverse origins? "We must not fail to observe, O Megillos and Kleinias, that there is a difference in places, and that some beget better men and others worse; and we must legislate accordingly."[35]

It is understood, too, that there are unpredictable factors that impose constraints on legislation. Calamities like war, poverty, disease, and natural disasters can overturn constitutions and rewrite laws. In that sense, chance and accident are "the universal legislators of the world."[36] The statesman, therefore, is like the navigator of a ship. He cannot control the wind and waves, but he must have the skill to recognize and seize favorable opportunities, steering as best he can toward his goal.

So, where to begin? "What, in heaven's name," muses the Stranger, "should be the first law our legislator will establish?"[37] Without waiting to hear what Kleinias and Megillos have to say, he answers his own question: "Surely the first subject he will turn to in his regulations will be the very first step that leads to the birth of children in the state: the union of two people in the partnership of marriage." Kleinias readily agrees that marriage must be regulated first because it is crucial to the nurture and education of future citizens.

The formation of citizens is so important to the common good, the Stranger continues, that parents need to be made aware of the close connection between the private and the public order. For this purpose, there should be a specially appointed official, the Law Warden, in charge of education. This office, he insists, will be the most important office in the city.[38] There must be also legislation to combat impiety and the corruption of the young. (Although Plato had regarded Socrates' execution for the crime of impiety as a grave injustice, he apparently did not deem it improper for the law to be concerned with that subject.)

Turning to the education of girls, he recommends that women should have much the same education as men.[39] Women are to share in the activities of the state to the fullest extent possible, and will be eligible equally with men for public honors.[40] Accordingly, it would be a great mistake for the legislator to neglect the formation of half the polis.

But not everything that pertains to the city's seedbeds of character and competence needs to be, or can be, regulated by legislation. Unwritten customs, according to the Stranger, "are the bonds of the entire social framework."[41] When soundly established and habitually observed, they "shield and preserve" the written law. "But if they go wrong," says the Athenian from bitter experience, "well, you know what happens when carpenter's props buckle in a house: they bring the whole building crashing down."

As the interlocutors ponder how law can foster sound customs and good habits, the conversation returns to education. Indeed, from the beginning to the end of *The Laws*, no matter what topic is under discussion, nurture and education repeatedly come to the fore. The ultimate concern in *The Laws* is not so much with the right laws for the state, but with the right formation for citizenship.[42] The Athenian continually brings the discussion around to the idea that the aim of law is to lead the citizens toward virtue, by developing their character. He stresses that the lawgiver has not only force but also persuasion at his disposal to accomplish this aim, and that a legislator for free men should try to devise the laws so as to win the voluntary understanding and cooperation of the citizens. At the same time, he recognizes that for this approach to work, the citizens, at least a good portion of them, have to be open to persuasion.

To illustrate these points, the Athenian compares the legislator who simply issues commands to a certain kind of doctor whom he calls the slave doctor.[43] The slave doctor, a slave himself, has learned what he knows of medicine by working as the servant of a doctor. His manner of practicing his profession is to make a hurried visit, to order whatever remedy experience suggests, and then to rush off to the next patient. By contrast, the free man's doctor begins by getting to know the patient, his history, his family, and his mode of life. He inquires searchingly into the disorder, and when he has obtained as much information as possible, he begins instructing the patient about what he must do to regain his health. The free man's doctor issues his prescriptions only after he has won the patient's understanding and cooperation.

Returning to the lawmaker, the Stranger asks: Should he merely issue a set of commands and prohibitions, add the threat of a penalty, and go on to announce another decree, without a word of encouragement or advice to those for whom he is legislating? This kind of law may be fit for slaves, he says, but surely a legislator for free men should try to devise his laws so as to create good will in the persons addressed and make them ready to receive intelligently the command that follows.

Interestingly, the question of the best type of regime is given rather short shrift once it is agreed that the rule of law is of paramount importance. "Whatever the form of government," says the Athenian, "where supreme power joins hands with wise judgment and self-restraint, there you have the birth of the best political system with laws to match."[44] And again, "The state in which the law is above the rulers, and the rulers are the inferiors of the law, has salvation, and every blessing which the gods can confer."[45] The message, in today's terms, seems to be that culture is prior to law, but that legal norms and institutions can exert some influence on culture, for better or worse.

Today, the specifics of the highly detailed code proposed by the three travelers for an ancient agricultural colony are of little more than historical interest. The project of making laws for a real city, as the Stranger recognizes, is always a work in progress. Circumstances will change, new challenges will arise. The passage of time will reveal the merits and flaws of legal arrangements, and from time to time, corrections will have to be made: "Do you imagine that there ever was a legislator so foolish as not to know that there are many things which someone coming after him must correct, if the constitution and the order of government is not to deteriorate but to improve the state which he has established?"[46] The laws may change, but what does not change are the recurrent processes of human knowing by which the laws can be tested, evaluated, and improved, always with a view toward "the freedom, unity and wisdom of the city."[47]

At a certain point, Kleinias, the practical politician, challenges the Athenian Stranger: "Can you show that what you have been saying is true?" The Stranger replies: "To be absolutely sure of the truth of matters concerning which there are many opinions, Kleinias, is an attribute of the gods not given to man. But I shall be very happy to explain what I think and to enter into discussion about it."[48] As night falls, and the conversation comes to an end, Megillos the Spartan urges the Cretan to entreat their wise friend to stay and help with the founding of the new city. Without the Athenian's assistance, he says he does not see how the project can go forward. Kleinias agrees. At last, a statesman who is open to the ideas of a philosopher! But the Stranger never responds and never speaks again. Plato's last dialogue ends with a resonating silence.

And yet, perhaps we are meant to hear in that silence an echo of what Socrates said just before his death when a grieving friend asked, "Where, Socrates, are we to get hold of a good singer of incantations— since you are abandoning us?"

"Greece is a vast land, Cebus," the old man replied. "I suppose there are good people in it—and there are many races of barbarians too. . . . You must search for him in company with one another, too, for perhaps you wouldn't find anyone more able to do this than yourselves."[49]

TWO

MARCUS TULLIUS CICERO

POLITICS IN A DYING REPUBLIC

More rare than athletes who have played both baseball and football
in the major leagues are individuals who have achieved great distinction
in both of the vocations that Aristotle deemed most choice-worthy.
Marcus Tullius Cicero, however, would hold a place of honor on any
list of superstars of politics and philosophy. If he had never risen to
eminence as a Roman orator, Senator, and Consul, he would still be
remembered for his contributions to the great Greco-Roman synthesis
at the base of Western civilization. And if he had never written on
philosophy, he would still be honored for his courageous efforts to
preserve the rule of law in the last years of the Roman Republic.

Cicero shared Aristotle's view that statesmanship and the pursuit
of knowledge were the highest callings for those who have the talent to
pursue them. But he parted company with the author of the *Politics* on
which was the superior choice. A true Roman, he never lost his desire
for public honor, and rarely faltered in his conviction that a life of
public service was "the course that has always been followed by the
best men."[1]

No philosophical discourse is so fine, he maintained, "that it deserves to be set above the public law and customs of a well-ordered state."[2] Following Aristotle's *Ethics*, he held that moral excellence is a matter of practice, and it seemed evident to him that its most important field of practice was in the government of the state. Philosophers, he said, can spend their whole lives spinning theories about justice, decency, and fortitude, but statesmen are the ones who must actually set the conditions to foster the virtues that are necessary to a well-functioning polity. "There can be no doubt," he maintained, "that the statesman's life is more admirable and more illustrious, even though some people think that a life passed quietly in the study of the highest arts is happier."[3]

Cicero's ideal statesman, however, was the man whose actions are illuminated by philosophy (by which he meant mainly ethics and political theory). The best statesman of all, at least for Rome, would be someone steeped in the city's history, someone who combined civilized values with "intimate knowledge of Roman institutions and traditions and the theoretical knowledge for which we are indebted to the Greeks."[4] In other words, someone like Marcus Tullius Cicero.

Though philosophy, as he told his son, was "indispensable to everyone who proposes to have a good career," it was always, for him, a handmaiden to politics.[5] Even philosophers, he said, have an obligation to concern themselves with public affairs, not only out of civic duty, but for the sake of philosophy itself, which requires certain political conditions in order to flourish.

Yet in times when he was excluded from political life or overcome with personal sorrow, he plunged into his philosophical studies with prodigious energy. Rarely has so much of the noble sort of ambition that the ancients called *thymos* been combined in one individual with such intense attraction to the *eros* of the mind. On occasions when Cicero's political fortunes were at low ebb, he could not help casting a glance down the path not taken. "Now that power has passed to three uncontrolled individuals," he wrote to his friend Atticus during the triumvirate of Caesar, Pompey, and Crassus, "I am eager to devote all my attention to philosophy. I only wish I had done it from the outset."[6] And in Cicero's dialogue *On the Republic*, the character of Scipio relates a dream in which he meets his deceased grandfather, the legendary general Africanus, who reminds him of the transience of worldly success: "Of what value, pray, is your human glory which can barely last for a tiny part of a single year? If you wish to look higher you will not put yourself at the mercy of the masses' gossip nor measure your long-term destiny by the rewards you get from men. Goodness herself must draw you on by her own enticements to true glory. In no case does a person's reputation last for ever; it fades with the death of the speakers, and vanishes as posterity forgets."[7]

Cicero's insistence on the primacy of politics perfectly reflected the ethos of Republican Rome. For over four centuries, the Romans had been famed for their skill in law and administration. By the time of Cicero's birth in 106 BC, the city had developed a sophisticated legal system and an elaborate form of mixed government that came to be known as republican. The most powerful branch in this regime was the Senate, whose members, traditionally drawn from old and wealthy patrician families, held office for life. Executive authority was wielded jointly by two Consuls who were elected annually. The population at large was represented by an assembly of Tribunes, who in Cicero's day were constantly agitating for more power.

The Romans were fiercely proud of their city's laws and institutions. Cicero gave the palm to the Greeks where philosophy was concerned, but when it came to government, he claimed, "I hold, maintain, and declare that no form of government is comparable in its structure, its assignment of functions, or its discipline to the one which our fathers received from their forebears and handed down to us."[8] Roman law, in his view, had reached such a degree of perfection that he could only shake his head in wonder at "how confused and almost ridiculous other systems of law are when compared with ours." His almost reverential appreciation for the genius of Roman jurists was shared a thousand years later by the European Renaissance legal scholars who re-discovered Roman law, pronounced it to be *ratio scripta*, "written reason," and adapted it to the needs of their own societies.

Due to the predominance of the Senate, the Roman "republic" was essentially a modified form of aristocracy or oligarchy, but it had the merits of placing some limits on the concentration of power and providing some checks and balances. It was a system, as Cicero saw it, that combined the best features of monarchy, aristocracy, and democracy, a system where "the Consuls have enough power, the councils of eminent citizens enough influence, and the people enough liberty." And most importantly, it established the principle, if not the consistent observance, of the rule of law.

Over Cicero's lifetime, however, the traditional system was collapsing. Structures that had worked well for a smaller, more homogeneous society were proving inadequate for the government of a vast expanding empire. At home, order and legality were constantly breaking down in a city wracked by civil wars, attempted coups, and popular unrest.

For an ambitious Roman citizen whose birth did not give him automatic entry into the circles of power, and who was not inclined toward a military career, the path to eminence lay through law and oratory, and the law courts were a proving ground. Cicero was the precocious firstborn son of a prosperous landowner in Arpinum, a country town some seventy miles southeast of Rome, close to present-day Montecassino.[9] The family belonged to the class of *equites*, well-to-do landowners and merchants who were increasingly aspiring to political influence in the capital. According to Plutarch, young Marcus Tullius acquired a reputation for cleverness as soon as he began to have lessons—so much so, that the fathers of the other boys often dropped by the school to hear him recite.[10] When he was old enough to pursue higher studies, his father's wealth and connections enabled him to place the gifted boy with the best teachers in Rome.

There Cicero studied rhetoric, philosophy, and law. Rome, then a bustling city of about 400,000 inhabitants, was full of distractions. But Cicero's poor digestion discouraged excesses of food and drink, and though he exercised for the sake of his health, he took no interest in games and sports. As for the company of courtesans, he told a friend in later years that, "even in my youth, I was not attracted by this sort of thing."[11] What did excite his imagination was the idea of a life crowned with public honor. He took his motto from a line in the *Iliad* where Glaucus recalls his father's exhortation, "Always to be the best and far to excel all others." His passion for recognition made him prone to self-aggrandizement, yet by all accounts he was free of envy, generous in his praise of others, and had a great gift for friendship. Plutarch tells us that he was "by natural temper very much disposed to mirth and pleasantry."[12]

Like many a law student today, Cicero complained about the long hours he had to spend on material that was often less than interesting. What he preferred was visiting the Forum, where large crowds flocked to see performances by the great orators of the day. He embarked on his own career as an advocate in his mid-twenties, and enjoyed considerable success, despite severe attacks of stage fright and a pedantic tendency that earned him the nicknames of "the Greek" and "the scholar." Around this time—the date is uncertain—he married Terentia, a well-born Roman woman whose dowry and family connections would greatly aid his efforts to break into politics. But just when he seemed well advanced on his chosen path, his health broke down under the stress he had imposed upon himself. As he later recounted:

> I was at that time very slender and not strong in body, and such a constitution, combined with hard work and strain on the lungs, were thought to be almost life-threatening. When friends and doctors begged me to give up speaking in the courts, I felt I would run any risk rather than abandon my hope of fame as a speaker. I thought that by a more restrained and moderate use of the voice and a different way of speaking I could both avoid the danger and acquire more variety in my style. And so, when I had two years' experience of taking cases and my name was already well-known in the Forum, I left Rome.[13]

Another factor in Cicero's decision to leave from Rome may well have been his desire to put some distance between himself and the powerful Roman dictator Lucius Cornelius Sulla, whose excesses he had had the temerity to criticize in the course of two lawsuits. In any event, the journey was as beneficial for his intellectual development as for his physical health. He traveled to Greece and Rhodes, where, together with a group that included his younger brother Quintus and his lifelong friend Atticus, he studied with the most famous philosophers and orators of the day. When he returned to Rome two years later, he was, he said, "almost another man."[14] He had learned to control his voice, his style was improved, his health was restored, and Sulla was in retirement.

Now he was ready to embark on the first stages of a political career. Within two years, he was elected a Quaestor, an official position that gave him membership in the Senate. The quaestorship involved a tour of duty in Sicily, where he gained respect for his honesty and diligence.

For Cicero personally, the high point of his Sicilian sojourn may well have been his discovery of the burial place of Archimedes, who had been killed by a Roman soldier during the siege of Syracuse in 212 BC, despite orders from the commanding general that the famous mathematician and inventor should be brought to him unharmed. According to legend, the soldier became enraged when Archimedes refused to accompany him, saying he had to finish working on a problem. When Cicero expressed a desire to visit the great man's tomb, Syracusan officials told him that they doubted it even existed. But Cicero insisted. He recalled reading somewhere that Archimedes had been interred under a monument inscribed with a few lines of verse and adorned with a sphere and cylinder (in commemoration of his discovery of the relation between the volume of a sphere and that of a cylinder of the same height).

One can sense the excitement in Cicero's description of how he found the tomb under a thick overgrowth of briars.

[A]fter taking a good look all round (for there are a great quantity of graves at the Agrigentine Gate), I noticed a small column rising a little above the bushes, on which there was the figure of a sphere and a cylinder. And so I at once said to the Syracusans (I had their leading men with me) that I believed it was the very thing of which I was in search. Slaves were sent in with sickles who cleared the ground of obstacles, and when a passage to the place was opened, we approached the pedestal fronting us; the epigram was traceable, with about half the lines legible, as the latter portion was worn away.[15]

Cicero permitted himself to boast that Syracuse, "one of the most famous of Greek cities, and once one of the most learned, would not have known the grave of its most brilliant citizen, if it had not learned it from a man of Arpinum." (Sad to say, the grave of Archimedes is nowhere to be found in twenty-first-century Syracuse.)

Upon returning to Rome after what he regarded with justifiable pride as a distinguished tour of duty in Sicily, Cicero learned that in politics, if not in friendship, out of sight is out of mind. He was shocked to realize that many people were unaware that he had been away, and that hardly anyone knew of his achievements in the service of Rome. Years later, he looked back with some humor at the self-important young man he once had been:

> To say the truth, I believed that people in Rome were talking of nothing but my quaestorship. At a time when the price of corn was very high I had sent over a large quantity; I was thought to have been civil to the men of business, fair to the traders, generous to the tax-farmers, upright to the provincials and everyone thought I had been most conscientious in all my duties; the Sicilians had devised unparalleled honours for me. So I left my province expecting that the Roman people would rush to reward me in every possible way. On my journey home I happened to reach Puteoli just at the time when it is full of fashionable people. I almost fainted . . . when someone asked me when I had left Rome and what was the news there.[16]

Then and there, he said, he resolved to make sure that Romans "should see me in the flesh every day. I lived in their sight, I was never out of the Forum; neither sleep nor my doorkeeper prevented anyone from gaining access to me."

Once resettled in the capital, Cicero quickly demonstrated that his interlude in Greece and Rhodes had been well spent. Though he never completely conquered attacks of stage fright, he established a reputation as the most brilliant advocate in Rome. The crowning achievement of his legal career was his victory over another celebrated orator, Hortensius, in a case in which Cicero successfully prosecuted one Gaius Verres for corruption in office while Verres was serving as a

Roman governor in Sicily. Cicero's energy in gathering evidence, his wit and eloquence in argument, and his courage in exposing the misdeeds of a powerful man won him wide admiration. Centuries later, Edmund Burke would take Cicero's speech "Against Verres" as the model for his own prosecution of Warren Hastings for high crimes and misdemeanors as Governor-General of India.

At the age of forty-three, Cicero reached the summit of the Roman political hierarchy by securing election as a Consul for the year 63 BC. This was an extraordinary achievement for a man from a provincial family that had never produced any senators. During his term as Consul (alongside a passive Co-consul), he rendered what he always regarded as his most important service to Rome by leading the suppression of the Catiline conspiracy, an attempted coup by a young aristocrat with a large popular following. In the course of restoring order, however, Cicero took a step that arguably violated his own principles as well as Roman traditions. He ordered five of the co-conspirators to be executed without trial. The executions had a semblance of legality, having been approved in advance by the Senate, and Cicero justified them as necessary to preserve public order in a time of emergency. But the decision earned him the lasting enmity of Catiline's supporters, among whom were some powerful and dangerous men.

The Catiline conspiracy, moreover, was only one manifestation of Rome's deepening social ills. Roman conquests abroad had expanded its dominion, enriching both the governing elite and the rising class of traders, but official corruption was rife, and so was popular unrest. The public treasury was drained by the expense of foreign wars; there was popular agitation for the cancellation of debts; and demobilized veterans were clamoring for their promised allotments. Periodic uprisings were put down with great brutality, but they did not cease. As Plutarch describes the mood, "Rome was in the most dangerous inclination to change on account of the unequal distribution of wealth and property. . . . There wanted but a slight impetus to set all in motion, it being in the power of any daring man to overturn a sickly commonwealth."[17]

The stage was thus set for three patrician leaders—Julius Caesar, Pompey, and Crassus—to seize power, styling themselves as champions of the people. In 60 BC, they formed a triumvirate, and began reducing the power of the Senate, the Consuls, and the Tribunes. Cicero's prestige was such that they invited him to join them as a fourth, but he declined to join an arrangement so plainly unconstitutional. They, in turn, declined to support him when cronies of Catiline took revenge by obtaining passage of a law—specifically aimed at Cicero—that retroactively sentenced to death or exile anyone who had condemned a Roman citizen to death without trial. Cicero fled to Greece; his property was confiscated, and his fine home on the Palatine hill was destroyed.

Pompey eventually pardoned him and recalled him to Rome, but Cicero's opportunities for political expression under the Triumvirate were restricted. It was in this period that he wrote his dialogues *De Republica* and *De Legibus*, consciously modeled on the two Platonic dialogues he most admired, the *Republic* and *The Laws*. In the former, Cicero dismissed Plato's ideal republic as imaginary and impractical, and presented his own vision of the ideal state: The Roman state, based on an unwritten constitution developed over centuries through trial and experience, with gradual improvements as a result of reflection on what had gone before. Unlike the laws of Greek cities, which were said to be the creations of divinely inspired lawgivers like Solon and Lycurgus, the Roman system was a collective achievement. It was "based upon the genius, not of one man, but of many; it was founded, not in one generation, but in a long period of several centuries and many ages of men."[18]

Prudently, Cicero avoided direct discussion of the current regime, confining himself to general expressions of regret for the vanished virtues and customs of former times. But his message was unmistakable. Resuming his own voice, rather than using one of the dialogue partners, he deplored that citizens and statesmen alike had forgotten that "the Roman state stands upon the men and morals of old":

Before our time, ancestral morality provided outstanding men, and great men preserved the morality of old and the institutions of our ancestors. But our own time having inherited the republic like a wonderful picture that had faded over time, not only has failed to renew its original colors but has not even taken the trouble to preserve at least its shape and outlines. What remains of the morals of antiquity, upon which the Republic stood? We see that they are so outworn in oblivion that they are not only not cherished but are now unknown. What am I to say about the men? The morals themselves have passed away through a shortage of men. It is because of our own vices, not because of some bad luck, that we preserve the Republic in name only but have long ago lost its substance.[19]

De Republica contains some of Cicero's most memorable prose. In the passages known as *Scipio's Dream*, Scipio is transported to a place high among the stars where he meets his late father who speaks to him of the best way of life:

Human beings were born on condition that they should look after that sphere called earth which you see in the middle of this celestial space. A soul was given to them out of those eternal fires which you call stars and planets. . . . You must not depart from human life until you receive the command from him who has given you that soul; otherwise you will be judged to have deserted the earthly post assigned to you by God. . . . Respect justice and do your duty. That is important in the case of parents and relatives, and paramount in the case of one's country. That is the way of life which leads to heaven and to the company here of those who have already completed their lives.[20]

From that place, says Scipio, "As I studied everything, it all seemed to me glorious and marvelous. There were stars we never see from here and their size was such as we never suspected; the smallest one was the one furthest from the heavens and closest to the earth and shone with borrowed light. The globes of the stars easily surpassed the size of the earth, and earth itself now seemed so small to me that I was ashamed of our empire, which touches only a little speck of it."

Dante would later pay homage to that passage in his *Divine Comedy* where, looking down on the earth from the summit of paradise, he says:

> I turned my eyes down through all the seven spheres
> And I saw this globe of ours such
> That I smiled at its mean appearance.
> And I approve that opinion as best which esteems it of least
> account; so that those who think of something else can be called
> righteous.[21]

The fruitful period of writing and reflection that yielded Cicero's best-known works came to an end when the Triumvirate decreed that all qualified ex-officials who had not yet governed a province should do so. As a former Consul, Cicero had no choice but to accept a foreign posting. To his annoyance, he was sent to remote Cilicia in the southern part of present-day Turkey. He made the best of the situation, however, conscientiously applying himself to administrative tasks, and consoling himself with the thought that the assignment was only of a year's duration.

Meanwhile, Rome was edging toward civil war. Caesar and Pompey had fallen out, Pompey aligning himself with the Senate and Caesar championing the cause of the people. Cicero preferred Pompey as more likely to restore the Republic, but he avoided open confrontation with Caesar, for whom he had more personal regard and with whom he shared intellectual interests. When Caesar emerged victorious from that conflict two years later, he once again solicited Cicero's support. But Cicero still could not bring himself to cooperate in what he viewed as the destruction of republican institutions.

During Caesar's dictatorship, Cicero continued with his literary work, keeping a low profile. But he missed his old life. To his son, he lamented, "Now that the Senate has been abolished and the courts annihilated, what work in keeping with my position is there for me to do either in the Senate or the Forum? Once I lived with great crowds around me, in the forefront of the Roman public eye. But now I shun the sight of the scoundrels who swarm on every side."[22] To his brother Quintus, Cicero gave full vent to his feelings of regret and frustration:

I am tortured, dearest brother, tortured, by the fact that we no longer have a constitution in the state or justice in the courts, and that at my age, when I ought to be at the height of my influence in the Senate, I am distracted by legal work or sustained by private study. And the eager hope I have had since I was a boy—'Always to be the best and far to excel all others'—has been destroyed. Some of my enemies I could not attack, others I have defended. I am unable to give free rein to either my opinions or my hatreds.[23]

Though Cicero did not participate in the conspiracy to assassinate Julius Caesar in 44 BC, he approved the coup as necessary. In the turmoil following that event, he emerged as a popular and widely respected elder statesman figure and was chosen as the spokesman for the Senate. In that position, Cicero, along with the surviving Consul, Mark Antony, was briefly one of the two most powerful men in Rome. But when Caesar's heir and adopted son, Octavian, began to challenge Antony, Cicero was again faced with a choice of which man to support when neither offered much hope for the preservation of republican institutions. The more Antony's ambitions revealed themselves, the more Cicero came to regret that Caesar's assassins had not disposed of Antony as well on the Ides of March.[24] But Octavian was an unknown quantity, only nineteen years old. Eventually, Cicero gambled on Octavian's youth and possible malleability. He began whipping up sentiment against Antony in a series of fourteen scathing speeches known as his Philippics.

Those polemics, brilliant as they were, proved to be Cicero's undoing. In a surprising turn of events, Octavian came to an understanding with Antony. Then, as Plutarch recounts, "The young man, once established and possessed of the office of Consul, bade Cicero farewell, and reconciling himself to Antony and Lepidus, joined his power with theirs and divided the government like a piece of property with them."[25] When Antony, eager for revenge, insisted that Cicero be put to death, Octavian did nothing to intervene. Once again, Cicero prepared to go into exile, but he did not move quickly enough. He was hunted down, captured, and killed in December 43 BC. His head and, by Antony's order, the hands that wrote the Philippics were cut off and put on display in the Forum.

Possibly Octavian felt some shame about his role in the affair, for, years later, when he was Augustus Caesar and ruler of the Roman Empire, he came upon his grandson reading a volume of Cicero's. As Plutarch tells the story, the boy attempted to hide the book under his clothes, but Augustus took the book and stood for a long time leafing through it. Then he handed it back to the boy, saying, "My child, this was a learned man, a learned man, and a lover of his country."[26]

The rich trove of Cicero's surviving letters—over 800 items, most of them never meant for publication—remains one of the most important sources of information about Roman life in the turbulent first century before Christ. Together with Cicero's writings on politics, these letters also provide a fascinating glimpse of how this ambitious "new man" thought about many of the issues that young persons with political aspirations ponder today.

"HOW SHOULD I 'PACKAGE' MYSELF?"

Every autumn, a remarkable metamorphosis takes place in American law schools, as the second- and third-year students ready themselves for the job market. As the fall foliage reaches the peak of color, the garb of future lawyers turns dark navy, charcoal grey, and basic black. The alterations in their clothing, hairstyles—and sometimes even teeth and noses—can be so drastic as to make it difficult to recognize the young man or woman one once knew. Occasionally, less often now than in the past, someone adopts a new name in time for it to appear on his or her diploma.

In Cicero's case, many of his friends urged him to change his surname, which they regarded as insufficiently dignified for a rising politician.[27] Apparently, the name derived from an ancestor who had a protuberance like a chick pea (*cicer*) on the end of his nose. It is some indication of young Marcus Tullius's self-confidence that he brushed off his friends' advice, declaring that he planned to make the name Cicero more famous than those of the celebrated statesman Scaurus (knobby ankles) and the military commander Catulus (puppy).

What Cicero did decide to change was his speaking style. It was not only the delicate state of his health, but a highly developed capacity for self-criticism that impelled him to interrupt his legal career after a promising start, and to devote two full years to refining his techniques and sharpening his intellect.

"POLITICS IS A DIRTY BUSINESS"

In late Republican Rome, as in present-day America, many of the most capable citizens were declining to enter public life, some out of disgust with the state of politics, others to take advantage of opportunities to live a private life in comfort and luxury. Epicurean philosophy was much in vogue among members of Rome's traditional ruling class, with its teaching that a wise man best preserves his freedom by avoiding involvement in public affairs. Cicero did not—indeed could not—dispute those who claimed that the Roman public square was filled with corrupt characters. Instead he turned their objection around, saying: "What stronger reason could brave and high-minded men have for entering politics than the determination not to give in to the wicked, and not to allow the state to be torn apart by such people?"[28]

Cicero's closest friend Atticus was one who opted for a life in the private sphere. Atticus was the heir to a great fortune, a man whose wealth, intelligence, amiability, and lineage would have assured him an easy entry into a political career. He was intensely interested in politics, and astute enough to be a valued advisor to Cicero, but he remained aloof from direct involvement in the controversies of the day, assuming the posture of a friend to all and ally to none. He survived with wealth intact through the civil wars and changing regimes of Late Republican Rome. As an old man, he cited Cicero's misfortunes as prime examples of the ingratitude, betrayals, and disappointments that an honest man was likely to meet in politics.[29] But for Cicero, if we can believe what he said in his preface to *De Republica*, all those disadvantages were outweighed by the honor and satisfaction of a life devoted to one's country and one's fellow men.[30]

"IS THE LIFE OF A POLITICIAN COMPATIBLE WITH A SATISFYING PRIVATE LIFE?"

In Cicero's case, the answer seems to have been "yes," in the sense that the satisfactions and disappointments of his personal life were of the sort that anyone could experience, in or out of the public square. His marriage to Terentia seems not to have been particularly close, but it lasted for thirty years before they divorced and went their separate ways. His son Marcus was something of a ne'er-do-well, but Cicero did his best to be supportive of him. His greatest source of joy was his daughter Tullia ("in face, speech and mind my very image").[31] Cicero delighted in her company and conversation, and nearly went mad with grief when she died at age 30 from complications of childbirth. He sent away his second wife Publilia, to whom he had been married only a few weeks when that tragedy occurred, apparently because she did not share his anguish.

Cicero did lament the loneliness of a life lived in the public eye, depending heavily on his brother Quintus and the loyal Atticus for counsel and companionship. On one occasion when both confidants were away from Rome, Cicero's letter to Atticus reminds one of Harry Truman's famous saying, "If you want a friend in Washington, get a dog."

> There is nothing I need so much at the moment as the one man with whom I can share all the problems which cause me some concern, that affectionate and wise friend with whom I can converse without hypocrisy, pretence or reserve. My brother is away, and where are you? I am so deserted by all that the only relaxation I have is spent with my wife, my dear daughter, and my darling son Cicero, for those self-seeking bogus friendships of mine exist in the bright light of public life, but they lack the rewards bestowed by my household. I go down to the Forum surrounded by droves of friends, but in the whole crowd I can find no one to whom I can make an unguarded joke or let out a friendly sigh.[32]

"WILL I LOSE SIGHT OF MY HIGHEST AIMS, BETRAY MY PRINCIPLES, EVEN LOSE MY SOUL AS I STRIVE TO GET AND KEEP PUBLIC OFFICE?"

Throughout his career, Cicero agonized about the kinds of concerns that keep many of the most principled young men and women from entering politics today. He struggled constantly with whether, when, and how far to compromise for the sake of advancing his most cherished cause—the preservation of the traditional system that he called republican. In "On Duties," he pondered the difficulty of deciding what to do when apparent right clashes with apparent advantage.[33] Some situations, he said, are perplexingly difficult to assess. Sometimes a course of action generally regarded as wrong turns out right. Sometimes a step that looks natural and right may turn out not to be right after all. Like Aristotle, who taught that in the realm of human affairs one can know only partially, and for the most part, Cicero said he belonged to the school of thought that requires one to seek the highest possible degree of probability, recognizing that the limitations inherent in political life make certainty impossible.[34] The statesman, unlike the philosopher, must act, and he must act within the range of what is possible, aiming for the best, while realizing that he must often settle for less.

On one occasion, after being criticized for vacillation, Cicero wrote to a friend, "Unchanging consistency of standpoint has never been considered a virtue in great statesmen. At sea it is good sailing to run before the gale, even if the ship cannot make harbor; but if she *can* make harbor by changing tack, only a fool would risk shipwreck by holding the original course rather than change it and still reach his destination."[35]

Cicero's career saw many changes of tack. They were viewed by some as prudent responses to shifts in the political environment, and were denounced by others as expedient, cowardly, or hypocritical. By his own account, there were occasions when he failed to live up to his own publicly professed standards. In private correspondence, he often berated himself for falling short of his own ideals. But he never abandoned his efforts to preserve republican principles from the encroachments of dictatorship on the one hand and mob rule on the other. Often he did so at great personal risk. In the end, his opposition to Antony cost him his life.

"COULD I REALLY MAKE A DIFFERENCE UNDER PRESENT CIRCUMSTANCES, OR ARE CONDITIONS SUCH THAT MY EFFORTS WOULD PROBABLY BE WASTED?"

Cicero does not seem to have fretted over these questions that are now so much discussed—even though, with hindsight, it is hard to see how anything that he might have done could have held back the forces that were destroying the institutions he valued. He always sought opportunities to shift probabilities in favor of republican laws and institutions, and seems only occasionally to have allowed himself to imagine that his efforts might be in vain. One day during Julius Caesar's dictatorship he wrote to a friend that "not even hope survives that things will at some time improve," yet a few days later we find him urging another correspondent "to contemplate, as I myself do, the obligation, if some sort of republic survives, of becoming a leader by virtue of the judgment of the citizens and the reality of the situation."[36] It was only toward the very end of his life, in his last letter to Atticus, that he conceded, "As for the Republic, even Hippocrates forbids medical treatment in hopeless cases."[37]

Though Cicero always thought of himself as first and foremost a statesman, his most significant legacy was arguably his compendium in Latin of the teachings of the various schools of Greek philosophy. He lived in an age when Greek and Roman traditions were coming together in a great dynamic synthesis that was to nourish Western philosophy, politics, and law for centuries. No one played a more essential role in forging that fertile synthesis than Cicero himself. His compendium was one of the most important means through which the heritage of Greek philosophy was preserved for posterity.

One dramatic example is Saint Augustine's famous account of how an encounter with a work of Cicero changed his life when he was nineteen years old:

> Following the usual course of study I had already come across a book by a certain Cicero, whose language (but not his message) almost everyone admires. That book of his contains an exhortation to study philosophy; it is called the *Hortensius*. This book indeed changed my whole way of feeling. It changed my prayers, Lord, to be towards you yourself. It gave me different plans and desires. Suddenly all vain aspirations lost their value; and I was left with an unbelievable fire in my heart, desiring the deathless qualities of wisdom. I began to rise up to return to you.[38]

Because Cicero made no claims to originality, he is sometimes paid the back-handed compliment of being called the world's most effective popularizer of Greek knowledge. But that is to greatly underrate his achievement. Only someone with Cicero's deep understanding of the works of the Greeks could have synthesized their leading ideas and methods, and only someone with his analytical and rhetorical skills could have related that body of knowledge to Rome's very different political conditions in a form that appealed to the practical-minded Romans.

What rendered this task especially difficult was the fact that the Latin of his day had neither the vocabulary nor the suppleness to render abstract speculative thought intelligible to Roman readers. An important part of Cicero's achievement was thus the expansion of the capabilities of the Latin language. Elizabeth Rawson, the author of a fine biography of Cicero, notes that the terms "quality," "essence," and "moral," (*qualitas, essentia,* and *moralis*), for example, come from Latin words first found in Cicero that were directly modeled on Greek originals.[39]

The magnitude of those intellectual accomplishments was recognized in Cicero's own lifetime by no less a personage than Caesar himself, who once said that Cicero merited greater laurels than a general because it was a greater thing to have extended the frontiers of the Roman genius than of its empire.[40]

Nor should one underrate Cicero's contributions to the fund of ideas about liberty, equality, limited government, and the rule of law that have become hallmarks of Western law and political theory. He gave memorable form and expression to the concept of a universal natural law applicable to all human beings (including slaves and foreigners). He held that there is a spark of divinity in man that gives dignity to every human being, and that requires all human beings to treat each other decently. He affirmed that all human beings are brothers, regardless of race or status. And he insisted on the social nature of human beings: "Our species is not made up of solitary individuals or lonely wanderers."[41] There is, he wrote, "an innate desire on the part of human beings to form communities. As I have said before, and it needs constant repetition, there is a bond of community that links every man in the world with every other."[42]

Eighteen centuries would pass before another man would achieve comparable eminence in politics, while leaving such a lasting mark on political philosophy. Edmund Burke, too, was a "new man," an outsider whose meteoric rise in politics was due not to wealth or birth, but to his own gifts and accomplishments. And as we shall see, Burke, like Cicero, ultimately failed to advance the cause that was closest to his heart.

THREE

Justinian, Tribonian, and Irnerius

HOW STATESMEN AND SCHOLARS RESCUED ROMAN LAW (TWICE)

Roman, remember by your strength to rule
Earth's peoples—for your arts are to be these:
To pacify, to impose the rule of law,
To spare the conquered, battle down the proud.
Aeneid, VI, 1151–1154

The Romans were set apart from all other peoples in the ancient world by their intense interest in law and administration. Greek philosophers wrote learnedly on politics, but ancient Greece had no specialized legal profession and no body of scholars who made a systematic study of law. Though some Greek cities, Sparta in particular, were known for good laws, none of them separated the administration of justice from other aspects of government.

Rome—no one knows just why—developed a distinctive set of legal arrangements that would become one of the wonders of the world. As early as the fifth century before Christ, the Romans began to arrange their hodge-podge of unwritten customs and official decrees into a coherent system. Over time, that system evolved into a sophisticated body of norms and procedures that would serve two great civilizations separated by over a thousand years—ancient Rome and Renaissance Europe. Remarkably, Roman law concepts still form the basis for the world's largest family of legal systems—those based on the Romano-Germanic civil law.[1]

The earliest known Roman codification, the Twelve Tables (ca. 450 BC), emphasized what today's lawyers call civil procedure. For example: "If a man call another to law, and he go not, he shall be seized"; "Where they settle the matter, let it be told"; "After mid-day, the cause shall be adjudged to the party present, if the other shall fail to appear." The rules it set forth were concise, formalistic, and simple. Yet, Cicero, looking back at the Twelve Tables centuries later, declared with patriotic pride, "They amuse the mind by the remembrance of old words, and the portrait of ancient manners; they inculcate the soundest principles of government and morals; and I am not afraid to affirm that the brief composition of the Decimvirs surpasses in genuine value the libraries of Grecian philosophy."[2] As examples of the "splendid laws" that originated in the Twelve Tables, Cicero cited the prohibition against legislation aimed at specific individuals and the requirement that rulings regarding a citizen's life can only be issued by the chief assembly.[3] Gibbon tells us that the Romans long revered those early laws, engraved them on tablets, and required young people to memorize them.[4]

As Rome became a busy commercial center, and later the hub of a vast empire, its legal system grew ever more complex. Eventually, there was a need for the specialized services of persons who knew their way around the system and could advise others. By the third century BC, a class of patricians known as jurisconsults had emerged. These legal experts were the first members of a species that future generations would bless and curse, but that no advanced society can do without: professional lawyers.

From the rise of the Roman Republic until the disintegration of its far-flung imperial domain, the city on the Tiber bustled with legal activity. The Forum not only served as a meeting place for popular assemblies that enacted laws, but was also the site of the law courts. In that once-magnificent space, where stray cats now roam among the ruins, the most important laws were publicly displayed on bronze plaques for all to see and know. On days when some silver-tongued advocate held forth, large crowds of spectators would gather there to enjoy the arguments. Cicero himself has left us a description of the scene that greeted a famous orator:

> When it is known that he is going to speak, the benches are crowded, the tribunal full, the clerks are influential in giving or allowing space, there is a crowd of bystanders, the jury is all anticipation. When the speaker rises, the bystanders signal for silence, there are frequent expressions of agreement and admiration. They laugh as he desires, they weep as he desires. Even from a distance it is possible to tell, though one does not know what is going on, that the speaker is a success, and a Roscius is on the stage.[5]

In the early years of the Republic, the leading advocates did not put much of a premium on technical legal knowledge. Like many of today's celebrated courtroom lawyers, they were hired mainly for their rhetorical skills. When they needed to be briefed on the finer points of law, they relied on the expert jurisconsults. Gibbon gives us a glimpse of the jurisconsults as they plied their trade in Republican Rome:

> On the public days of market or assembly the masters of the art were seen walking in the Forum, ready to impart the needful advice to the meanest of their fellow-citizens, from whose votes, on a future occasion, they might solicit a grateful return. As their years and honors increased, they seated themselves at home on a chair or throne, to expect with patient gravity, the visits of their clients, who at the dawn of the day, from the town and country, began to thunder at their door. The duties of social life and the incidents of judicial proceeding were the ordinary subject of these consultations, and the verbal or written opinion of the jurisconsults was framed according to the rules of prudence and law.[6]

For most of the Republican period, the jurisconsults enjoyed less prestige than orator-advocates like Hortensius and Cicero. The orators, in
fact, regarded detailed knowledge of the law as somewhat beneath
them. Cicero is supposed to have boasted that he could, if he wished,
make himself a jurisconsult in three days.[7]

The influence and status of the jurisconsults grew, however, along
with Rome's prosperity and administrative apparatus. By the time the
Republican era drew to a close, the jurisconsults had acquired such a
monopoly on technical information and legal experience that their
services were indispensable, not only in connection with litigation, but
for drafting documents and resolving disputes about property, inheritance, contracts, sales, loans, mortgages, agency, liability for damage,
and a host of other matters. Law schools were established, and legal
treatises began to appear. With the growth of the Roman empire, professional judges replaced the lay arbiters and assemblies before whom
the great orators had performed. The career magistrates, known as
praetors, regularly turned to the jurisconsults for advice, especially in
cases involving novel or difficult issues. Through this advisory role,
which often took the form of drafting opinions for the magistrates, the
jurisconsults kept in close touch with the courts. Their prestige
attained its peak under the Emperor Augustus when the formal opinions of officially certified jurisconsults were made binding on judges
in civil cases.

From its relatively primitive beginnings in the Twelve Tables,
the law of Rome matured into an impressive body of practical wisdom. Over a thousand years later, the English common law would
evolve in much the same incremental fashion, as decisions in concrete cases were collected and systematized. In Rome, this process
of systematization reached its fullest development in what is known
as the Classical period of Roman law, beginning in the early second
century AD.

The Classical period saw the emergence of a high legal culture—a
"learned and splendid age of jurisprudence," as Gibbon called it.[8]
Eminent jurists produced treatises in which they arranged and classi-
fied general principles drawn from opinions rendered by jurisconsults
to praetors. Among them, the names of Ulpian, Papinian, and Gaius

are chiefly remembered. These writers developed a distinctive vocabulary and style, coining maxims and terms of art that caught on and endured. "Their philosophic spirit," wrote Gibbon, "mitigated the rigor of antiquity and simplified the forms of proceeding."[9]

Papinian, perhaps the greatest of the classical jurists, was also the first lawyer known to have been put to death for refusing to endorse a monarch's misdeeds. This distant forerunner of Thomas More was executed in 212 AD by the Emperor Caracalla after he declined to write a legal opinion justifying Caracalla's assassination of his brother and co-emperor with whom he did not wish to share the throne. Gibbon, recounting the tale, tells us that even the philosopher Seneca had once lowered himself to compose such an opinion letter, but that Papinian "did not hesitate between the loss of life and that of honor."[10] Gibbon wrote admiringly that, "Such intrepid virtue which had escaped pure and unsullied from the intrigues of courts, the habits of business and the arts of his profession, reflects more lustre on the memory of Papinian than all his great employments, his numerous writings, and the superior reputation as a lawyer which he has preserved through every age of the Roman jurisprudence."

At its height, classical Roman law constituted a useful body of knowledge of a kind the world had not seen before. The work of the jurisconsults in that period was described by the twentieth-century scholar John Henry Wigmore as "of momentous significance, for it marks the dawn of legal science in the world."[11] Never before had jurists drawn general principles from the mass of rules and decisions and arranged them into a system that carried forward the best practices of the past, promoting predictability while leaving room for adaptation to new circumstances.

The Classical period of Roman law came to an end in the era of anarchy, invasions, plague, and civil wars that began around 235 AD. For a time, the legal profession continued to expand, but its professional standards deteriorated. In Gibbon's portrait of a declining profession in a dying empire, there is much to make a modern lawyer wince:

After a regular course of education, which lasted five years, the students dispersed themselves through the provinces in search of fortune and honors; nor could they want an inexhaustible supply of business in a great empire already corrupted by the multiplicity of laws, of arts, and of vices. . . . The honor of a liberal profession has indeed been vindicated by ancient and modern advocates, who have filled the most important stations with pure integrity and consummate wisdom; but in the decline of Roman jurisprudence the ordinary promotion of lawyers was pregnant with mischief and disgrace. The noble art, which had once been preserved as the sacred inheritance of the patricians, was fallen into the hands of freedmen and plebeians, who, with cunning rather than with skill, exercised a sordid and pernicious trade. Some of them procured admittance into families for the purpose of fomenting differences. . . . Others, recluse in their chambers, maintained the gravity of legal professors, by furnishing a rich client with subtleties to confound the plainest truth. . . . The splendid and popular class was composed of the advocates, who filled the Forum with the sound of their turgid and loquacious rhetoric. Careless of fame and of justice, they are described for the most part as ignorant and rapacious guides, who conducted their clients through a maze of expense, of delay, and of disappointment; from whence, after a tedious series of years, they were at length dismissed, when their patience and fortune were almost exhausted.[12]

In the chaos that accompanied the invasion of the western Roman empire by Germanic tribes, nearly all the ancient legal sources were permanently lost. Of the vast Roman legal inheritance, accumulated over the ten centuries from the Twelve Tables to the sack of Rome in 410 A.D., the only law book that survives today in relatively complete form is Gaius's *Institutes*, a short textbook for law students. That work, too, disappeared for centuries until a nineteenth-century German scholar discovered it on a palimpsest, an ancient parchment that had been over-written by a medieval monk.[13]

How, then, does it happen that we know as much as we do about the legal system that served the ancient Romans for a thousand years?

The answer involves a collaboration between an extraordinary statesman and an extraordinary scholar: Justinian I, the Christian Emperor
of Byzantium, and his chief legal advisor, Tribonian.

By the time Justinian ascended to the throne of the eastern Roman
Empire in 527 AD, the empire in the West had long been vanquished.
Roman law was still applied in the Eastern realm, but the problem of
access to legal materials was severe. As Gibbon described the situation, "the infinite variety of laws and legal opinions had filled many
thousand volumes, which no fortune could purchase and no capacity
could digest. Books could not easily be found; and the judges, poor in
the midst of riches, were reduced to the exercise of their illiterate discretion."[14] The administration of justice was in such a shambles that
Justinian, who had studied jurisprudence himself, determined to
make its reform a top priority.

To bring order out of accumulated legal chaos, Justinian called
upon the most learned legal scholars of the East—professors, practicing lawyers, and judges. He placed the whole enterprise under the
direction of one Tribonian, a man of such remarkable gifts that Gibbon
compared him to Francis Bacon: "This extraordinary man . . . was a
native of Side in Pamphilia; and his genius, like that of Bacon,
embraced as his own, all the business and knowledge of the age."[15]
Tribonian's writings ranged over philosophy, political theory, poetry,
and astronomy, as well as law. A talented, ambitious man of low birth,
Tribonian had worked his way up through the legal profession to
become the Emperor's chief legal advisor. Along the way, he accumulated a fair number of enemies who accused him of taking bribes, and,
at least according to Gibbon, there was some evidence that he had
occasionally been "swayed by gifts in the administration of justice." It
was also rumored that he harbored a secret aversion to the Christian
faith. But the Emperor's confidence in him never wavered.[16]

One of Justinian's first acts as emperor had been to appoint a
commission to prepare a new legislative code suitable for the circumstances of the time. That task, which required sifting through a moun-
tainous accumulation of imperial legislation, was accomplished with
remarkable speed, thanks in part to Tribonian, who was one of the
commission's most diligent members. The new code went into effect

in 530, replacing all previous legislation. In recognition of Tribonian's work on the codification commission, he was given the office of Quaestor, with the duty of drafting new legislation.[17]

Historians disagree about whether it was Justinian or Tribonian who then conceived the idea of synthesizing the enormous bulk of Roman legal material in their possession with a view toward making it more usable. But there is no doubt about the Emperor's enthusiasm for the project. In December 530, disregarding legal experts who protested that the task would be impossible, and that it would take ten years just to read the material, Justinian launched the project that would assure his lasting fame. He appointed Tribonian the president of a sixteen-member commission to prepare a comprehensive digest of the opinions of the most important Roman law writers from the past.

The formal instructions given by Justinian to Tribonian began by noting the magnitude and difficulty of the task ahead:[18]

> *THE EMPEROR CAESAR FLAVIUS JUSTINIANUS—*
> *PIOUS, FORTUNATE, RENOWNED, CONQUEROR AND*
> *TRIUMPHER, EVER AUGUSTUS—GREETS TRIBONIAN*
> *HIS QUAESTOR:*

> *Governing under the authority of God our empire which was delivered to us by the Heavenly Majesty, we both conduct wars successfully and render peace honorable, and we uphold the condition of the state. . . .*

> *1. Whereas nothing in any sphere is found so worthy of study as the authority of law, which sets in good order affairs both divine and human and casts out all injustice, yet we have found the whole extent of our laws which has come down from the foundation of the city of Rome and the days of Romulus to be so confused that it extends to an inordinate length and is beyond the comprehension of any human nature. . . .*

> *2. . . . In our haste to extricate ourselves from minor and more trivial affairs and attain to a completely full revision of the law, and*

to collect and amend the whole set of Roman ordinances and present the diverse books of so many authors in a single volume (a thing which no one has dared to expect or to desire) the task appeared to us most difficult, indeed impossible.

Nevertheless, Justinian continued, he was determined to undertake this daunting task, "relying upon God, who in the magnitude of his goodness is able to sanction and to consummate achievements that are utterly beyond hope."

Then, addressing Tribonian directly, he told the jurist that he had been chosen to direct the project because of his excellent work on the Code. Expressing confidence in Tribonian's judgment on how to proceed, he continued, much as a U.S. president today would address the chairperson of a new presidential council:

[W]e commanded you to select as colleagues in your task those whom you thought fit, both from the most eloquent professors and from the most able of the robed men of the highest law court. These men have now been brought together, introduced into the palace, and accepted by us on your recommendation; and we have entrusted to them the execution of the entire task, on the understanding that the whole enterprise will be carried out under your own most vigilant supervision.

He then laid out the task in general terms, saying, "We therefore command you to read and work upon the books dealing with Roman law, written by those learned men of old to which the most revered emperors gave authority to compose and interpret the laws, so that the whole substance may be extracted from them, all repetition and discrepancy being as far as possible removed, and out of them one single work may be compiled, which will suffice in place of them all." At the same time, he ordered the preparation of an elementary introductory textbook "so that the immature mind of the student, nourished on simple things, may be more easily brought to knowledge of the higher learning."

For the next three years, under Tribonian's supervision, the team of legal experts culled what they considered to be the most valuable material from some two thousand legal writings from all previous periods. They engaged in a careful process of selection and rejection, with Justinian looking over their shoulders and, by his own account, "constantly inquiring about the work in progress and acquainting Ourselves with what was doubtful." In the end, they produced a work of fifty "books" with their contents arranged under 432 topical headings. That work is now known as Justinian's *Digest*, or, in continental Europe, by its Greek name, the *Pandects*. Obedient to the Emperor's instructions, a small committee composed of Tribonian and two distinguished law professors also prepared a primer for law students. Modeled on the *Institutes* of the classical jurist Gaius, that text is known as Justinian's *Institutes*.

In December 533, in his formal address of thanks to the Tribonian commission upon completion of their work, Justinian singled out the concise *Institutes* for special praise. "As your wisdoms are aware," he said, law students had long been floundering in a sea of indigestible material. "[O]ut of all the great multitude of legal writings, extending to two thousand books and three million lines, students, on the advice of their teachers, made use of no more than six books, and those confused and very rarely containing laws of practical use; the other books had gone out of use and become inaccessible to everyone." Now, with the *Institutes* as the basis for all legal studies, the "treasures of the law" would be available to all who desired to know them. The wisdom of the ancient jurists had been channeled from all its "muddy sources into one pure reservoir by the agency of Tribonian, that glorious man, magister and ex-quaestor of our sacred palace and ex-consul, and also two of your number: Theophilus and Dorotheus, most eloquent professors." Thanks to these men, he confidently predicted, future lawyers "will prove themselves to be leading orators and servants of justice; in legal process they will be equally supreme as advocates and judges, successful everywhere and at all times."

On the same day, Justinian presented the *Digest* to the Senate and the population at large, describing it as one of the crowning achievements of his reign: "This third consulship, which God has granted to us, is the most splendid, since during it the peace with the Persians was confirmed; the book of laws, the like of which is not to be found among any of Our predecessors, was composed; and in addition a third part of the inhabited world—we are speaking of the whole of Libya—was added to Our empire."

After praising each member of the commission by name, and discussing the contents of the *Digest* in a way that displayed his own considerable legal knowledge, Justinian acknowledged that no system of law, no matter how well-designed, could anticipate the challenges of new and changing circumstances: "The character of human law is always to hasten onward, and there is nothing in it which can abide forever, since nature is eager to produce new forms. We therefore do not cease to expect that matters will henceforth arise that are not secured in legal bonds."

Concerned lest "interpretation" should undermine the great work he had accomplished, he declared that the *Digest* henceforth would have the force of law; that the old books were now superseded and must no longer be consulted; and that all adaptation to new circumstances must be accomplished by imperial legislation alone. Then, in a burst of legal hubris, he added, "No one, of those who are skilled in the law at the present day or shall be hereafter, may dare to append any commentary to these laws for fear lest their verbosity may cause such confusion in our legislation as to bring some discredit upon it." That imperial command, however, proved to be as futile as the order of the Persian King Ahasuerus who is said to have sent his soldiers to beat the waves of the sea into submission.

Once the *Digest* was completed, Justinian ordered Tribonian and his colleagues to begin work on a completely new Code, even though the ink had hardly dried on the Code of 530. In succeeding years, Justinian continued to find time for law reform amidst his military campaigns and public works (including the construction of the imposing basilica of Santa Sophia, now a museum in Istanbul). The intense period of legal activity in Byzantium came to an end only with the death of Tribonian in an outbreak of bubonic plague in 542.

The *Institutes* and the *Digest*, together with the *Code* and the *Novels* (new legislation produced after the Code), are known collectively as the *Corpus Juris Civilis*. The *Novels* were primarily concerned with the day-to-day affairs of the realm and are now mainly of historical interest. Among their features were improvements in the status of women and slaves, punishments for homosexual acts, and limitations on the rights of pagans, heretics, and Jews.[19]

Contemporary scholars of Roman law are generally as critical of Byzantine legislation as they are admiring of Roman law of the Classical period. Cambridge legal historian H. F. Jolowicz's description of the Justinian Code and Novels is withering. They were characterized, he wrote, by an insistence upon equity—not "in the restrained manner of the classical jurists, who conceived of *aequitas* as the principle of justice pervading the whole law, but with an arrogant impatience of legal subtleties. . . . [T]he Byzantine lawyer is not always capable of doing anything more than reversing the decision which he finds inequitable; he cannot put a new principle in place of the old."[20] Byzantine law was "humane" in the sense of "protecting those whom it considers weak against those whom it considers strong," but displayed "an almost pathetic confidence in the power of legislation to do away with evils of an economic character by mere prohibition."[21]

Justinian's *Digest*, by contrast, was to have lasting significance.[22] The famous opening chapter of Book I ("Justice and Law") illustrates the treatise's characteristic blend of classical Roman legal principles with Greek and Christian thought. The volume begins with a description of law as "the art of goodness and fairness."[23] Jurists are described as the priests of that art, quoting Ulpian: "For we cultivate the virtue of justice and claim awareness of what is good and fair, discriminating between fair and unfair, distinguishing lawful from unlawful, aiming to make men good not only through fear of penalties but also indeed under allurement of rewards, and affecting a philosophy which, if I am not deceived, is genuine, not a sham."

Justice is defined as "a steady and enduring will to render unto everyone his right. The basic principles of right are: to live honorably, not to harm any other person, to render to each his own. Practical wisdom in matters of right is an awareness of God's and men's affairs, knowledge of justice and injustice."[24]

Book I also introduces the distinction between public law (pertaining to the organization of the state and its relations with its subjects) and private law (governing the relations of subjects among themselves). It then proceeds to distinguish within private law between the *jus civile*, the law that a nation applies to its own citizens, and *jus gentium*, the law "which natural reason has established among all human beings." In succeeding volumes, the *Digest* goes on to treat in detail the sources of law, the status of persons, the duties of public officials, the administration of justice, civil procedure, evidence, restitution, agency, sales, sureties, gifts, wills and inheritance, guardianship, relations between masters and servants or slaves, debtors and creditors, all aspects of property, usufructs, servitudes, liability for damage to persons or property, criminal law, and military law.

Most importantly, the *Digest* and *Institutes* became the principal sources for the remarkable revival of Roman law that took rise in the eleventh century, spreading from northern Italy throughout continental Europe. It is sobering to realize that, were it not for Justinian and Tribonian, the entire corpus of Roman law would almost certainly have been lost forever. Yet, thanks to the collaboration between the Emperor and the scholar, Gibbon could say, "The vain titles of the victories of Justinian are crumbled into dust; but the name of the legislator is inscribed on a fair and lasting monument."[25]

That monument and its contents, the Roman law, came perilously close to vanishing with the Lombard, Slav, and Arab invasions that followed the reign of Justinian. In the disorder and localism of the Middle Ages, there was simply no use for a body of legal material as sophisticated as the Justinian compilations. The work disappeared for five hundred years, and might well have suffered the fate of the priceless works of antiquity that were lost in the destruction of the famous library of Alexandria. As Gibbon unkindly pointed out, "If such was the fate of the most beautiful compositions of genius, what stability could be expected for the dull and barren works of an obsolete science? The books of jurisprudence were interesting to few and entertaining to none; their value was connected with present use, and they sunk forever as soon as that use was superseded."[26]

It would be a mistake to suppose, however, that Europe was completely without Romanist legal influence during the Middle Ages. Roman conquerors and administrators, after all, had once been all over Europe, and many of the peoples they subjugated had been, to a certain extent, "Romanized."[27] Although Roman law and legal science were left stranded by the collapse of the way of life that had produced them, crude versions of Roman legal rules mingled with the customary law of the Germanic tribes. The laws of the petty kingdoms that rose and fell during the Middle Ages are sometimes described by historians as "Romanized customary laws," and sometimes as "barbarized Roman laws." The Roman element thus served both as a strand of continuity and a latent, potentially universalizing factor in what was later to become the Romano-Germanic legal tradition of continental Europe.

Toward the end of the eleventh century, a chance event led to a momentous change in the entire European legal landscape. The event was the discovery near Pisa of a manuscript copy of the *Corpus Juris Civilis*. That a single copy had somehow survived was in itself remarkable. That it was found at the very moment when Europe was ready to make use of it was fortuitous. European societies were just beginning to emerge from economic and social stagnation. Medieval customary law was not up to the challenge of meeting the host of legal needs produced by the revival of commerce and the gradual return of political order. Merchants, for example, required devices to assure the security of transactions and efficient methods of resolving disputes when legal arrangements broke down. The discovery of the Justinian compilations enabled a group of northern Italian scholars to rescue the Roman legal inheritance from oblivion, and to give it a second life.

Renaissance jurists embraced the Roman legal legacy with the same awestruck admiration that Thomas Aquinas, Maimonides, and Averroes brought to the ancient Greek philosophers. The center of the legal Renaissance was the city of Bologna, where a brilliant young scholar named Irnerius began to lecture on the Justinian *Digest* in 1088. Irnerius became a veritable evangelist for the legal accomplishments of antiquity, lauding Roman law as *ratio scripta*, written reason. Drawing ever larger audiences, he proclaimed the superiority of Roman law to the diverse welter of customs and decrees that had accumulated during the Middle Ages.

From Bologna the new learning spread to other parts of Italy. Soon, students began to arrive from all over Europe to hear the

Bolognese jurists hold forth on the *Corpus Juris Civilis*. Among these learned doctors of the law was Giovanni Calderini, whose well-educated daughters often took over his lectures when he was away from the city on diplomatic missions. Novella and Bettina Calderini were the world's first female law professors. According to local legend, they were so beautiful that they lectured from behind a screen in order to avoid distracting the students.

Classes were generally held in the professor's home, or, in the case of the most popular teachers, in an outdoor meeting place. Legal education was responsive to its consumers to a degree that today's students and professors would find difficult to imagine. The professors were hired and paid by the students, who fined them if they were unprepared or late to class, and fired them if they failed to perform up to expectations.

A major problem, however, with studies based on a five-hundred-year-old compilation of still more ancient texts was that several parts of the *Digest* were obscure. Many of the institutions and problems they treated were unfamiliar. The first generation of Bolognese legal scholars, therefore, made it their business to try to accurately interpret and explain the text. They became known as Glossators because of the annotations (glosses) they made on the margins of the *Digest*. Their memory is still honored in Bologna, where the elaborate marble *Tombe dei Glossatori* in the Piazza San Domenico and Piazza Malpighi are among that city's most imposing monuments.

The work of the Glossators in turn became the basis for the efforts of a second generation, the Commentators, who set about adapting the principles of Roman law to the circumstances and needs of their own society. They probed deeply into the rationale and underlying principles of Roman legal arrangements in order to discern their applicability to contemporary problems. Bartolus (d. 1357) is remembered as the most eminent of the Commentators.

Like the jurisconsults of Roman times, the Commentators were legal practitioners who were often called upon to give opinions in court proceedings. They were thus instrumental in bringing the revived Roman law into the everyday practice of law. Leading Commentators also wrote treatises that were influenced by the new spirit of rational inquiry and speculative dialectic that pervaded the work of Aquinas and others.

Well into the fifteenth century, law students continued to flock to Italy by the thousands from all parts of Europe—Paris and Oxford, Prague and Heidelberg, Cracow and Copenhagen. This phenomenon represented yet another example of fruitful collaboration between scholars and statesmen, for many were sent by their rulers to acquire the new legal learning so that it could be taught in their home universities and put to use in their courts. Many of these men entered the administrations of princes, municipalities, and the Church. In continental Europe (but not in England, where a powerful legal profession barred the door) a fusion took place between the medieval Romano-Germanic customary laws and the new learning based on the revived Roman law. To varying degrees, this amalgam formed the base from which all of today's civil law systems emerged.

Roman private law, refined by ancient jurisconsults, rescued by Justinian and Tribonian, revived by Bolognese Glossators and Commentators, was welcomed in Renaissance Europe. Remarkably, it won wide acceptance, not as the command of a sovereign, but on its own merits as a system of "written reason" that met the needs of increasingly complex societies. The widespread use of Roman law principles as starting points for legal reasoning by continental European courts came to be known as the "reception of Roman law." As legal historian Alan Watson put it:

> From the later eleventh century to the codification movement of the eighteenth century the most important event in western legal development was the celebrated Reception of Roman law. This occurred slowly, over a long period of time, at different times in different places and with different degrees of intensity. But what emerged was everywhere the same: a system of private law that is recognizably modern; a system with a considerable input from Roman law on substance; more especially, on structure; above all, on concepts.[28]

For early modern Europe, the practice of deciding disputes through analysis of specific problems in light of a principle based on reason and experience represented the possibility of escaping from both custom and arbitrary command—at least in the realm of private law.

The collaboration between Justinian and Tribonian was of such lasting importance that Napoleon consciously chose to imitate it when he commissioned the codification of French law. In emulation of Justinian, Napoleon appointed a four-man team headed by Jean Portalis, the best jurist of his day, to prepare a civil code that would legally unify France. As a young lawyer under the old regime, Portalis had first achieved recognition for his brilliance in advocacy and later as a learned writer who took his philosophical bearings primarily from Montesquieu.[29] No less a personage than Voltaire had praised one of Portalis's legal opinions as "a real treatise of philosophy, legislation and political morals."[30] Portalis was imprisoned during the Terror phase of the French Revolution, but survived to continue his legal career and eventually to attract the attention of Napoleon who appointed him to the Council of State.

When he undertook the supervision of the preparation of the Civil Code in 1803 at age 57, Portalis was completely blind due to cataracts in both eyes, but he threw himself into the project with vigor, aided by a remarkable memory. His colleagues not only acknowledged his preeminent role in the process, but entrusted him with writing the Report that presented the Code to the world. In the many countries where the French Civil Code was received, that report is still regarded as a masterpiece of legal literature.

The provisions of the new French code incorporated the results of a profound intellectual, political, and social revolution, but the draftsmen closely followed the traditional Roman framework they found in Justinian's *Institutes*. Like Justinian, Napoleon himself hovered over the drafting process. He personally contributed some of its most innovative provisions, such as those permitting divorce by mutual consent and the establishment of filiation by adoption.

Once the Civil Code of 1804 was complete, Napoleon vainly attempted, as Justinian before him had done, to protect it from distortion through interpretation and commentary. At his insistence, the Code specifically provided that all prior laws were abrogated, that judges were forbidden to announce general rules when deciding cases, and that judges must not refuse to decide a case "on the pretext that the law is silent, obscure, or incomplete."[31] The wise Portalis, however, knew full well that the development of the law could not be so easily forestalled. At the beginning of the drafting process, he had written: "How can one hold back the action of time? How can the course of events be opposed, or the gradual improvement of mores?"[32] Napoleon lived long enough to realize that Portalis was right, but unlike Portalis, he did not regard the process with equanimity. As commentaries accumulated and judges began to re-introduce elements of the old law in the guise of interpretation, the Emperor is supposed to have remarked ruefully that, after Hercules had cleaned the Augean stables, "there were replacements."

In exile on St. Helena, Napoleon called the French Civil Code a greater achievement than all his military conquests: "My true glory is not that I have won forty battles; Waterloo will wipe out their memory, but my civil code will live forever."[33] And indeed, though France has had many constitutions, the Napoleonic Civil Code, much amended, remains in effect. It is still considered by many to be the true constitution of France.

Just as ancient Roman law had been introduced into the conquered territories of a vast empire, the French Civil Code was imposed by Napoleon and his armies on Belgium, the Netherlands, parts of Poland, Italy, and the western regions of Germany. Later, in the colonial era, France further extended her legal influence—to parts of the Near East, to Northern and sub-Saharan Africa, Indochina, Oceania, French Guyana and the French Caribbean islands. It speaks volumes for the genius of Portalis and his colleagues that the influence of French law outlived both the Napoleonic conquests and French colonialism. The Code was so widely admired that most of those former colonies and conquered territories retained it even after French armies and colonial governments had departed. It was also influential in many countries that had been untouched by French military or colonial power.

Today, Justinian's compilation lives on as part of the genetic inheritance, so to speak, of the world's largest family of legal systems. As explained by Alan Watson:

[T]he *Corpus Juris Civilis* has been without doubt the most important and influential collection of secular legal materials that the world has ever known. The compilation preserved Roman law for succeeding generations and nations. All later Western systems borrowed extensively from it. But even more significantly, that strand of the Western tradition encompassing the so-called civil law systems—the law of Western continental Europe, Latin America, the parts of Africa and other continents which were former colonies of continental European powers, and to some extent Scotland, Quebec, Louisiana, Sri Lanka and South Africa—derives its concepts, approaches, structure, and systematics of private law primarily from the long centuries of theoretical study and putting into practice of the *Corpus Juris Civilis*.[34]

What a remarkable tribute to the practical wisdom and ingenuity of the ancient Romans who devised so many useful methods for regulating the relations of citizens with one another!

The body of law that governs the relations between citizens and the state, however, was another matter. Nearly all the Roman jurisprudence that was received and incorporated into later legal systems concerns private law—contracts, torts, property, procedure, remedies, and the like. Public law, the rules that involve the state in its various functions, was regarded as the preserve of the prince, prudently left aside by jurists. When Niccolò Machiavelli sat down in the sixteenth century to write a book of advice for new princes, neither Roman law nor Greek philosophy figured prominently in his calculations.

FOUR

Advising the Prince

THE ENIGMA OF MACHIAVELLI

Niccolò Machiavelli's position as a Florentine civil servant and roving diplomat gave him a front row seat from which to observe politics in action. Unlike Plato, who ventured only sporadically into public life, Machiavelli enjoyed a political career that was remarkably successful so long as his friends were in power. While still a young man, Machiavelli exercised major civic responsibilities in his native city, and was entrusted with diplomatic missions that brought him into contact with the leading military and political figures of his time.

And what a turbulent time it was. All during Machiavelli's life (1469–1527), the Italian peninsula was wracked by warfare among its numerous city-states, duchies and principalities. These local wars, mostly fought by hired mercenaries, weakened the Italian states and made them tempting targets for foreign incursions from France, Spain, and Austria. Political turmoil within the various cities increased their vulnerability.

Florence was no exception. In 1494, rebels aided by France overthrew the city's ruling family, the Medici, and established a republic.

The new regime was dominated for a time by a charismatic Dominican friar, Girolamo Savonarola, whose studies of Roman history had led him to believe that republican government would foster virtue among the citizens. Savonarola had gained a large following by preaching against the spread of vice and worldliness, even daring to speak out against immorality in the notoriously corrupt court of Pope Alexander VI. In 1497, he organized a famous "bonfire of the vanities" in which items associated with moral laxity—mirrors, cosmetics, fancy dresses, lewd books, pictures, and statues—were piled up and burned in the Piazza della Signoria. It is said that many valuable works of art, including some by Botticelli, were committed to the flames.

Before long, however, the Florentines were as fed up with the monk's moral severity as they had been with Medici corruption. As one historian put it, Savonarola "desired a free government to promote religious reform; and the Florentines accepted religious reform, only for the better consolidation of a free government."[1] So when irate members of the papal Curia called for their insolent critic to be silenced, the city fathers were only too ready to cooperate. They arrested the over-zealous reformer and charged him with heresy. In 1498, Savonarola himself was burned to death in the Piazza della Signoria. The Florentines threw his ashes into the Arno, and resumed their old ways. For the next fourteen years, however, Florence enjoyed the broadly representative republican form of government that he had helped to put in place.

Enter twenty-nine-year-old Niccolò Machiavelli. His genteel family had provided him with a good education, but their impecunious circumstances meant that he would have to make his own way in the world. As it happened, his lack of connections proved to be an asset in the eyes of the new Florentine government. They offered a staff position to Machiavelli in preference to others who had more experience but also carried more political baggage.

His intelligence, energy, and readiness to take on any assignment were such that the city officials entrusted him from the beginning with important responsibilities.[2] He soon gained a promotion to the post of Secretary to the city's Ten of War, the body responsible for foreign and diplomatic relations. In that capacity, he traveled far and wide, gathering information and writing reports related to the security of Florence. He did this job so well that he became the trusted right-hand man of Piero Soderini, who in 1502 had been named the head (*Gonfaloniere*) of the Florentine republic.

Over the years, Machiavelli's diplomatic missions brought him to the courts of King Louis XII of France, the Borgia Pope Alexander VI, the Medici Pope Julius II, the formidable Countess of Forlì Caterina Sforza, and the Holy Roman Emperor Maximilian. As he went about his business, he observed the workings of the various types of government, studied the character of powerful leaders, and reached certain conclusions about how political power could be won, maintained, and lost.

Of all the personages he encountered, none fascinated him more than Cesare Borgia, a larger-than-life figure whose military prowess, cunning, and ruthlessness awed and terrified his contemporaries. Cesare was the illegitimate son of Pope Alexander VI, and with his father's aid had assembled a dominion for himself by conquering a number of towns in central Italy. In the process, he made liberal use of bribes, torture, and murder to eliminate opposition.

Despite the man's legendary cruelty, he struck Machiavelli as a leader who might be strong enough to unite warring Italian factions and repel foreign armies. In a confidential report to the Ten of War after his first meeting with Cesare Borgia, Machiavelli, then only twenty-seven, described him as "superhuman in his courage" and enormously self-confident. He told his superiors that Cesare was a man "who must now be regarded as a new power in Italy."[3] The report went on to warn the Florentine rulers that:

> This lord is most splendid and magnificent and is so vigorous
> in military matters that there is no undertaking so great that it
> does not seem a minor thing to him; he never ceases from
> seeking glory or enlarging his state, and he fears no effort or
> danger: he arrives in a place before it has been noticed that he
> set out from another; his soldiers love him; he has recruited
> the best men in Italy; and all of this makes him victorious and

formidable, to which we should add that he is perpetually lucky.[4]

The brutal soldier's fortunes swiftly declined, however, when both he and his father were stricken with tertian fever, a severe form of malaria, in the summer of 1503. Pope Alexander VI died after only three days of illness, and Cesare was left too debilitated to deal effectively with an unexpected event that created a serious challenge to his power. Pope Alexander's successor, Pius III, had been a compromise candidate acceptable to the Borgia faction in the papal conclave. Pius died suddenly, however, after just twenty-six days in office. Unfortunately for Cesare, one of the leading candidates to succeed the short-lived pontiff was an implacable enemy of the Borgias—Giuliano della Rovere, who had been forced by Alexander to live in exile for ten years.

Cesare, though weakened by illness, still wielded considerable influence among the Cardinal-electors. Machiavelli, who was present in Rome as an observer, reported to the Florentine Signoria that "Duke Valentino" (a reference to Cesare Borgia's title of Duke of Valentinois) "is much cultivated by those who wish to be Pope . . . and many cardinals have been to talk to him every day in the Castle, so that it is thought that whoever becomes Pope will be indebted to him, and he lives in hope of being favored by the new Pope."[5]

Della Rovere, determining that he would need Cesare's support, swallowed his pride and made a number of promises, including that Cesare would be appointed to head the papal armies. Inexplicably, the man who himself had broken any number of promises took the bait. In one of the shortest conclaves on record, Giuliano della Rovere was elected Pope Julius II.

Machiavelli scented trouble ahead as soon as he heard of the arrangement. "The Duke," he wrote to his superiors, "allows himself to be carried away by his brave confidence, and believes that other people's words are more to be relied upon than his own."[6] Surely, he pointed out, della Rovere could not have forgotten his grievances against Alexander VI so quickly that he now looks forward to an alliance with the son.[7] And indeed, Cesare Borgia had met his match in duplicity. Not only did Julius II renege on his promise, but as soon as he felt secure in his position, he arranged for Cesare's arrest and banishment to his native Spain. Cesare Borgia died in the service of the King of Navarra at the age of thirty-one.

From the rise and fall of Cesare Borgia, Machiavelli drew a number of lessons. In *The Prince*, written years later, he still found much to commend:

> When all the actions of the duke are recalled, I do not know how to blame him, but rather it appears to me that I ought to offer him for imitation to all those who, by fortune or the arms of others, are raised to government. . . . He who considers it necessary to secure himself in his new principality, to win friends, to overcome either by force or fraud, to make himself beloved or feared by the people, to be followed and revered by the soldiers, to exterminate those who have power or reason to hurt him, to change the old order of things for the new, to be severe and gracious, magnanimous and liberal, to destroy a disorderly soldiery and to create new, to maintain friendship with kings and princes in such a way that they must help him with zeal and offend with caution, cannot find a more lively example than the actions of this man.[8]

Nor did Machiavelli, in retrospect, condemn Cesare's horrifying acts of cruelty. The Borgian's career, rather, prompted him to reflect on the perils of confusing statecraft with private morality and to argue that a prince must sometimes be cruel to individuals in order to be kind to the many:

> Cesare Borgia was held to be cruel, nonetheless his cruelty restored the Romagna, united it, and reduced it to peace and to faith. If one considers this well, one will see that he was much more merciful than the Florentine people, who so as to escape a name for cruelty, allowed Pistoia to be destroyed. A prince, therefore, so as to keep his subjects united and faithful, should not care about the infamy of cruelty, because with very few examples he will be more merciful than those who for the

sake of too much mercy allow disorders to continue from which come killings or robberies; for these customarily harm a whole community, but the executions that come from the prince harm one particular person.[9]

Machiavelli had nothing but disdain, however, for Cesare's failure to use his influence to prevent della Rovere from being elected Pope. In Machiavelli's view, the mistake that led to Cesare's undoing was to underestimate the gravity of the threat that Julius II would pose to him: "Whoever believes that among great personages new benefits will make old injuries be forgotten deceives himself."[10]

Let us note in passing that art lovers should be grateful for Cesare's lapse, for it was Julius II who commissioned the Sistine Chapel ceiling by Michelangelo and Raphael's famous painting known as the *School of Athens*, along with many other masterpieces of art and architecture.

Machiavelli, however, cared little for such things. Curiously for a man with such a lively intellect, he seems to have had no interest in the explosion of creativity that was taking place all around him—even though he lived among the greatest Renaissance artists and architects. His own boss, Soderini, in fact, was the patron who commissioned Michelangelo's *David*. According to Pasquale Villari, the Florentine author of a nineteenth-century biography, the fine arts "had no visible influence" on Machiavelli's character or intellect.[11] Villari tells us:

> When in Rome he never made a single remark on the grandeur of the ancient or contemporary works before his eyes. Neither did those surrounding him in Florence ever seem to arouse his attention, for no word of his records the great artistic events taking place there. . . . Yet these events were mainly owed to the initiation of the Gonfalonier, Soderini, whose government gave a strong impulse to the arts and warmly fostered them.[12]

Machiavelli's only mention of his extraordinary artistic contemporaries is a sarcastic reference to Filippo Brunelleschi, who designed Florence's famous Duomo. In his *Florentine Histories*, Machiavelli recounts how this "architect of great genius" persuaded the Florentines that they could conquer Lucca by constructing a dike on the river Serchio and flooding the enemy city.[13] The plan backfired spectacularly, flooding the Florentine camps instead, and cutting them off from their target.

Machiavelli's indifference to the visual arts seems surprising in view of his love of literature, but perhaps can be explained by the intensity of his political interests. Some evidence to that effect is the remark in his *Discourses*, that men who admire classical art and architecture would do better to study classical history from which they could draw useful lessons.[14] He seems, like Lyndon Johnson, to have lived for politics.

Machiavelli had no blind spot, however, when it came to observing the successes and failures of the powerful. One lesson that Machiavelli himself appropriated from Cesare Borgia's military successes was that an army drawn from the citizenry will often have an advantage over hired soldiers because native sons are less likely to flee when the going gets tough. After convincing the Florentines to form a citizen militia, he himself led the city's forces in a successful attack on their old enemy Pisa.

The tireless civil servant prospered along with his patron until 1512, when Soderini was deposed and Florence once again came under the rule of the Medicis. Machiavelli was unsparing in his criticism of Soderini for underestimating his opponents and thus bringing about his own downfall. Like Cesare Borgia, Soderini had been overly confident. Unlike Cesare, he was an ethically scrupulous man who "believed he would overcome with his patience and goodness" the appetite of the Medicis to return to power. To his protégé's dismay, he was insufficiently ruthless in dealing with the threat his enemies posed: Though "fate and the ambition of those who struck him gave him the opportunity to eliminate them, nonetheless he never turned his mind to doing it." Soderini's unwillingness to take drastic and extralegal measures, Machiavelli observed, may have been "wise and good," but the result was that he allowed good to be crushed by evil. By failing to realize that "malignity is not tamed by time or appeased by any gift," and "through not knowing how to be like Brutus, he lost not only his fatherland but his state and his reputation."[15]

With the ouster of Soderini, Machiavelli found himself at the age of forty-three without a job. To make matters worse, he was arrested and imprisoned on suspicion of complicity in a plot against the Medicis. Lacking any direct proof of Machiavelli's guilt, his captors attempted to extract a confession from him by means of a form of torture known as the *strappado*.[16] His hands were tied behind his back with cords attached to a pulley suspended from the ceiling. From this position, he was dropped suddenly and suspended just short of the floor. Although subjected to this procedure six times, he did not incriminate himself. Only a remarkable stroke of luck brought his ordeal to an end: the election of a Medici to the papacy. In celebration of the elevation of their illustrious relative Giovanni, the Medici rulers of Florence pardoned all those who had been imprisoned on suspicion of plotting against them.

Upon his release from prison, Machiavelli was allowed to retire with his wife and five children to a small family farm outside Florence. There, he spent the last fourteen years of his life in straitened circumstances, writing the works that would assure his place in Italian literature and Western political thought. As summed up by biographer Roberto Ridolfi, "There have been few Italian authors, even among the greatest, able to reach the heights in more than one literary genre. Machiavelli was supreme or left a profound mark on almost all those which his genius explored."[17]

His literary achievements did not console Machiavelli, however, for the loss of a role in the public sphere. In a letter to his friend Francesco Vettori, he gave an entertaining but rueful description of the life into which fortune had plunged him:

> I rise in the morning with the sun, and go into a wood that I am having cut, where I remain two hours in order to check the work done the day before and to pass the time with the woodcutters, who always have some argument at hand among themselves or with their neighbors. . . .
>
> Leaving the wood, I go to a spring and from there to my bird-snare. I have a book with me, Dante or Petrarch or one of the

lesser poets like Tibullus, Ovid or the like. I read about their amorous passions and their loves, I remember my own, and I revel in these thoughts for a while. I then move on up the road to the inn. I speak with those who pass, and I ask for news of their area; I learn many things and note the different and diverse tastes and ways of thinking of men. Lunchtime comes, when my family and I eat that food which this poor farm and my meager patrimony permit. After eating, I return to the inn; there I usually find the innkeeper, a butcher, a miller and two bakers. With these men I waste my time playing cards all day, and from these games a thousand disagreements and countless offensive words arise, and most of the time our arguments are over a few cents; nevertheless, we can be heard yelling from as far away as San Casciano. Caught this way among these lice, I wipe the mold from my brain and release my feeling of being ill-treated by Fate; I am happy to be driven along this road by her, as I wait to see if she will be ashamed of doing so.[18]

It was not in Machiavelli's character, however, to wait passively for Fate to change her mind. He never ceased trying to reenter public life, making numerous attempts to ingratiate himself with the new rulers of Florence. He celebrated the ascension of Giovanni de' Medici to the papacy as Leo X by composing a fulsome poem in the new pontiff's honor. He planned to dedicate *The Prince* to Giuliano de' Medici, but later dedicated it to Lorenzo de' Medici when Lorenzo succeeded Giuliano as heir to the family's Florentine interests. At the conclusion of his homage to Lorenzo, he added this plea, "And if Your Magnificence will at some time turn your eyes from the summit of your height to these low places, you will learn how undeservedly I endure a great and continuous malignity of fortune."[19]

Toward the end of his days, Machiavelli's efforts to gain the favor of the Medicis won him a few official assignments, but the family never entrusted him with important public responsibilities. One of the crumbs that fell from the Medici table was the task of persuading a certain Franciscan Friar to preach in the Florence cathedral during Lent. That mission caused a good deal of amusement among

Machiavelli's friends, who knew him as a world-class carouser. One of them cracked that sending bad boy "il Machia" to find a preacher was like sending Pacchierotto, a notorious Florentine homosexual, to secure a beautiful wife for a friend.[20]

In the political writings that won him fame, Machiavelli presented himself, and many have seen him since, as a great discoverer. Just as the explorers of his time were extending the frontiers of the known world, he pioneered a new political science, based not on high ideals, but on what he considered to be more solid ground. At the beginning of his *Discourses on Livy*, he proclaimed, "I have decided to take a path that has not yet been trodden by anyone."[21] He elaborated on that boast in *The Prince*, dismissing—in the name of realism—all the ancient writers who had "imagined republics and principalities that have never been seen or known to exist in truth."[22]

That pretension to superior realism was more than a little disingenuous. With his knowledge of the classics, Machiavelli certainly knew that men like Plato, Aristotle, Cicero, Augustine, and Aquinas were far from naïve about political realities. In the course of outlining an ideal polity in *The Republic*, and a "second-best" regime in *The Laws*, the participants in Plato's dialogues show they are well aware of how chance, circumstances and human failings can confound the best efforts of statesmen. At the very beginning of *The Laws*, there is a discussion of the obstacles that bedevil even the best efforts to establish good government: Not only are cities always in undeclared war with one another, but human beings are always at war within themselves, torn between reason and passion.

Nor was Machiavelli by any means the first to warn of the dangers of political naïveté. In Plato's "Seventh Letter," he tells us that the downfall of his friend Dion was entirely due to underestimating the wickedness of his enemies, thus illustrating the danger for good men when they deal with men who are evil and intemperate.[23] Dion was too intelligent to be entirely blind to the character of his foes. But, according to Plato, he was like a ship captain who sees an approaching storm without gauging the full extent of its fury; he failed to grasp "how high a pitch of general wickedness and greed" the men who opposed him had reached. True, Plato had offered little by way of pragmatic advice to statesmen. But Cicero, long before Machiavelli, had already criticized him for that, calling for philosophy to be more attentive to political practice.

So in what way did Machiavelli break new ground? As he saw it, he was blazing new trails in political theory by deliberately repudiating the insistence of the classical writers on the centrality of virtue. Ancient thinkers like Plato, Aristotle, Cicero, and Augustine had just as many opportunities as Machiavelli to observe politics and human behavior at their seamiest. But they kept searching for the best way to achieve man's highest goals, realizing that human efforts will always fall short of the ideal. To Machiavelli, that approach, if taken seriously by states-men, was a prescription for disaster. Asserting, rather than proving, the inadequacy of classical (and, by implication, biblical) thought, he maintained that the ancients had demanded too much of human nature. There is so great a distance, he wrote, "from how one lives to how one should live that he who lets go of what is done for what should be done learns his ruin rather than his preservation: for a man who wants to make a profession of good in all regards must come to ruin among so many who are not good."[24] Politics, he maintained, should be based on empirical observation, taking men as they are and not as they ought to be.

But what does it mean to be realistic about human nature? To the ancients, "taking men as they are" meant understanding that human beings are endowed with reason as well as subject to passion. It meant, further, that statesmen must be concerned with fostering conditions that enable us, individually and collectively, to achieve self-control, act virtuously, and achieve happiness. "Just as man is the best of the ani-mals when completed," Aristotle wrote, "when separated from law and adjudication, he is the worst of all."[25] Nurture, education, and law were thus indispensable aids to men and political communities in their quest for the good life. Augustine anticipated Machiavelli in a sense, by doubting that reason, law, nurture, and education would be enough to enable human beings to overcome the defects in human nature. That, in his view, would require conversion and the help of divine grace. Augustine's answer to the problem of the weakness of human will—the problem of original sin, as he would have put it—was faith, hope, and charity. Faced with our frequent failure to do what we know is right, his Christian proposition was to keep aiming for the highest standards, striving all the while to discern and cooperate with the divine will.

Machiavelli's solution was to lower the bar. In his view, the selfish passions predominate over reason so regularly that it makes no sense to prescribe goals that are unattainable by most people most of the time. Men, he wrote, are "ungrateful, fickle, pretenders and dissemblers, evaders of danger, eager for gain."[26] Thus a ruler, especially a new one, should be aware that people have "less hesitation to offend one who makes himself loved than one who makes himself feared; for love is held by a chain of obligation, which, because men are wicked, is broken at every opportunity for their own utility."[27] The political conclusion he drew, as nicely put by philosopher Ernest Fortin, was that "everyone would be better off if moderate ideals and absolute expectations were substituted for the absolute ideals and moderate expectations of the ancients."[28]

Accordingly, in Machiavelli's catalog of the qualities of a good statesman, wisdom yields to canniness, and virtue (*virtù*) appears mainly with its secondary connotations of courage and political skill. In one of the passages that helped to make the author's name an adjective, he wrote, "it is necessary to a prince, if he wants to maintain himself, to learn to be able not to be good, and to use this and not use it according to necessity."[29] Though circumstances and accidents place many matters beyond the prince's control, a bold prince will know how to recognize and seize opportunities: "Fortune is a woman, and it is necessary, if one wants to hold her down, to beat her and strike her down. And one sees that she lets herself be won more by the impetuous than by those who proceed more coldly."[30]

With moral virtue out of the way, there was little need to discuss nurture and education. Machiavelli left no doubt, moreover, that his scorn for building imaginary kingdoms extended to the kingdom of God. While he maintained that religion is important for the maintenance of a polity, he regarded a religion that exalts humility over the spirit and strength of active men as too effeminate to be politically useful.[31] (He did not consider it necessary to name the religion he had in mind.) A prince, he advised, should seem religious, but it would be inexpedient for him to be so.[32] All this was presented in language that still ranks among the finest examples of Italian prose.

Regarding the point of view according to which a prince who followed Machiavelli's counsels would imperil his immortal soul, Machiavelli says nothing. "His silence" on that point, wrote Quentin Skinner, "is eloquent, indeed epoch-making; it echoed around Christian Europe."[33] We can glimpse his views on the subject, however, in his ribald play, *Mandragola*, where the "hero," a young man scheming to seduce a virtuous matron, exclaims to his co-conspirator:

> And there are so many good men in hell! Are you ashamed to go there? Face your lot; flee evil, but, not being able to flee it, bear it like a man; don't prostrate yourself, don't degrade yourself like a woman.[34]

Machiavelli's insouciance toward religion, legendary among his friends, continued into his last illness, when he spoofed Cicero's account of Scipio's vision in which the true reward of a noble leader appears to be an eternal life of happiness and contemplation. Machiavelli told the companions gathered around his bed that he, too, had had a dream—in which he saw the saints on their way to Heaven and the great philosophers of antiquity on their way to Hell. In a final burst of bravado, he declared he would be happier in Hell, where he could discuss politics, than in Heaven, where he would surely be bored.[35] Although some biographers say he died a few days later "after confessing his sins to one Friar Matteo," others dismiss that story as a pious invention.[36]

Still, Machiavelli's "dream" of Hell as an eternal seminar does remind us of how deeply he venerated the classical philosophers whom he famously attacked. It is hard not to be moved by the conclusion of the letter he sent to Vettori shortly after he had been banished from Florence by the Medicis. After describing his daytime hours spent in performing menial chores, chit-chatting with neighbors, and day-dreaming about old loves, Machiavelli wrote:

> When evening has come, I return to my house and go into my study. At the door I take off my clothes of the day, which are

covered with mud and mire, and I put on my regal and courtly garments; and decently reclothed, I enter the ancient courts of ancient men, where, received by them kindly, I feed on the food that alone is mine, and that I was born for. There I am not ashamed to speak to them and to ask them the reasons for their actions; and they, in their humanity, reply to me. And for the space of four hours I feel no boredom, I forget every pain, I no longer fear poverty, death does not frighten me. I deliver myself entirely to them.[37]

For some readers, the charm of that passage may be dimmed by other letters where Machiavelli boasts of past, present, and hoped-for adulterous adventures. Nevertheless, the letters as whole reveal their author in all his complexity, a creature of reason and passion, animated not only by personal ambition but by the love of learning and a vision of a united Italy free of foreign domination.

Nearly five hundred years have passed since the appearance of *The Prince,* yet Niccolò Machiavelli and the book that made him famous remain an enigma. A lively debate continues over the meaning of his works. Was he bad on the surface, but really a great republican and patriot whose shocking treatise has been misunderstood, as some biographers have stoutly insisted?[38] Or was he, as Harvey Mansfield said on the occasion of his 2007 Jefferson Lecture, bad on the surface, but even worse underneath?[39]

In his fascinatingly detailed biography, Villari presented a spirited defense of his fellow Florentine, whom he described as "the least understood and most calumniated personality that history has ever known."[40] Villari maintained that Machiavelli's dream of unifying Italy and driving out her foreign rulers was "the holiest of objects," one that would have been "impossible to achieve . . . without recurring to the immoral means practised by the statesmen of the time."[41] Machiavelli's "ruling thought", Villari claimed, was that Italian independence would have "led to the re-establishment of morality," and indeed was "the only possible way of political and moral redemption."[42] Yet even Villari concedes that Machiavelli avoided the important question of "whether the excessive immorality of the means employed may not, even while momentarily grasping the desired end, sap the very foundations of society, and render in the long run all good and strong government an impossibility."[43]

Machiavelli's defenders are correct that he did not teach that the end always justifies the means, nor that politics should be an entirely "value free" science. Those who maintain he has been misunderstood and misjudged point out that the most complete exposition of his thought on politics and government is found, not in *The Prince*, but rather in the *Discourses on Livy*. There, he posits the Roman Republic as an ideal, and condemns official oppression that is not aimed at promoting the internal stability of the polity and securing its protection from foreign enemies. The *Discourses* do not, however, differ significantly from *The Prince* in their message about human nature and the role of virtue in politics.

Cynical political positions (such as that justice is merely the will of the stronger) were well-known to the ancients. But propositions that Plato had placed in the mouths of Thrasymachus and others to serve as foils for Socrates became guidelines for action in Machiavelli's new science. He was, as Mansfield has observed, "the first political philosopher not merely to lack respect for the just, the noble, and the sacred, or even to *show* his lack of respect—but actually to *advise* all others to act without respect."[44]

Nevertheless, it is important to keep in mind that *The Prince*, the work upon which the author's reputation is mainly based, was addressed to the challenges faced by *new* princes. At the beginning of the book, Machiavelli explicitly notes that the situation of hereditary rulers whose families have ruled for generations is quite different. Those princes, he says, have far fewer difficulties in maintaining their states, for even if they are men of mediocre ability, it generally suffices simply "not to depart from the order of [their] ancestors."[45] The situation is different in the case of a prince who comes to power without traditional legitimation. For him, everything will depend on a combination of luck and skill, and it is to such a man that Machiavelli's most famous work is addressed.

Whether one concludes that Machiavelli was, underneath it all, better or worse than he appears on the surface, one thing is clear. As is often the case when ideas migrate from political theory into law and government, what traveled fastest and furthest from Machiavelli's imagination was not the whole of his thought but certain arresting fragments that could pass for realism—if one believes that the ideal and the real are always distinct. These fragments took root in the minds of other thinkers who came to believe that it was "realistic" to trash faith in ideals, to denigrate the power of faith and reason to overcome passion, and to neglect the political importance of nurture and education.

In the present age of great governmental bureaucracies, it would be interesting to know more about what Machiavelli, so full of advice for princes, would have advised persons like himself whose vocation for politics lies in various forms of government service. But the only evidence we have on that matter comes from a letter he wrote in his later years to a young man named Rafaello Girolami, who had just been made an envoy to the Emperor Charles V in Spain. It was a plum assignment, one that Machiavelli himself would have relished, but one that could never be his under the Medicis.

He counseled Girolami that it is important for an ambassador to have a reputation for trustworthiness in order to be able to negotiate effectively. But since there are times when he cannot tell the truth, he needs to learn to dissemble and to "conceal a fact with words." He must work hard to be well-informed about the matters to be negotiated and develop skill in discerning the true intentions of others, for everyone can be expected to dissemble. He must diligently gather information by finding and cultivating the gossipy individuals that are present in every court. The best way to get information, the veteran diplomat told the novice, is often to begin by giving some yourself. He concluded by telling Rafaello that one should always present his opinions to his own ruler as objective analyses of the evidence, and he even suggests a formula for doing so: "Considering then everything about which I have written, prudent men here judge that the outcome will be such and such."[46]

Machiavelli's approach to public service was certainly different from that of Plato who, when confronted with the corruption of the rulers of his own city and later with the unteachability of Dionysius II of Syracuse, simply retreated from involvement in public affairs. Throughout his life, Plato seems to have followed the policy outlined in his *Seventh Letter*: "When your country appears to you to be following the wrong course, you should say so, unless your words are likely to fall on deaf ears, or lead to the loss of your life. When it is not possible to introduce good government without driving men into exile or putting them to death, the wise man should keep quiet and offer up prayers for his own welfare and for that of his country."[47] To anyone who aspires to advise princes—as Plato tried to do, and Machiavelli did—Plato's counsel was that they should never pander to power: "When government is being carried on in the right course, it is the part of a wise man to advise such people. But when rulers flatly refuse to move in the right path and order their counselors to advise them only about how their aims can most readily be accomplished, I should consider unmanly one who accepts the duty of giving such forms of advice, and one who refuses it to be a true man."[48] One wonders whether Machiavelli, *il Machia*, ever measured himself by Plato's standards for manliness.

Neither Plato nor Machiavelli provide much guidance regarding the everyday dilemmas that public servants, high and low, confront on a regular basis. As any university professor can attest, countless young men and women today are drawn to public life through their desire, as they say, "to make a difference," but they agonize over whether they can maintain their integrity in a political career. The more decent they are, the more they agonize.

The result, as Aristotle observed long ago, is that virtuous people often decline to enter public service. They worry about such questions as: How should one comport himself or herself as a member of a regime that may be far from being even second best? How much should one compromise for the sake of getting and keeping a position from which one might be able to have influence on the course of events? How much should one compromise for the sake of achieving a higher political goal? Are private morality and political morality distinct, and if so, what principles should govern political action?

In our increasingly interdependent planet, ridden with conflicts far more dangerous than those of Renaissance Italy, the need for public servants who can negotiate such moral minefields with wisdom and integrity is more urgent than ever. It is hard to resist the conclusion of the classical philosophers that no polity can afford to neglect the nurture and education of future citizens and statespersons.

It was Machiavelli's challenges to classical political ideas, however, that captured the imaginations of the early modern political philosophers—even though the author of *The Prince* provided little grounding for the propositions he advanced so boldly. For a root-and-branch attack on biblical, classical philosophical, and customary traditions, political theory would have to await one of Machiavelli's most audacious followers, Thomas Hobbes. What Machiavelli had merely asserted, Hobbes set out to prove scientifically.

FIVE

THE SCHOLAR VS. THE STATESMAN

THOMAS HOBBES AND EDWARD COKE

Whhe the flow of ideas between the forum and the tower has often benefited denizens of both worlds, the relationship has also been marked by episodes of outright conflict—none more acrimonious than the vendetta carried on by the philosopher Thomas Hobbes (1588–1679) against one of England's most learned statesmen, Edward Coke (1552–1634). Though the two men never actually met (Coke was at the end of his career when Hobbes began to turn his attention from science to political philosophy), the philosopher's zeal to discredit the eminent jurist and parliamentarian amounted to an obsession. To understand why Coke became Hobbes's *bête noir* is to gain an appreciation of the warnings by philosopher-statesmen like Cicero and Edmund Burke against divorcing political theory from political practice.

Edward Coke is chiefly remembered today for the courageous words he spoke to King James I on a November morning in 1608.[1] The King had summoned Coke, then Chief Judge of the Court of Common Pleas, in order to settle a long-simmering turf war between the law courts and the ecclesiastical courts. The rivalry between the two judicial systems had come to a head when Coke issued a writ forbidding a Church tribunal to rule on secular issues governed by the common law. For the Archbishop of Canterbury, that assault on his jurisdiction was the last straw. He appealed directly to the King.

On the appointed day, both judge and prelate presented their sides to King James at Whitehall Palace with a crowd of curious courtiers looking on. The Archbishop asked the King to block Coke's order, arguing that the sovereign had the power, if he pleased, to take any case away from the courts and decide it himself.

Coke had the temerity to deny that was so. "The King," he insisted, "cannot take any case out of any courts and give judgment upon it himself." He maintained that, according to the law and custom of the realm, cases within the jurisdiction of the law courts were to be decided by those courts alone.

King James himself then intervened, saying that it was his understanding that the law was founded upon reason. He remarked that members of the legal profession had no monopoly on reason: "I and others have reason as well as the judges." Coke respectfully acknowledged that "God had endowed his Majesty with excellent science and great endowments of nature." But, he continued, "his Majesty was not learned in the laws of his realm of England, and causes which concern the life or inheritance or goods or fortunes of his subjects are not to be decided by natural reason, but by the artificial reason and judgment of the law, which law is an art which requires long study and experience before that a man can attain to the cognizance of it."

King James was quick to see where that line of argument could lead, and he did not like what he saw. If that were so, he indignantly pointed out, the King himself would be under the law! Such a proposition, he declared menacingly, would be treasonous to affirm. Coke responded by quoting a saying attributed to the thirteenth-century jurist Henry Bracton, that the King ought not to be under any man, but under God and the law (*quod Rex non debet esse sub homine sed sub Deo et lege*). At that, the King fell into such a rage that Coke escaped being sent to the Tower of London only after the intervention of a powerful kinsman and his own abject apology.

Coke's tense encounter with King James did not end his judicial career right away, but it escalated a series of conflicts over the extent of royal power that eventually led to his removal from the bench. Those conflicts came to a head in 1616, when King James summoned all his judges and asked them whether they would stay a lawsuit if the King so ordered. All of the judges said they would, except Coke, who said that "when that case should be, he would do that should be fit for a judge to do."[2] Coke's enemies, among them Francis Bacon, a staunch defender of the King's positions, took the occasion to urge his dismissal, and a few months later he was dismissed by a writ giving no reasons.[3]

Coke then went on to become a member of the House of Commons where he defended the prerogatives of Parliament against the Crown as vigorously as he had insisted on respect for the jurisdiction of the law courts.

By 1621, an exasperated James I had had enough. He threw the seventy-year-old Coke into prison for responding to a royal reprimand with a ringing affirmation of Parliament's role in protecting English freedoms:

> The privileges of this House is the nurse and life of all our laws, the subject's best inheritance. If my sovereign will not allow me my inheritance, I must fly to Magna Charta and entreat explanation of his Majesty. Magna Charta is called . . . the Charter of Liberty because it maketh freemen. When the King says he cannot allow our liberties of right, this strikes at the root. We serve here for thousands and tens of thousands.[4]

After keeping Coke in the Tower of London for seven months without books or any comforts, the King gave in to advisors who persuaded him that he could not detain the old man further without cost to his own prestige.[5] To the sovereign's great annoyance, the arrogant lawyer "had become an oracle amongst the people."[6] "Throw this man where you will," complained James, "he falls upon his legs."[7]

The unrepentant Coke then returned to Parliament, where he played a prominent role in drafting the Petition of Right of 1628, a classic statement of certain "rights of Englishmen" (no taxes to be imposed without parliamentary consent, no subject to be imprisoned without cause, soldiers not to be quartered in the houses of citizens, and martial law not to be imposed except in time of war).

Today, Coke is revered as a courageous champion of the rule of law. The words he immortalized—*non sub homine sed sub Deo et lege*—are firmly ensconced in the Anglo-American legal heritage. Among lawyers, he is remembered for an illustrious legal career in which he distinguished himself first as a successful barrister, then as Attorney General under Queen Elizabeth and later James I, then as a judge, and finally as a member of Parliament. Over the course of his long career, he authored a number of legal writings, including the monumental treatises that he called *Institutes* in tribute to Justinian. Coke's *Institutes* stood for nearly three centuries as one of the most authoritative sources for the study of English law. Many of his judicial decisions are still regarded as legal landmarks, especially the opinion in *Dr. Bonham's Case*, a forerunner of *Marbury v. Madison* in which the U.S. Supreme Court claimed the power of judicial review.

In his own time, he was as popular as he was controversial. Men and women alike were attracted by his "youthful enthusiasm" and sparkling conversation "mixing mirth with wisdom."[8] He was wealthy and handsome, "delighting in good clothes, well worn, and being wont to say that the outward neatness of our bodies might be a monitor of purity to our souls." Sir Francis Bacon's animosity toward him was personal as well as political, for Bacon had lost out to Coke in the courtship of one of the great beauties of the day. The victory was a Pyrrhic one, however, for the widowed Coke's marriage to Lady Elizabeth Hatton was marked by unseemly public disputes and ended in a bitter separation.

In view of the intense speculation that attends every new appointment to the United States Supreme Court today—about whether and how the nominee will change upon donning judicial robes—it is interesting to ponder the transformation of Edward Coke when he was appointed to the bench at the age of fifty-four.

During the previous twelve years, he had served as Attorney General under two sovereigns. In that office, his principal responsibility had been to track down and prosecute "Papist traitors," a charge he pursued with relentless zeal and small attention to procedural niceties. Even his contemporaries, according to legal historian Theodore Plucknett, sometimes felt he had overstepped all bounds.[9] In keeping with the customs of the time, he did not scruple to use torture to extract information and confessions.[10] Nor did he flinch at the grisly punishment for treason—which he described with evident relish in his summation to the jury in the 1606 trial of the Gunpowder Plot conspirators.

The just punishment of Guy Fawkes and his associates in the plan to blow up Parliament, said Coke, would unfold as follows:

> To be drawn to the place of execution from his prison, as being not worthy any more to tread upon the face of the earth whereof he was made. Also for that he hath been retrograde to nature, therefore is he drawn backward at a horse-tail. And whereas God hath made the head of man the highest and most supreme part, as being his chief grace and ornament, he must be drawn with his head declining downward and lying so near the ground as may be, being thought unfit to take the benefit of the common air. For which cause he shall also be strangled, being hanged up by the neck between heaven and earth as deemed unworthy of both or either; . . . then is he to be cut down alive, and to have his privy parts cut off and burnt before his face as being unworthily begotten and unfit to leave any generation after him. His bowels and inlayed parts taken out and burnt, who inwardly had conceived and harbored such horrible treason. After, to have his head cut off, which had imagined the mischief. And lastly his body to be quartered and the quarters set up in some high and eminent place, to the view and detestation of men and to become a prey for the fowls of the air.[11]

Coke's friends and foes alike were astonished later that year when the ruthless prosecutor seemed to become a different person upon his appointment as Chief Judge of the Court of Common Pleas. Even his generally admiring biographer Catherine Drinker Bowen found it remarkable that Coke as a judge and legislator risked his life more than once "for the very principles he seems at first to have betrayed, principles which today we take for granted: a prisoner's right to public trial and the writ of habeas corpus, a man's right not to be jailed without cause shown, his right against self-incrimination in a court of law."[12]

Undoubtedly, a major factor in what people considered a dramatic turnabout was simply that the role of an advocate is different from the role of a judge. But Coke seems also to have been influenced by the fact that James I had made it clear soon after ascending to the English throne that he intended to insist on the royal prerogative far more than Queen Elizabeth had done.

In any case, Coke's transformation was far from total. In his role as judge, he still resorted on occasion to his old repertoire of advocate's tricks, bending precedent this way and that, tossing in a bit of Latin to muddy the waters. Nor did he ever relinquish the "fanatical bias" against Catholics that his enemies called the "soft spot in Coke's head."[13] Yet, once he became a judge, he never wavered from his course where the fundamental principles of English law and government were concerned.

Why then, one may wonder, did Thomas Hobbes single out the greatest English jurist of the seventeenth century for vituperative condemnation?

To begin with, the times were changing. While Coke, born in 1552, had stood on the brink of the modern era, Thomas Hobbes was fully immersed in the new age from the moment of his birth. Western Christendom had been transformed by Reformation and religious wars, by the rise of nation-states on the continent, by geographic and scientific discoveries, and by the diffusion of ideas through printing. By the end of his long life, Hobbes had witnessed the Thirty Years' War in Europe (1618–1648); civil war in England (1642–1648), the beheading of Charles I in 1649; the brutal military dictatorship of Oliver Cromwell (1649–1658); and the unstable Restoration of the English monarchy under Charles II (1660).

For a man of Hobbes's lively mind and diffident temperament, those were both the best and worst of times. Best, because science was his first love and his position as tutor and traveling companion to noblemen brought him into contact with great thinkers like Galileo and Kepler, whose discoveries opened vast intellectual horizons for him; worst, because of his nervous disposition. Hobbes never pretended to be a courageous man. In fact, he often claimed that the specter of the Spanish Armada near the coast of England had so alarmed his pregnant mother that she delivered him prematurely, causing him to be born "a twin with fear."[14] He unabashedly confessed that in 1640, when civil war was imminent and many defenders of the King's cause decamped for the continent, "I was the first of those that fled."[15] His aversion to risk served him well, for he survived dramatic regime changes, was blessed with loyal patrons and friends, and lived a vigorously productive life until age ninety-one.

All things considered, it is hard to blame Hobbes for placing an especially high value on peace and social stability. His political solution, however, put him squarely at odds with practically everything that Edward Coke had stood for. As elaborated in his celebrated work, *The Leviathan* (1651), Hobbes's prescription for good government involved nothing less than submission to an all-powerful sovereign.

Hobbes's defense of absolute sovereignty begins with an image of man's pre-political condition as so miserable that one would do almost anything to get out of it. The natural state of human beings, he memorably wrote, is one of perpetual war of all against all where life is "solitary, poor, nasty, brutish, and short."[16] So long as there is no "common power to keep them all in awe," people exist in a condition where there is no industry, no agriculture, no arts and letters—only "continual fear and danger of violent death."[17] In the world according to Hobbes, human beings are far from being naturally sociable and political, as the ancients maintained. He envisioned the state of nature as populated by solitary creatures, driven by fear and desire and posing a constant threat to one another. Lacking any sort of government, they are naturally free. But with deadly peril lurking behind every tree, that kind of freedom offered few benefits.

Hobbes also maintained that humans are naturally equal, women along with men.[18] (He was perhaps the first important political philosopher to advance that proposition, explicitly rejecting the traditional views held by Aristotle and others.) Hobbes's notion of equality, however, challenges widely held modern assumptions about what it means to say that "all men are created equal." Equality for him had nothing to do with the juridical equality that Roman law granted to all free citizens, and even less relation to the radical Christian teaching that "among you there is neither male nor female, Jew nor Greek, slave nor free." For Hobbes, natural equality simply meant that in the state of nature, no one is strong or smart enough to be safe from deadly peril. Even a weaker, dumber person can kill a stronger man by stealth when he sleeps, or by ganging up with others.[19] In the state of nature, as Hobbes imagined it, nothing is good or evil, just or unjust. Everyone has only one "natural right," namely, to do whatever is necessary to preserve his life.[20]

Anticipating demands for proof of his dour hypotheses, Hobbes invited doubtful readers to look within themselves, and to test his view of human nature by their own experiences: Even though you live in a society with policemen and courts, he asks, don't you lock your doors when you go out? And don't you lock up your valuables to protect them—even from members of your own household?[21]

The state of nature in his account is so dangerous that human beings are driven into society, not because they are sociable, but for the sake of self-preservation. What enables them to organize their exit from the state of nature is their possession of reason.[22] But taking leave of Plato, Aristotle, Aquinas, and others who understood reason as a means of controlling man's passions, Hobbes understood it as a faculty that is in the service of the passions. "Thoughts are to the Desires," he wrote, "as Scouts, and Spies, to range abroad, and find the way to the Things Desired."[23] And while the classical philosophers regarded reason as representing the possibility of orienting human desires toward some good, Hobbes taught that "good" and "evil" are just names that people give to the objects of their desires and fears.[24] "For there is no such *Finis ultimus* (utmost aim), nor *summum bonum* (greatest good) as is spoken of in the books of the old moral philosophers."[25]

Reason, in Hobbes's sense, tells human beings that they can escape from their miserable natural condition by entering into a contract "to confer all their power and strength upon one man, or upon one assembly of men," thus creating "the great Leviathan" who "hath the use of so much Power and Strength . . . that by terror thereof, he is enabled to form the wills of them all to peace at home and mutual aid against their enemies abroad."[26]

In exchange for the security provided by a common power, men must give up the precarious liberty and equality they possessed in the state of nature. Henceforth, their relations will be regulated by law, which is nothing more or less than the command of the sovereign. With the advent of government, justice and injustice now enter Hobbes's picture for the first time, but nothing is just or unjust in civil society except as commanded by the sovereign.[27]

Hobbes was ready for the objection that this exchange of one's natural liberty for life under an absolute sovereign does not sound like a good deal. He knew it would strike many people as asking too much of the citizen and giving too much power to a ruler who might make the citizen's life miserable. His answer was that nothing is worse than "the miseries, and horrible calamities, that accompany a civil war; or that dissolute condition of master-less men, without subjection to laws, and a coercive power to tie their hands from rapine, and revenge."[28] People who think otherwise, he said, are looking at the world through magnifying glasses where every little injury is enlarged, when what they really need is a telescope "to see far off the miseries that hang over them, and that cannot, without such payments, be avoided."

As a practical matter, he added, a wise sovereign will make good laws, even though nothing he does can be called unjust.[29] For the one right that we do not relinquish when we enter civil society is the natural right to do whatever is necessary for our self-preservation, including disobedience to the sovereign.

Though Hobbes was a vigorous defender of absolute sovereignty, his emphasis on consent as the basis of government did not endear him to the various holders of power in his lifetime. That idea—government based on consent—was too subversive of rule by divine right to appeal to royalists. And Hobbes's theory of natural right was hardly calculated to win him friends among Cromwellians, parliamentarians, or restorationists. "Neither the antiquarianism of Parliament nor the mysticism of divine right," wrote Plucknett, "had any meaning for the dry, penetrating, but narrow, mind of Hobbes."[30] In all quarters of the forum, there was suspicion of a man who taught that the social contract no longer held if the regime failed to fulfill the purpose for which it was created: "The obligation of subjects to the sovereign is understood to last as long, and no longer, than the power lasts, by which he is able to protect them."[31] Thus, at the end of the day, the power of the absolute sovereign *is* limited in the Hobbesean scheme. It is limited by the power that created it, the power of the subjects who, in consenting to government, never relinquish their natural right to self-preservation.

The Colossus that blocked reception of Hobbes's ideas in his own country's political system was the massive English legal and constitutional tradition that Edward Coke had both defended and personified. In the English forum—the world of judges, legislators, and practicing lawyers—Hobbes's advocacy of absolute sovereignty found no traction. It clashed with a long tradition of hard-won limitations on royal power, dating back to the struggles between king and nobles that had produced Magna Carta in 1215. Moreover, Hobbes's idea of law as mere command was profoundly at odds with the concept of the common law as the time-honored "custom of the realm." In Hobbes's day, the judge-made common law was by far the principal source of law, punctuated only sporadically by statutes and royal decrees.

By labeling Coke's theories false and seditious, Hobbes was attacking the unwritten English constitution itself. Not even the rule of law was spared. The maxim that the sovereign is *sub Deo et lege*, Hobbes charged, is so subversive of government that it should be considered one of the chief diseases that can afflict a commonwealth.[32] The sovereign, he argued, cannot be subject to the civil laws, "for, having power to make, and repeal laws, he may when he pleases free himself from that subjection, by repealing those laws that trouble him, and making of new; and consequently he was free before."[33] As for ideas of "higher law," they just represent the opinions of men, and since men do not agree on their content, they can hardly be regarded as offering guidance, much less as binding.

As far as the famous "rights of Englishmen" were concerned, Hobbes denied that English subjects have any inalienable rights, apart from self-preservation. "[I]t is an easy thing," he wrote, "for men to be deceived, by the specious name of liberty; and . . . to mistake that for their private inheritance and birthright."[34] Well aware of the long-standing tradition to the contrary, Hobbes blamed continental learning for planting mischievous ideas in English minds. He charged that the Romans ("who had been taught to hate monarchy") had done great mischief by suggesting that liberty had something to do with controlling the sovereign.[35]

Even worse in Hobbes's view were those Christians who try to excuse disobedience to the sovereign on religious grounds. Though he never mentions Thomas More who went to his death rather than acknowledge the supremacy of Henry VIII as head of the English Church, he surely had More in mind when he wrote that the claim that one's duty to God takes precedence is "so evident a lie, even in the pretenders' own consciences, that it is not only an act of an unjust, but also of a vile, and unmanly disposition."[36] The true liberty of a subject, he insisted, lies only in doing what the sovereign has not forbidden.[37]

In a move guaranteed to further alienate the English legal profession, Hobbes flat out repudiated the traditional idea of law as the custom of the realm, legitimated by long use and acceptance. It is only ignorance, he scoffed, that leads people to make custom the guide for their actions. When lawyers do so, calling it precedent, they are acting "like little children that have no other rule of good and evil manners, but the correction that they receive from their parents and masters."[38] Then, in order to avoid declaring nearly all existing English law illegitimate, Hobbes prudently conceded that long usage could become law, but only with the consent of the sovereign, which could be signified by silence.[39]

To lawyers, that line of argument was patently disingenuous, for it rested on a deliberate misunderstanding of what English jurists meant when they spoke of custom and precedent. To members of the profession, those terms did not signify blind adherence to what was done in the past. Rather, they evoked a developing body of judicial decisions that afforded predictability by treating like cases alike, but permitted the adaptation of time-tested principles to new circumstances. That open-ended process, of course, leaves considerable wiggle room, enabling Hobbes to point out an area where Coke was undeniably vulnerable. Lawyers, Hobbes unkindly remarked, often shuttle back and forth between arguments based on reason and those based on precedent, depending on what seems expedient to them at the moment.[40] They cite precedent when their rational arguments are weak, but resort to reason when they wish to circumvent inconvenient precedents.

Leaving no legal monument undesecrated, Hobbes also took aim at Coke's oft-quoted claim that "Nothing contrary to reason is lawful, for reason is the life of the law; nay the common law itself is nothing else but reason."[41] For Hobbes, the question was: Whose reason? Coke had made his own answer quite plain. For him, the reason of the law was what he called corporate reason, an extended collaborative dialogue, a group achievement. It was, as he memorably put it, "an artificial perfection of reason gotten by long study, observation and experience . . . fined and refined [over the ages] by an infinite number of grave and learned men."[42] The common law, to Coke and his fellow jurists, was a dynamic, potentially self-correcting, system of practical reason that develops as judges adapt the accumulated experience of the past to new circumstances, case by case.

That concept of law cut no ice with Hobbes. "Long study," he pointed out, "can confirm errors." The "reason of the law," he said, is not the reason of scholars or "some subordinate judges," but rather "the reason of this our artificial man the Commonwealth, and his Command, that maketh Law."[43] The decisions of judges are law only by virtue of the tacit consent of the sovereign. "Law," properly speaking, is "the word of him that by right hath command over others."

Hobbes's concept of reason as calculation in the service of desires prevented him from recognizing that the common law tradition was a living, operating model of the mode of reasoning that was embodied in Plato's dialogues. Dialectical reasoning is a dynamic process that builds on common sense, but subjects common sense to continuous critical evaluation. Like scientific method, the dialectic method attends to available data and experience, forms hypotheses, tests them against concrete particulars, weighs competing hypotheses, and stands ready to repeat the process in the light of new data, experience, or insight. But, unlike the method of the natural sciences, dialectical reasoning in the human sciences begins with premises that are doubtful or in dispute. It ends, not with certainty, but with determining which of opposing positions is supported by stronger evidence and more convincing reasons.

That, of course, makes this type of reasoning unsatisfying to persons like Hobbes who take their bearings primarily from pre-quantum-theory physical sciences. It was Hobbes's contention that the skill of making and maintaining governments was just as much of a science as mathematics.[44] Accordingly, when he turned his attention from science to political theory, he made it his business to scientifically prove the novel propositions about human nature and politics that his predecessor Machiavelli had only asserted.

But as Aristotle famously pointed out in *The Ethics*, one cannot expect the same degree of precision in the human sciences as in the natural sciences: "It is the mark of an educated man to look for precision in each class of things just so far as the nature of the subject admits; it is evidently equally foolish to accept probable reasoning from a mathematician and to demand from a rhetorician scientific proofs."[45] In the realm of human affairs, he advised, we must be content "to indicate the truth roughly and in outline, and in speaking about things which are only for the most part true and with premises of the same kind to reach conclusions that are no better" (to which the common-law lawyer or modern social scientist might add that it is no small thing to reach conclusions that are "for the most part true"!). Nor is it a small thing that dialectical reasoning, with its constant recursive self-scrutiny, provides the common-law tradition with a limited but real capacity to resist, and correct for, bias and arbitrariness.

The Leviathan made its author a towering figure in the intellectual revolution that launched modern political thought by severing it from its classical, biblical, and customary roots. But his lack of impact on the politics of his day must have rankled with the old philosopher. For he never was able to let go of his antagonism toward Coke. Coke had been everything that Hobbes was not—a mover and shaker in tumultuous times, a courageous political actor, and a thinker who was deeply in touch with the most enduring elements of the British constitutional heritage.

At the very end of his life, the old philosopher launched a final assault against the legacy of his deceased antagonist. He devoted an entire work, the *Dialogue between a Philosopher and a Student of the Common Laws of England* (published posthumously in 1681), to the points on which he had disagreed with Coke.[46] One searches this peculiar tract in vain for anything that was not already said in *The Leviathan*. In fact, one searches in vain for genuine dialogue. It is little more than an imaginary conversation in which a philosopher who sounds like Hobbes triumphantly delivers a series of "gotchas" to a lawyer who sounds like a defanged Coke.

Given his obsession with Coke, it is noteworthy that Hobbes in all his works scarcely mentions the thinker with whom he had most in common. Though Machiavelli has received the lion's share of credit or blame for the new political science grounded in the idea of men as they are and not as they ought to be, Hobbes believed that he, with his scientific approach, was the first real political philosopher.[47]

Certainly, a case can be made that it was Hobbes who did more to lend respectability to the cynical ideas about man, reason, law, and justice that Plato had put in the mouths of Sophists as mere foils for Socrates. In fact, the reclusive Hobbes, who never actively engaged in politics, was a more thorough and relentless trasher of traditions than his more notorious Florentine predecessor. Though timid by his own account when it came to physical danger, Hobbes was fearless in attacking dead philosophers. Unlike Machiavelli, who had more than a little admiration for the classical thinkers whose theories he rejected, Hobbes gave them no quarter. Their false ideas about liberty, in his view, had done so much harm that it would have been better for the world if their works had perished: "There was never anything so dearly bought, as these Western parts have bought the learning of the Greek and Latin tongues."[48] While the skeptical Machiavelli had deplored the softness of Christian religion and smiled at the innocence of Christian believers, Hobbes ridiculed their stupidity: "Fear of power invisible, feigned by the mind, or imagined from tales publicly allowed [is] religion; not allowed, superstition."[49]

Moreover, as we have seen, Hobbes's attacks were not limited to the "old moral philosophers" and traditional religion. Less noticed, but no less radical, was his full-bore assault on custom. That was one source of authority that even Machiavelli had never bothered to question. For Machiavelli, the sense of fitness that—for better or worse— arises from long usage was simply a fact of life in society. Much of the novelty of *The Prince*, in fact, is due to the author's exploration of the problem of establishing political order where customary legitimation is absent.[50]

Machiavelli made a crucial distinction between princes whose families had ruled over a territory for generations and those princes who are new to power. It was the new prince—the upstart—to whom his book was primarily addressed. The ruler of a hereditary principality, he wrote, has much less need to worry about holding on to his position, for he has the weight of tradition on his side so long as he is careful not to upset long-standing usages.[51] Even if a hereditary ruler should happen to be ousted by a usurper, his chances of regaining power are aided by the fact that the people are "accustomed to his lineage." (This is so, Machiavelli wryly observed, even though a search into the pedigree of a hereditary prince might lead back to a successful usurper whose misdeeds had been long forgotten). A new prince, in contrast, will have a more difficult time of it, especially if he is a conqueror. Much of Machiavelli's counsel to new princes consisted of advice on how to preserve the state until such time as the new regime has acquired the support of custom.

Hobbes, by rejecting the authority of custom, struck at the very heart of the rule-of-law tradition, and, in his desire for peace and stability, embraced the idea of law beloved by despots everywhere: the command of the sovereign backed up by the armed might of the state.

Hobbes was also profoundly influential in rationalizing the revolution wrought by Henry VIII. Before Henry, authority in the Christian world had been divided between Church and State, and dispersed among countless smaller groups that Hobbes likened to "wormes" in the body politic.[52] In his zeal to establish the unity of authority and to eliminate competing loyalties Hobbes rationalized and justified what we now know as totalitarian regimes.

The sinister implications of Hobbes's "scientific" prescriptions for good government practically guaranteed their cool reception in the English forum. In the judgment of historian Peter Laslett, it was the abstract nature of Hobbes's ideas that prevented their implementation in England:

> After he had written, [political theory] became entirely different, but the political habits of his countrymen were changed not one little bit. . . . The reason for his historical ineffectiveness is not far to seek. A man who can say, as he did, that "the skill of making and maintaining Commonwealths, consisteth in certain rules, as doth Arithmetique and Geometry; not (as tennis play) on practice only," lacks what might be called a sense of policy.[53]

More likely, however, it was the dissonance between Hobbes's ideas and English rule-of-law traditions that prevented their acceptance. The powerful legal profession, in particular, was sublimely indifferent to the philosopher's concepts of law and government. To English and American lawyers of the seventeenth and eighteenth centuries, "law" meant first and foremost the common law, the massive accretion of court decisions in which generations of judges, "living oracles" as Blackstone would call them, declared and developed the principles that constituted the custom of the realm. Within this body of law, supplemented from time to time by parliamentary enactments and royal decrees, the rights of Englishmen had taken shape, and had been preserved through many a trying time, as well as through profound social and economic changes.[54] In the minds of those who counted—the landed gentry and the rising entrepreneurial class alike—the idea of the rule of law was linked to security of property, and security of property in turn was regarded as an essential part of what made it possible for Englishmen to be free. As Coke had put it, "The common law is the best and most common birth-right that the subject hath for the safeguard and defence, not only of his goods, land, and revenues, but of his wife and children, his body, fame, and life also."[55] The very durability of the common law, Blackstone would later claim, "endeared it to the people in general, as well because its decisions were universally known, as because it was found to be so excellently adapted to the genius of the English people."[56]

All this was perfectly understood by John Locke, who, as we shall see, had enormous influence on statesmen, especially in the United States. For Hobbes, law had been the instrument of the sovereign; for Locke, as for Coke, law was a bulwark of the citizens' liberties.

SIX

JOHN LOCKE

THE DON HEARD ROUND THE WORLD

Until a chance medical errand brought thirty-something John Locke into the company of political leaders, he fully expected to spend his entire life as an Oxford don. Yet, by the time of his death in 1704, he had played a key role in the great public events of his time, and produced a political tract that would affect far more people than any of his philosophical writings. Though Locke never held high public office himself, he exerted considerable influence as an adviser to prominent men, first through his association with the Earl of Shaftesbury during the turbulent reign of Charles II, and later as the confidant of Lord John Somers, a leading figure in England's transition to constitutional monarchy. Locke's modest but independent means gave him the freedom to be his own man in those roles, as well as to pick and choose among the various official posts that were offered to him. It was a life that Machiavelli would have envied, except for the absence of wenching and carousing.

Little in Locke's early years suggested that he would become a public personality. As a young man, he set his sights on an academic career, believing that scholarship was the only thing at which he could excel—and excel he did at rhetoric, philosophy, and medicine.[1] Though his wide-ranging interests extended to political questions, all indications were that he would spend his entire life in the relatively cloistered setting of an Oxford college. In 1659, with England in upheaval following the death of Oliver Cromwell, Locke, then twenty-seven, remained aloof, writing that "all these tossings have served but to rock me into a pleasant slumber, whilst others dream of nothing but fire, sword and ruin."[2] The following year, he became a lecturer at Christ Church, Oxford, keeping up his study of medicine while teaching Greek, rhetoric, and philosophy. A short period of service as secretary to an English envoy on a mission to Germany in 1665 was sufficiently stimulating to cause him to consider repeating that sort of experience, but for the most part his world remained bounded by the university and his family home in Somerset.[3]

One day in 1666, however, Locke was asked by a physician friend to bring some medicinal waters to a patient suffering from a chronic liver ailment. That house call would change his life. The patient was Lord Ashley, King Charles II's Chancellor of the Exchequer, soon to become the Earl of Shaftesbury. Ashley was not only one of the most powerful personages in England, but also a man of extensive learning and lively intellectual curiosity. He was so impressed with Locke that he sought further conversations with the young gentleman, and eventually brought him into his household as a tutor, secretary, and personal doctor. In the latter capacity, Locke soon rose even higher in Ashley's estimation. When the great man developed a life-threatening infected cyst in his liver, Locke devised a daring treatment that involved the insertion of a drain through the abdominal wall. It was a risky procedure, given the primitive state of surgery at the time—not to mention the fact that young Mr. Locke was not completely credentialed in medicine.[4] But it succeeded in restoring the patient to health.

Ashley began to entrust Locke with responsibilities that gave him an insider's knowledge of politics and government. As his patron rose in the court of Charles II, the modest don found himself immersed in a second career. In 1672, Ashley became the Earl of Shaftesbury, and a few months later the King appointed him Lord Chancellor, then the most important position in the government. Locke was given an official post overseeing ecclesiastical matters under Shaftesbury's supervision, and from time to time was dispatched on confidential diplomatic missions. As the Lord Chancellor's "assistant pen," Locke's influence grew. He drafted numerous reports, analyses, letters, and public papers, and assisted in the preparation of a constitution for the colony of Carolina.[5]

Shaftesbury's fortunes declined, however, when he fell out of favor with Charles II over the religious issues that were agitating the kingdom. The King's toleration and evident sympathy for Catholic dissenters displeased the Earl, who, according to historian Maurice Cranston, was "one of the most passionate anti-Catholics in English history."[6] Shaftesbury was suspicious of the King's alliances with Catholic powers in Europe, and alarmed by the possibility that the King's brother James, a Catholic, might succeed to the throne.[7] Eventually, Shaftesbury's views and activities brought him under suspicion as a possible enemy of the Crown, and in 1675 he lost his offices. At that juncture, he turned his efforts toward building up the constitutionalist organization that would become known as the Whig party.

Upon his patron's downfall, Locke, who shared the Earl's antipathy to all things Popish, withdrew from public life.[8] For a time, he went his separate way, keeping in touch with Shaftesbury by correspondence. He spent the next four years in France, pursuing his philosophical and scientific studies.

On returning to England in 1679, Locke found the country in turmoil over James's imminent ascension to the throne. Shaftesbury and his Parliamentary allies were engaged in fighting for an "exclusion bill" that would assure a Protestant succession. It was during this tumultuous period, 1679–1680, that Locke composed much of the *Two Treatises of Government*. He concealed that controversial manuscript among his medical books, disguising it, with wry humor, under the title *De Morbo Gallico* ("Of the French Disease").[9]

In 1681, Charles II forestalled passage of the exclusion bill by dissolving Parliament, and began cracking down on his opponents. Shaftesbury, who had been up to his lace jabot in intrigues, became a prime target. He was indicted for treason, but was released when a Whig grand jury dismissed the charges. Fearing another arrest with a possibly fatal outcome, the Earl fled to Holland. By that time, it was dangerous to be known as an associate of Shaftesbury's, and Locke, too, sought refuge in Holland.

There he devoted much of his time to his major philosophical work, the *Essay Concerning Human Understanding*. But he kept up contacts with his political acquaintances, many of whom were also in exile. In 1685, the worst fears of the exiles were confirmed when James II became King of England. For Locke it seems to have been a time of anxious reflection on his choice of vocation and his future. He had given up his position at Oxford, and Shaftesbury, the man with whom he had cast his lot, had died in 1683. According to biographer Roger Woolhouse,

> His association with Shaftesbury had been a partial cause of his not pursuing a career as a physician, and it had led to his losing the one home he had had independently of Shaftesbury's patronage (and even that was now over). It had 'confounded the quiet I always sought,' and in the end had led him, so he had complained, into 'a storm,' in the course of which he had lost his place at Christ Church, with its guarantee of rooms for himself and his books, and of maintenance (about 25 pounds per annum), and 'which I always so valued, as the highest convenience for a retired single life, that the keeping of it (which was always my great care) was what most satisfied me in the not getting other things.'[10]

If Locke had died in this period, Mark Goldie points out, "he would have left scarcely a mark on the historical record, the suspect servant of a fallen aristocratic courtier."[11]

Hope returned to Locke and his fellow exiles, however, as they realized that the reign of James II was highly unstable. The expatriate community in Holland became a hotbed of revolutionary activity, and John Locke was in the thick of it. Maurice Cranston, commenting on a portrait of him done in this period, saw in it "the face of a man of affairs, . . . almost, one might have said, a politician's face," adding that, by that time, "In his own devious and unobtrusive way, Locke *was* a politician, advising and prompting behind the scenes the men who took the stage itself."[12] Evidence is scarce as to the nature and extent of Locke's involvement in plots to oust King James, but at the very least he seems to have been instrumental in obtaining financial support for the insurrectionists.[13]

The exiles did not have long to wait before the stage was ready to be taken. In the "Glorious Revolution" of 1688, James II was forced to abdicate, and in the following year, James's Protestant daughter Mary and her husband, William of Orange, accepted the English throne on terms set by Parliament. Though many biographies state that Locke was among the triumphant band who returned on the ship that carried the future Queen Mary from Holland to England, Woolhouse dismisses that "pleasant and pervasive idea" as erroneous.[14] Locke was not yet ready to step into the spotlight.

It was in the following year that John Locke, at age fifty-seven, came into his own, both as a public intellectual and a major political force. Up to that time, none of his major works had appeared in print, but 1689 saw the publication of all three of his best-known writings, the *Essay Concerning Human Understanding*, the *Letter Concerning Toleration*, and the *Two Treatises on Government*.[15]

The *Essay* brought him immediate acclaim.[16] The books on toleration and government, however, were published anonymously, probably because the political situation in England was still unsettled. James II was rallying his supporters in Ireland, and so long as there was a possibility of his return, it would have been risky for Locke to put his name on works that not only debunked the claim of rule by divine right, but advocated toleration for every religion except Catholicism. Locke's attitude toward religion, as summed up by Goldie, was characterized by "an 'anti-formalism' that accented virtuous conduct rather than creedal or ceremonial dogma; a distaste for sectarians and 'enthuasiasts' (whatever their legitimate claims to toleration); and a horror of Roman Catholicism both as a theological monstrosity and a threat to civilized society."[17]

Even after James's forces were defeated in the Battle of the Boyne in 1690, the *Two Treatises* remained somewhat radioactive. At first glance, the book's preface sounded highly respectful of the King. It recited that the author's purpose was "to establish the throne of our Great Restorer, our present King William; to make good his title in the consent of the people." But the phrase "consent of the people" had powerful implications. Moreover, the preface went on to speak of "natural rights," praising "the people of England, whose love of their just and natural rights with their resolution to preserve them, saved the nation when it was on the very brink of slavery and ruin." Locke could hardly have expected that such a radical book, with its open endorsement of a right of resistance, would become the favorite reading of the new sovereign.

In fact, William of Orange, once on the throne, was fast becoming more interested in the prerogatives of the Crown than in those of Parliament. To the dismay of the Whigs who had supported him, the country's first constitutional monarch began to lean toward the Tories.[18]

Locke, meanwhile, had reached the summit of his political career. Many of his old friends had become members of Parliament, and he was now recognized as the intellectual leader of the Whigs. Among the men who turned to him frequently for advice on matters of state was Lord John Somers, a masterful negotiator who had played the leading role in securing Parliament's acceptance of the abdication of James II. Somers had gone on to preside over the drafting of the Bill of Rights of 1689, and was now a dominant figure in the government.[19]

Though a worsening case of asthma required Locke to move to the country in 1691 for the sake of better air, he continued his political activities through a voluminous correspondence and made regular visits to London. His prestige, plus his modest personal means, enabled him to be selective about the many offers of public positions that now came his way. He accepted a place as Commissioner of Appeals for Excise, which yielded a comfortable income, but on two occasions declined posts that were personally offered to him by the King himself. Though the exact nature of the royal proposals is not known, they are thought to have involved foreign affairs, probably ambassadorships and perhaps even Secretary of State.[20] Explaining to Lord Somers his reasons for "begging his Majesty to think of some fitter person, and more able to serve him" in one of these posts, Locke wrote:

> My temper, always shy of a crowd of strangers, has made my acquaintances few, and my conversation too narrow and particular, to get the skill of dealing with men in their various humours, and drawing out their secrets. Whether this was a fault or not to a man that designed no bustle in the world, I know not. I am sure it will let your Lordship see that I am too much a novice in the world for the employment proposed.[21]

Locke did, however, accept appointment in 1695 as a member of the Commission on Trade and Plantations, a position that involved him to some extent in the administration of England's slave-owning colonies. As many have pointed out, Locke's occupancy of this post, plus the investments he once held in the slave-trading Royal Africa Company, left a blot on his credentials as a philosopher of freedom.[22] Though Locke never addressed the "glaring contradiction between his theories and Afro-American slavery," Woolhouse suggests that "the selling of his African investments fifteen years before composing the *Second Treatise* indicates a change of mind on the legitimacy of slavery."[23]

Locke's declining health forced him to give up his position on the Trade and Plantations Commission in 1700, but he kept up his correspondence and writing until 1704, when he died a famous man at the age of seventy-two.

Locke's influence extended far beyond his own lifetime and his own country. To note what did and did not migrate from his works into the political movements of a later day is to gain an appreciation for the power of Locke's language, symbols, and stories as well as for his teaching that all governments derive their just powers from the consent of the governed. Nowhere were the effects of his ideas more pronounced than in England's breakaway colony, the United States, where they affected the way that generations of Americans would think about law and government. As Thomas Pangle has pointed out, those effects were so powerful that they tended to overwhelm, or to impress their own image upon, other important elements of the American story:

> [I]n the generations after Locke, lesser men of all stamps of opinion and sect felt increasingly the compulsion to explain their views using Lockean ideas: and this means that they were induced, often only half-consciously, to transmit even their most traditional opinions in drastically modified versions. By the late eighteenth century, the largely Lockean consensus on political first principles . . . was so strong that only a few articulate Americans still sensed a need to thrash out the deep doubts imbedded in the lingering legacies of biblical and classical thought.[24]

The ideas of Locke's that traveled furthest and fastest are mainly to be found in the second of his *Two Treatises of Government.* The First Treatise, where he demolished Sir Robert Filmer's defenses of rule by divine right, was soon forgotten. It was in the second book where Locke set himself the more challenging task of finding "another origin of political power . . . than what Sir Robert F. has taught us."[25] Like Hobbes, he began by telling a reverse Garden-of-Eden story where man starts out in a condition that is filled with many woes, until, by using his reason, he arranges his escape into a better life.

In Locke's version of the tale, however, the state of nature with its "innocent delights" is not quite so grim, nor is the remedy for its disadvantages so drastic, as Hobbes would have had it. Human beings do not always pose a deadly threat to one another, for the "law of nature" teaches them that they should not harm one another, and—except when self-preservation is at stake—they should act "to preserve the rest of mankind."[26] So long as there is no common power to enforce that principle, however, it is up to each individual to serve as judge and "executioner of the law of nature."[27] Therein lies the problem: With so many private enforcers running around, life in the state of nature is "very unsafe, very unsecure," and fraught with many "inconveniences."[28] Although the state of nature is not a state of war, it is so precarious that it can easily degenerate into one. Nor is the state of nature confined to some distant historical or imaginary past. In

Locke's view, the state of nature is always just below the surface of civil society, ready to break out whenever a common power is lacking or ineffective.

Locke did not hold, as Hobbes had done, that human beings enter civil society merely out of fear of violent death. They are also drawn by an inclination for the society of others, and by the desire for all the good things that law and government make possible—agriculture, commerce, industry, arts, comfort, and leisure.[29]

While Locke did follow Hobbes in locating the origin of government in consent, he and his allies in the struggle for constitutional government were in no way disposed to accept submission to an absolute sovereign as a reasonable price to pay for escape from the state of nature. Though life in the state of nature was "unsafe," the freedom and "innocent delights" that men enjoy in their natural condition were not to be lightly exchanged for life under a sovereign power. "I desire," Locke wrote, "to know what kind of government that is, and how much better it is than the state of nature."[30] In opposition to Hobbes, who had held that there are no pre-political rights except the right to self-preservation, Locke taught that men establish governments to protect their natural rights to life, liberty, and property.[31]

The inclusion of property in that trilogy was to have far-reaching consequences, especially in the United States. Locke's famous chapter on property is the very centerpiece of the *Second Treatise*. There, he begins by presenting his theory of the origin of individual ownership in the state of nature. It is "very clear," he says, that, in the beginning, God gave the world "to mankind in common"; no one had exclusive dominion over the plants, the animals, or the land.[32] Yet even then there was property—for "every man has a property in his own person," and in the "labour of his body, and the work of his hands."[33] As for the things held in common, they were of little use to anyone until he could establish exclusive right to them.[34] That was accomplished, Locke postulated, when a man "mixed his labor" with a thing by removing it from its natural state. By picking the apple, catching the fish, or bringing down the deer, a man made them his property—"at least where there is enough, and as good left in common for others."[35]

The same was true for appropriation of land by tilling, planting, and cultivating. In support of his theory, Locke pointed to the customary rules that even today favor first takers of fish and game, and he argued from reason that God could not have meant for the goods of the earth to remain unused and unproductive.[36]

So deeply has Locke's emphasis on property rights penetrated American legal consciousness that in 2001 the U. S. Supreme Court explained its rejection of the contention that a State can redefine property rights in such a way as to forestall future takings claims by saying, "The State may not put so potent a Hobbesian stick into the Lockean bundle."[37]

After making his case that property rights are anterior to government, Locke went on to discuss property as we know it—property in civil society where ownership is regulated by law. The reader is suddenly whisked from the state of nature, where everyone may take what he or she needs, to societies like Locke's and ours where some people have much more than they need while others have less. Strangely missing is any transition explaining how human beings got from mixing their labor with fruits and nuts to a situation where lands are divided by metes and bounds. All Locke says is that human beings "incorporated, settled themselves together, and built cities, and then, by consent, they came in time to set out the bounds of their distinct territories, and agree on limits between them and their neighbors, and by laws within themselves settled the properties of those of the same society."[38] Along the way, he reasons, they must have consented to the unequal possession of the goods of the earth even while in the state of nature, for they began to use money, and money has its value only from consent.[39]

It all sounds very orderly and peaceful. One hardly notices that the author has glided over some important matters, such as the role of force in some of these acquisitions. In a later chapter, Locke does discuss conquest, denying that it can serve as a legitimate basis for government.[40] But he is silent on the problem of the legitimacy of titles to land acquired by conquest.

In passages guaranteed to make the entrepreneurs among his readers feel good, Locke provides them with his version of the theory that a rising tide lifts all boats. God may have originally given the world to all in common, but since he cannot be supposed to have meant for it to remain uncultivated, we must assume that "he gave it to the use of the industrious and rational."[41] Persons who work hard, make land productive, and invest their profits are benefactors, contributing to the betterment of all: "He who appropriates land to himself by his labor, does not lessen but increases the common stock of mankind."[42] That theory, as philosopher Ernest Fortin pointed out, "was a clever one indeed, for by reconciling selfishness with altruism, it enabled everyone to reap the rewards of virtue without going to the trouble of acquiring it."[43] In what Pangle has rightly called Locke's "most radical departure" from traditional teachings about property, there is total silence concerning the way in which the duty of charity limits the absoluteness of property rights.[44]

Locke's property chapter set the stage for a move that was to have great significance for later developments in America. Announcing that he would use the word "property" to designate collectively "Lives, Liberties, and Estates," Locke declared that the preservation of property, in this capacious sense, is the "great and *chief end*" for which men come together into commonwealths."[45]

Property, then, is not only a natural right that exists prior to the formation of organized society, it is *the* prototypical right, standing even for life and liberty. Why property should have been selected to bear this extraordinary weight presents something of a puzzle. Equally puzzling, in the case of a careful philosophical thinker like Locke, is the lack of rigor in his argumentation. Why did he leave so many important issues untreated when he skipped from the state of nature to civil society? What did he mean by his frequent references to natural law, references that were deeply at variance with the *Essay on Human Understanding*, where he maintains that there are no innate principles of justice or morality? What was the basis for his assertion that human beings have property rights in their bodies?

That this latter proposition was hardly self-evident is apparent from the fact that the contrary idea was and is deeply entrenched in continental European legal systems, where an individual's right to the protection of personal autonomy and bodily integrity is recognized, but not in terms of ownership. In fact, the human body is treated as *hors de commerce*, and not subject to ownership by anyone.[46] To treat one's body as one's property also creates certain logical difficulties, for ordinarily if one owns something, one is able to dispose of it by gift or sale. In the case of one's body, however, that would lead in a direction few modern thinkers would want to take. Can one sell oneself into slavery?

Locke was well aware that the property metaphor entailed problems. Since he decidedly did not want to back into a Hobbesean bargain, much less to sanction selling oneself into slavery, he had to specify that freedom, in his view, did not include the power to enslave oneself: "For a man, not having the power of his own life, cannot, by compact, or his own consent, enslave himself to any one, nor put himself under the absolute, arbitrary power of another, to take away his life, when he pleases. Nobody can give more power than he has himself, and he that cannot take away his own life, cannot give another power over it."[47]

It helps to understand Locke's choice of property to stand for lives, liberties, and estates if one approaches the *Second Treatise* as a political tract rather than as a philosophical work. Locke's principal aim—both when he began writing the *Two Treatises* (probably around 1679), and when he polished and published the book after the Revolution of 1688—was to assist in justifying the transition from relatively unfettered royal power to constitutional monarchy. In doing so, he drew on the skills he had acquired first as a teacher of rhetoric, and later as ghost writer for the politically adroit Shaftesbury. To help delegitimate absolute monarchy, Locke found it useful to postulate the existence of natural rights that exist prior to and independent of the sovereign state. (That, of course, was precisely why Hobbes had condemned theories of natural rights: they gave people ideas "of licentious controlling the actions of their sovereigns."[48]) Then, to fortify the case for limited government, Locke portrayed the protection of those natural rights as the very reason for government's existence.

As a rhetorician, Locke knew that property, in seventeenth-century English society, was a terrific candidate for the paradigmatic pre-political right. His likely readership, after all, would have been composed predominantly of two classes of property owners: holders of landed estates and members of the rising merchant class. Neither group was likely to support a revolution that placed everything up for grabs. For them, property was a suitable proxy for lives and liberties as well as estates. Both of Locke's main audiences would have been apt to regard life and liberty as significantly dependent on property, and thus to see governmental protection of property as going a long way toward securing their lives and freedoms.

But if *Two Treatises on Government* is primarily a political tract, there is another puzzling omission. Why did Locke not draw upon the long history of English constitutionalism to support his arguments for limited government? Why not invoke Magna Carta? Why not cite Lord Edward Coke's brave insistence that the sovereign is "under God and the law"? Why not call upon the ancient "rights of Englishmen"? And the hard-won prerogatives of Parliament and the courts? Locke's failure to appeal to these venerable traditions is strange, for they would have resonated strongly with his readership. Since Locke's Preface to the *Two Treatises* refers to a middle section that was lost, it is possible that some such arguments were made. As matters stand, however, the omission is simply a mystery.

Whether arguments based on English traditions were lost or simply never included, Laslett seems correct in surmising that this very abstraction from English history helped to give Locke's work its extraordinary transnational appeal: "Neither Machiavelli, nor Hobbes, nor Rousseau succeeded in making the discussion of politics so completely independent of historical example, so entirely autonomous an area of discourse, yet Locke has affected the everyday activity of practising politicians more perhaps than any of them."[49] That such abstraction was not without dangers, however, would be pointed out by Edmund Burke—after some of Locke's ideas (notably the right to resist) had migrated to France, where they were stripped down, radicalized, and shipped back to England.

As a figure who simultaneously pursued the vocations of scholarship and statesmanship, leaving his mark in both areas, Locke's occasional reflections on the relationship between the two ways of life are of particular interest. In the *Essay on Human Understanding*, his comment on an ancient controversy reveals his appreciation for the role of practical wisdom in human affairs: "Notwithstanding these learned

disputants, these all knowing doctors, it was to the unscholastic statesmen that the governments of the world owed their peace, defense, and
liberties."[50] Later, in an unfinished work on human understanding, he
mused further on the need for theory to be rooted in practical knowledge and for common sense to develop the means to critique its own
contents. Both the man of action and the man of contemplation are
diminished, he said, if they remain shut up in their own worlds: "They
have a petty traffic with known correspondents in some little creek:
within that they confine themselves and are dexterous managers
enough of the waters and products of that corner . . . but will not venture out into the great ocean of knowledge, to survey the riches that
nature hath stored other parts with, no less genuine, no less solid, no
less useful than what has fallen to their lot in the admired plenty and
sufficiency of their own little spot, which to them contains whatever is
good in the universe."[51]

Although Locke recognized that theory and practice are as indispensable to one another as the two blades of a scissors, numerous
discrepancies between his political writings and his philosophical
works reveal that he was not always able to accomplish a happy marriage between theoretical and practical knowledge. Nor was Locke,
with his religious prejudices, exempt from the various biases that he,
as the author of the *Essay on Human Understanding*, well knew could
distort one's perception of data, one's reasoning processes, and one's
judgment.

Few scholars or statesmen, however, have bridged the worlds of
forum and tower as successfully as he, or with such lasting influence.
His political views, shaped in the thick of struggles to establish parliamentary government in England, have echoed down through the centuries wherever autocratic rule has been challenged by the principle of
government based on the consent of the governed. His successful col-
laborations with the leading political figures in England's transition to
constitutional government testify to the benefits of keeping political
theory in close touch with practical politics and vice versa. The same
cannot be said of Jean-Jacques Rousseau who prided himself on his
lack of experience in the forum, yet whose theories influenced a wide
assortment of political actors.

SEVEN

JEAN-JACQUES ROUSSEAU

POLITICAL PHILOSOPHY WITHOUT POLITICS

*I shall be asked if I am a prince or a legislator, to write on
politics. I answer that I am neither, and that is why I do so.*
Rousseau, The Social Contract, *Book I*

One day in 1799, Napoleon Bonaparte paid a visit to the grave of
Rousseau on the estate of the Marquis René Louis de Girardin at
Ermenonville. Pausing in front of the tomb, the First Consul remarked
to his host, "It would have been better for the peace of France if this
man had never lived."[1] "But why, Citizen Counsel?" Girardin wanted
to know, adding, "It was he who prepared the French Revolution. I
should have thought it was not for you to complain of the French
Revolution." Napoleon was silent for a while and then replied: "Well,
the future will tell us whether it would have been better if neither I nor
Rousseau had ever lived."

Jean Portalis, the jurist Napoleon chose to supervise the preparation of the French Civil Code, took a similarly dim view of the author

of *The Social Contract*. How much better it would have been for the nation, he lamented, if the revolutionaries had taken their theories from the practical-minded Montesquieu rather than the "false speculative philosophy" of Rousseau.[2]

Just two years before the French Revolution, the political writings of Montesquieu had found a most respectful reception among the framers of the United States Constitution. But in late eighteenth-century France, Montesquieu's works, replete with counsels to moderation, were not the stuff to set a revolutionary heart on fire. The French "men of '89" found their slogans and inspiration in the works of a rank outsider—the brilliant, eccentric, Jean-Jacques Rousseau. In the heady days leading up to the fall of the Bastille, stirring passages from Rousseau's works were read aloud to wild applause on the street corners of Paris. "It would be difficult," a Parisian journalist wrote, "to cite a single revolutionist who was not transported over these anarchical theories, and who did not burn with ardor to realize them."[3]

Whether for better or worse, and despite his unfamiliarity with the actual workings of government, Jean-Jacques Rousseau was to have a profound influence, not only in France, but on the forum and the tower throughout the world. He was, as Paul Johnson has pointed out, the very archetype of a new phenomenon—the secular intellectuals who emerged in the eighteenth century to fill the vacuum left by the decline of clerical influence and to offer themselves as guides for the diagnosis and cure of social ills.[4] Voltaire gained the ear of Prussia's Frederick the Great; Diderot was a regular correspondent of Catherine the Great of Russia; and the Austrian Emperor Joseph II instituted reforms based on the theories of the school of French economists known as the physiocrats. But none of those celebrated thinkers had the magic of the self-taught upstart from Geneva.

From the moment he burst upon the scene, Rousseau challenged the smug superiority of Voltaire, D'Alembert, Diderot, Turgot, and other *philosophes* who immodestly called themselves *les Lumières*, the enlightened ones. In 1749 the Academy of Dijon offered a prize for the best essay on the question, "Has the restoration of the sciences and the arts contributed to the improvement of the mores?" No doubt they expected the contestants to vie in counting the ways that "enlightenment" had raised the level of culture. By the middle of the eighteenth century, advances in science and technology had fueled enormous faith in progress. It was widely believed that the human race was emerging from a long night of ignorance and superstition into an era when Reason at last would conquer age-old social and political problems. It was something of a sensation, therefore, when the palm went to an unknown thirty-eight-year-old who answered the Academy's question with a resounding "No."

In the essay now known as his "First Discourse," Rousseau contended that manners and morals had declined as the arts and sciences had advanced. The arts had encouraged sensuality and license, while science had set up strange gods against true religion. Reason had been elevated over feeling; learning was prized more than plain goodness and honesty. City people looked down on country folk, and the rich more than ever lorded it over the poor. Political writers spoke less of virtue than of commerce. Society was overrun with scribblers who "smile contemptuously at such old names as patriotism and religion, and consecrate their talents and philosophy to the destruction and defamation of all that men hold sacred."[5] What is learning without virtue? Rousseau asked. What progress can there be without progress in goodness? The essay was suffused with secularized echoes of pious writers who had elaborated on Paul's words to the Corinthians: "Where is the wise man to be found? Where the scribe? Where is the master of worldly argument? Has not God turned the wisdom of the world into folly?"[6]

Those comments, as John Stuart Mill wrote a century later, "exploded like bombshells" amidst the prevailing views of day, "dislocating the compact mass of one-sided opinion."[7] Rousseau's merit, in Mill's view, was not that his interpretations were sounder than those he criticized. "On the contrary," said Mill; but the critique had administered a "salutary shock" to mainstream thought, causing its elements "to recombine in a better form with additional ingredients."

The "First Discourse" was followed by a cascade of writings in which Rousseau challenged the scientific rationalism of Voltaire and other well-known intellectuals. In the space of twelve years, the eccentric outsider produced a stream of works that made him the preeminent critic of modernity. Yet he was no traditionalist. Through his elevation of feeling over reason, he became the leading prophet of the coming age of romanticism. In the hands of Rousseau, secularized biblical and modified classical themes were deployed in a powerful critique not only of the faith in reason that was the hallmark of the epoch, but of all existing governments, and of the individualism of English thinkers like Hobbes and Locke.

Rousseau was born in Calvinist Geneva in 1712, the son of a watchmaker and a mother who died from complications of childbirth. When the boy was ten, his father placed him in the care of an uncle who in turn sent him to live with a country pastor. These men provided him with a haphazard education, but the precocious youth never received any formal schooling. At fifteen, he quit an unhappy apprenticeship to an engraver, and struck out on his own for the nearby Duchy of Savoy. There, a parish priest commended the wandering lad to the hospitality of a woman of good works in Annecy.

Warmhearted Madame de Warens, the estranged wife of a landowner, was not your usual church lady. Though a convert to Catholicism and pious in her way, she did not believe in original sin, or Hell, or that it could be sinful to follow one's natural impulses. She took a fancy to the clever, awkward boy, and he developed an enduring attachment to her. Rousseau spent several formative years as a sort of cavalier-servant, and occasional sexual partner, to this woman, whom he called *Maman*. Under her protection, he read voraciously, gained a sense of his extraordinary mental powers, and learned enough about music to support himself as a copyist and teacher.

In 1744, after holding various menial positions—footman, tutor, secretary—in well-to-do households here and there, Rousseau settled in Paris, determined to be independent. There he became friendly with Diderot, and began his lifelong liaison with Thérèse Le Vasseur, a laundry maid in his residential hotel. According to the well-known story in Rousseau's *Confessions*, each of the five children born of this union was abandoned to a foundling home shortly after birth. The writer whose works had extolled the child-centered family explained to posterity that he had insisted on this "solution," over

Thérèse's tearful protests, because he was too poor to provide for children, and that, besides, they would have interfered with his study and work.[8]

(Rousseau's biographers, though skeptical of much of his autobiographical material, have always taken that tale at face value. There is reason to suppose, however, that the long-suffering Thérèse may not have complied with her consort's wishes. She and her ever-present mother treated their brilliant patron, in many respects, like a child or ward. They did not hesitate, for instance, to make financial arrangements with Rousseau's friends behind his back.[9] It would have been quite in character for them, faced with his refusal to accept parental responsibility, to have placed the babies with members of their large, extended Catholic family.)

Rousseau's circumstances improved greatly after he won the Dijon prize. His cheeky, contrarian "First Discourse" brought him not only literary fame, but an entrée into polite society where, however, he would never be at ease. That essay was followed by his discourses on "Inequality" (the "Second Discourse") and "Political Economy," both destined to be landmarks in political philosophy. *Julie, ou la Nouvelle Héloïse*, which appeared in 1761, became one of the best-selling novels of the eighteenth century. *The Social Contract*, the chief source of the ideas and phrases that would capture the imaginations of revolutionaries, and *Émile*, his enormously influential work on education, were both published in 1762.

That extraordinary burst of creativity was followed by a long period of physical and mental decline, the former mostly due to an agonizing disorder of the urinary tract, and the latter aggravated by persecution for blasphemies that Catholics and Calvinists alike discerned in his work. Despite the sufferings, real and imagined, of his later years, Rousseau managed to produce the *Confessions, Dialogues,* and *Reveries of a Solitary Walker*, all published posthumously.

After his death in 1778, Rousseau's popularity soared to new heights. *Julie* and *Émile* continued to attract a wide readership, especially among women, while his political writings made him a cult hero to the leaders of the French Revolution. *The Social Contract* went through thirty-two editions between 1789 and 1799, including a pocket edition for soldiers, and collections were made of his most memorable epigrams.[10]

When the Revolution entered its radical phase, it was the ideas and catchphrases of Rousseau, shorn of their ambiguity and subtlety, that—more than those of any other writer—dominated the thinking and speaking of the insurgents. The revolutionaries' rhetoric, Tocqueville would later observe, "was borrowed largely from the books they read; it was cluttered up with abstract words, gaudy flowers of speech, sonorous clichés, and literary turns of phrase."[11] The Revolution, he went on, had been conducted in the spirit of the political writers whom its partisans admired: "Our revolutionaries had the same fondness for broad generalizations, cut-and-dried legislative systems, and a pedantic symmetry; the same contempt for hard facts; the same taste for reshaping institutions on novel, ingenious, original lines." The result, in Tocqueville's judgment, "was nothing short of disastrous; for what is a merit in the writer may well be a vice in the statesman and the very qualities that make great literature can lead to catastrophic revolutions."

Even today, Rousseau remains the preeminent expounder of challenging ideas about human beings, nature, politics, and history that must be reckoned with one way or another. Whether one finds him disturbing or stimulating, it is nearly impossible to remain unaffected by him. Like Plato and Nietzsche, he saw deeply into the most important questions and wrote about them so beautifully that, love him or hate him, we all stand in his shadow. As Allan Bloom once put it in a lecture at Boston College, "His influence was overwhelming, and so well was it digested into the bloodstream of the West that it worked on everyone almost imperceptibly."

Rousseau's influence on political thought extended far beyond France and its Revolution. His early modern predecessors, Machiavelli, Hobbes, Locke, and Spinoza, had broken with the virtue-based political theories of the ancients and developed theories of government based on human nature as they thought it really was, rather than as it ought to be. Rousseau attacked their new science of politics at its foundations. He began his "Discourse on Inequality" by scoffing at previous attempts to account for the origins of government by describing what human beings must have been like in the "state of nature."

In the mythic tales told by Hobbes and Locke, mankind had progressed from "a horrible state of war" (Hobbes) or from a very precarious, "very unsafe" existence (Locke) into a more secure way of life in organized society. According to Rousseau, such accounts had it exactly backward. Those English writers had failed to understand the natural condition of man, he claimed, because they "carried over to the state of nature ideas they had acquired in society; they spoke about savage man but they described civilized man."[12] The complex fears and desires they attributed to our early ancestors could only have been produced by society. (In this, it must be said, he had been anticipated by Montesquieu, who had already taken Hobbes to task for attributing "to mankind before the establishment of society what can happen but in consequence of this establishment.")[13]

Rousseau then presented his own version of pre-history as universal truth: "O man, of whatever country you are, and whatever your opinions may be, listen: Behold your history as I have thought to read it, not in books written by your fellow creatures, who are liars, but in nature, which never lies."[14] The earliest human, as Rousseau imagined him, was a simple, animal-like creature, "wholly wrapped up in the feeling of [his own] present existence."[15] He was not inherently dangerous to his fellows, as Hobbes had claimed. Rather, he led a "solitary," "indolent" life, satisfying his basic physical needs, mating casually without forming ties.[16] He possessed a "natural feeling" of compassion for the suffering of other sentient beings that made him unwilling to harm others, unless (a big unless) his own self-preservation was at stake. He was not naturally endowed with reason, but existed in an unreflective state of pure being. The transition from this primitive state into civil society represented a "loss of real felicity," in Rousseau's view, rather than an unambiguous step forward.

Rousseau next took aim at the social contract theories of his predecessors. As he saw it, what drew human beings out of their primeval state was not rational calculation leading to agreement for the sake of self-preservation (as Hobbes had taught), but rather a quality he called "perfectibility."[17] Previous thinkers, he claimed, had failed to pay sufficient attention to the distinctively human capacity to change and develop, to transform oneself and to be transformed.[18] In other words, they failed to consider the implications of the fact that human nature itself has a history. Or that human beings, through their capacity to form ideas, can to some extent shape that history. These were the insights of the "Discourse on Inequality" that won the admiration of such a dissimilar personality as Immanuel Kant and stirred the historical imaginations of Hegel and Marx.

With the development of human faculties, Rousseau continued, came language, family life, and eventually an era when families lived in simple tribal groups. That centuries-long stage of communal living, succeeding the state of nature and preceding organized society, "must have been the happiest and most stable of epochs" which only a "fatal accident" could have brought to an end.[19] That accident was precipitated by the ever-restless human mind. The invention of agriculture and metallurgy led inevitably to the state of affairs where human beings lost their self-sufficiency and came to depend on one another for their survival. ("It is iron and wheat which have civilized men and ruined the human race.")[20]

In striking contrast to Locke, who taught that property was an especially important, pre-political right, Rousseau wrote:

> The first man who, having enclosed a piece of ground, bethought himself of saying *This is mine*, and found people simple enough to believe him, was the real founder of civil society. From how many crimes, wars and murders, from how many horrors and misfortunes might not any one have saved mankind by pulling up the stakes, or filling up the ditch, and crying to his fellows, "Beware of listening to this imposter, you are undone if you once forget that the fruits of the earth belong to us all, and the earth itself to nobody."[21]

Continuing his attack on Hobbes and Locke, and following Montesquieu, Rousseau charged that it was civil society, not nature, which gave rise to a state of affairs that was always in danger of degenerating into war. Civil society begat governments and laws, inequality, resentment, and other woes. Governments and laws "bound new fetters on the poor, and gave new powers to the rich; which irretrievably destroyed natural liberty, eternally fixed the law of property and inequality, converted clever usurpation into unalterable right, and, for the advantage of a few ambitious individuals, subjected all mankind to perpetual labor, slavery and wretchedness."[22] It would be absurd to suppose, he went on, that mankind had somehow consented to this state of affairs where "the privileged few . . . gorge themselves with superfluities, while the starving multitude are in want of the bare necessities of life."[23]

Though Rousseau's evocative imaginary depictions of primitive societies were to swell the tide of nineteenth-century romantic "nostalgia" for the simple life, he himself insisted that there was no escape from history. There was no going back, he explained, because human nature itself had changed: "The savage and the civilized man differ so much . . . that what constitutes the supreme happiness of one would reduce the other to despair."[24] Natural man had been sufficient unto himself; man in civil society had become dependent on his fellows in countless ways, even to the point of living "in the opinions of others."[25] Reprising the theme of his Dijon essay, Rousseau concluded that modern man, though surrounded by philosophy, civilization, and codes of morality, had little to show for himself but "honor without virtue, reason without wisdom, and pleasure without happiness."[26]

The radical character of Rousseau's political thought is nowhere more apparent than in his treatments of reason and human nature. Together with early modern and Enlightenment thinkers, he rejected older ideas of a natural law discoverable through right reason. But by insisting that human beings are not naturally endowed with reason, he struck at the very heart of the Enlightenment project. Like Hobbes, he rejected the classical view that human beings are naturally social or political. But by exalting individual solitude and self-sufficiency, he set himself apart from his fellow moderns, anticipating the hyper-individualism of a much later age—our own.

Not without justification, then, did Bloom in his Boston College lecture call the "Discourse on Inequality" "the most radical work ever written, one that transformed the way people thought about the world." This one essay contained the germs of most of the themes that

Rousseau would develop in later works, and that would be further elaborated by others who came under his spell. Rousseau's lyrical descriptions of early man and simple societies fueled the nineteenth-century popular romantic revolt against classicism in art and literature. His criticism of property, together with his dark view of the downside of mutual dependence, made a deep impression on the young Karl Marx.

The central thesis of the "Second Discourse," that the most serious forms of injustice had their origins in civil society rather than in nature, foreshadowed Rousseau's famous charge at the beginning of *The Social Contract* that virtually all existing governments were illegitimate: "Man is born free; and everywhere he is in chains."[27] Having raised the explosive issue of legitimacy, and sensing that Europe's old regimes were about to crumble, Rousseau turned to his most ambitious project to date: the question of how better governments might be established. "I want to see," he wrote, "if, in the civil order, there can be some legitimate and solid rule of administration, taking men as they are and the laws as they can be."[28]

Like many critical theorists before and since, Rousseau was less successful at developing a positive political vision of his own than he had been at spotting flaws in the theories of others. In *The Social Contract*, he framed the problem of good government as that of finding a form of political association which would protect everyone's person and property, but within which each person would remain as free as before. The solution he devised was an agreement by which everyone would give himself and all his goods to the community, forming a state whose legislation would be produced by the will of each person thinking in terms of all (the "general will"). The state's legitimacy would thus be derived from the people, who, in obeying the law, would be obeying themselves.

That solution to the problem of legitimate government would obviously require a special sort of citizen, a "new man" who could and would choose the general will over his own interests, or the narrow interests of his group. The concept of the general will thus links *The Social Contract* to Rousseau's writings on nurture, education, and morals, particularly *Émile*, which contains his program for forming the sentiments of the young so that they will retain their natural goodness while living in civil society.

The legitimate state, as Rousseau imagined it, would need not only virtuous citizens, but an extraordinary "Legislator" who could persuade people to accept the rules necessary for such a society. Law in the properly constituted state would be, among other things, an instrument of transformation: "He who dares to undertake the making of a people's laws ought to feel himself capable of changing human nature."[29]

Rousseau had learned from the classical philosophers, however, that good laws can take root only amidst good customs. The law "which is not graven on tablets of marble or brass, but on the hearts of the citizens," he said, is "the most important of all, the real constitution of the state."[30] That insight led Rousseau, like Plato, to emphasize the pedagogical function of law. With morality and custom, he wrote, "the great legislator concerns himself in secret, though he seems to confine himself to particular regulations; for these are only the arch, while manners and morals, slower to arise, form in the end its immovable keystone."[31]

It was implicit in *The Social Contract* that many existing societies were already beyond help. "What people," Rousseau asked, "is a fit subject for legislation?"[32] His answer was not encouraging to revolutionaries bent on overthrowing unjust regimes: "One which, already bound by some unity of origin, interest, or convention, has never yet felt the real yoke of law; . . . one in which every member may be known by every other, and there is no need to lay on any man burdens too heavy for a man to bear; . . . one which is neither rich nor poor, but self sufficient. . . . All these conditions are indeed rarely found united, and therefore few states have good constitutions."[33]

Once a legitimate state is established, it needs to be maintained and defended. Here, the plot darkens. According to Rousseau, there should be no "particular associations" competing for the loyalty of citizens; religion should be subject to political control; and those who refuse to conform to the general will would have to be "forced to be free."[34]

Rousseau was given two opportunities to apply his ideas to concrete political situations when groups in Poland and Corsica invited him to draft constitutions for their countries. But by that time his health had begun to decline. Neither of his efforts to put his theories into practice was ever implemented.[35] That would not have surprised Cicero who held that little can be expected from sages who attempt to step into politics after spending their lives remote from the hurly-burly where the art of statecraft is acquired.[36]

In the unfinished *Constitutional Project for Corsica*, however, we gain a revealing glimpse of how the author of *The Social Contract* envisioned the implementation of its prescriptions. Rousseau wanted the leader of the group that commissioned the draft to convene the inhabitants of the island and administer to them an oath of adherence to the social pact. The speech he drafted for that occasion began with these words: "Corsicans be silent: I am going to speak in the name of all. Let those who will not consent depart, and let those who consent raise their hand."[37] The oath itself would have required each male citizen to swear: "I join myself—body, goods, will, and all my powers—to the Corsican nation; granting to her the full ownership of me—myself and all that depends upon me. I swear to live and die for her, to observe all her laws, and to obey her lawful Chiefs and Magistrates in all things conformable to the Law."[38] That, as Conor Cruise O'Brien observed, "is pretty much how Robespierre understood the matter."[39] In many ways, as Paul Johnson would later point out, the State that Rousseau envisioned for Corsica "anticipated the one the Pol Pot regime actually tried to create in Cambodia, and this is not entirely surprising since the Paris-educated leaders of the regime had all absorbed Rousseau's ideas."[40]

The contrast between Rousseau's program in *The Social Contract* and the practical ideas that guided the American Founders could hardly be more striking. The legacy of the most influential political *thinker* of the eighteenth century is thus at odds with the era's greatest political *achievement*—the design for government framed by men who believed that good governments could be based on reflection and choice.[41] The pragmatic authors of *The Federalist* had their own clear-eyed understanding of human nature with its potency and its limitations. They knew that human beings are creatures of reason *and* feeling—capable of good and evil, trust and betrayal, creativity and destruction, selfishness and cooperation. In Madison's famous formulation: "As there is a certain degree of depravity in human nature which requires a certain degree of circumspection and distrust, so there are other qualities in human nature which justify a certain portion of esteem and confidence."[42]

It should be noted however, that Rousseau and his most discerning readers, especially Tocqueville, served the world's democratic experiments well as sources of constructive criticism. They were instrumental in keeping alive the classical insight that a healthy polity cannot be sustained without virtuous citizens and good customs. They have been among the main contributors to the classical critique of liberalism that has sustained, enriched, and corrected the excesses of democratic states. At the same time, however, liberal democracy has been menaced by Rousseau's most illegitimate offspring—not the descendants of his abandoned children who, one hopes, may still be thriving somewhere—but those political figures who bridle at authority themselves, yet advocate authoritarian measures to force others to be free.

Generations of scholars have attempted to resolve the seeming contradictions in Rousseau's political writings, notably between his passionate attachment to natural freedom and his complacency about the state that compels nonconformists to be free. Rousseau himself thought the ideas in *The Social Contract* could work only in a small homogeneous polity like Geneva or possibly Corsica.[43] He opposed revolution, and was generally pessimistic about the possibility of changing bad institutions.

But in the worlds of politics and culture, what Rousseau actually said or meant was of less consequence than the emotional responses his writings stirred. Rousseau's critique of existing governments was heady stuff. The subtlety of his political thought was masked by his fluid, seductive literary style. His writings thus became a reservoir of ideas and slogans from which individualists and communitarians, revolutionaries and conservatives, moralists and bohemians, constitutionalists and Marxists drew freely and selectively. Vulgarization of his thought sheared off his deep historical pessimism, with the result that his influence at the popular level was overwhelmingly to the Left where, ironically, it fed the nineteenth-century cult of progress.

Though Rousseau was the leading secular thinker of the Counter-Enlightenment, his "defense" of religion shows how firmly he stood within the modern horizon of his antagonists, and how he extended that horizon. Voltaire and others, much impressed by the natural science of their day, mounted an offensive against what they called clericalism but by which they meant Christianity in general and Catholicism in particular. They portrayed organized religion as an impediment to progress and a bastion of bigoted ignorance. Rousseau gained more credit than he deserved for reproving their contempt of religion in his "First Discourse," for he was no friendlier to traditional religion than they. His childhood exposure to Calvinism and his brief later passage through Catholicism left him with a vocabulary and a critical stance, but little more. Where Christianity was concerned, he seems to have unquestioningly accepted the reigning opinion among the secular learned men of his time.

He made his views about organized religion clear in *Émile* and *The Social Contract*, so clear in fact that he was forced to flee from both Swiss and French authorities. The Savoyard vicar in *Émile* sounded much like Rousseau himself. He argued that the presence of religion in society should be welcomed, but not the religion of the day. Rejecting *both* reason and revelation, he proclaimed that, "The essential worship is that of the heart. God does not reject its homage, if it is sincere, in whatever form it is offered to him."[44] The religion that Rousseau "defended" was a radically subjective one based on inner sentiment—a belief system rooted in being true to one's own feelings. It was the religion of Madame de Warens.

That private, inner religion was well-suited for the ideal polity outlined in *The Social Contract*. Once a truly legitimate state has been constructed, Rousseau argued, religion would be helpful in shoring it up—ideally, a patriotic "civil religion."[45] Sharing Hobbes's belief in the need to discourage organized competitors for loyalty to the state, Rousseau held that a well-constituted state could be tolerant of religious activity so long as it was primarily inward and private. Unlike Luther and other reformers, he was uninterested in correcting the defects of institutional religion. He came not to support their critique, but to push it to the limit.

Morality, in Rousseau's view, was rooted in neither reason nor revelation, but in the natural feeling of compassion. Indeed, he is in an important sense the father of the politics of compassion. As we now know, however, compassion is a shaky foundation on which to build a just society. Compassion, unlike charity, is not a virtue acquired by self-discipline and habitual practice. It is only a feeling, and a fleeting one at that. It yields not only to self-preservation, but to self-interest.

It was the expression of Rousseau's ideas as much as the ideas themselves that won admiration from a surprising assortment of readers. Both Marie-Antoinette and Robespierre were devotees, though not to the same works. Even Napoleon had to confess that, as a youth, he had been captivated: "Until I was sixteen, I would have fought for Rousseau against the friends of Voltaire."[46] Tocqueville wrote that Rousseau, with Pascal and Montesquieu, was one of the three writers with whom he "lived a little every day."[47]

Julie marked the rise of the romantic literary genre that celebrates the primacy of feeling and the beauties of nature, while the *Confessions* did the same for the modern literature of self-revelation. Taken out of context, his passages on the communal existence of peoples, his evocation of a lost happy childhood of the human race, and his stress on the importance of religion found wide and disparate audiences, as did his critiques of the commercial mentality, the institution of private property, and the conquest of nature. The new human sciences of anthropology and psychology and the modern understanding of history are all in his debt.

Yet not all of his insights were original. He had a large unacknowledged debt to Montesquieu. He borrowed heavily, though haphazardly, from classical and biblical sources to criticize the reigning dogmas of his age. The extent of his obligation was not always apparent, for he was adept at "translating" traditional wisdom into language that appealed to secular intellectuals. Though his skepticism about the benefits of progress in the arts and sciences was at odds with widely held views among educated men of his time, such attitudes were common among the women who were his closest friends, and in popular devotional literature.

Madame de Stael once remarked of Rousseau, "He had nothing new, but he set everything on fire."[48] Though exaggerating his lack of originality, she did not overestimate the magic of his prose. Rousseau was a consummate stylist, the father of the sound-bite, a phrase-maker par excellence. He was able to give many different kinds of readers the impression that he understood and empathized with their deepest concerns. Above all, he tapped into *ressentiment* as no writer had done before. All the humiliations he had suffered in his life, all the pettiness and vice he had observed in the households of the ruling classes, lent power to his prose. Many others before and since have written about the plight of the disadvantaged and the injuries of class, but Rousseau remains, as Judith Shklar once put it, the "Homer of the losers."

By Rousseau's own lights, however, his influence was different from, even opposite to, what he had hoped. His philosophical ideas, he frequently insisted, were only for the few, and the writings containing them could not be understood unless read in relation to one another—and more than once. The teaching of the "First Discourse," for instance, is not that the sciences and the arts are unworthy pursuits, but that their spread to the public at large, their vulgarization, had had a corrupting effect—by destabilizing customary morality and fostering skepticism. The best education for ordinary folk, Rousseau held, was education aimed at the formation of healthy sentiments.

But no writer can control how and by whom his works are read. Discerning readers like Tocqueville and Kant were stimulated by Rousseau. To them, his writings were sources of enrichment and challenge, not least because, in his borderline mystical way, he carried forward to the new science of politics important insights from classical and biblical thought. Many activists who were "influenced" by Rousseau's political ideas, however, probably never read even one of his works in its entirety. More often than not, Rousseau's writings seem to have affected the emotions of his readers more than their intellects. As Jacques Maritain, who detested Rousseau, pointed out, Rousseau, more than any other writer, gave voice to the longings of his times:

[S]uch men are prophets of the spirit of the world, prophets of below, who concentrate in their heart the influences which work in the deeps of wounded humanity during a whole epoch. They then proclaim the age which is to follow them, and at the same time discharge on the future with prodigious strength those influences which have found their unity in them. They act on men by an awakening of emotional sympathies. . . . They spread around them the contagion of their self, the waves of their feelings and their instincts, they absorb people into their temperament.[49]

What is one to make of a body of thought so ambiguous and so influential as that of Rousseau? Rousseau's native genius enabled him to acquire a good grasp of one of the two great pre-modern intellectual traditions. He learned enough from the ancient Greeks to mount a powerful critique of narrow scientific rationalism, but not enough to appreciate the more capacious form of reason that infused classical, biblical, and legal traditions alike with dynamism. Like the Enlightenment thinkers he criticized, Rousseau rejected the moral and intellectual traditions that had nourished his own genius. He thus failed to see that what he called "perfectibility" was rooted in man's innate desire to know, the desire that gives rise to the never-ending, recurrent operations of questioning, experiencing, understanding, and choosing. Ironically, philosophical works that he intended for the few fostered popular skepticism and relativism, while his writings addressed to the many promoted a revolt against reason even among philosophers.

This prodigiously gifted, gravely flawed genius of the eighteenth century was at his best when he reminded his proud contemporaries of the limitations of science and politics. He sounded an early, much-needed warning that material progress does not necessarily bring moral progress. He helped to keep alive the classical insight that good government requires moral foundations. He gave vivid expression to the plight of the poor and marginalized. But the practical effects of his political ideas in France were alarming enough to prompt Napoleon's observation that it would have been better for the country if Rousseau had never lived. Philosopher-statesman Edmund Burke, to whom we next turn, wrote in 1790 that "were Rousseau alive and in one of his lucid intervals, he would be shocked at the practical phrenzy" of the revolutionaries who claimed to be inspired by his works.[50] Rousseau's political ideas were "so inapplicable to real life and manners," said Burke, "that we [in England] never dream of drawing from them any rule for laws or conduct."[51]

EIGHT

EDMUND BURKE

MAN ON A TIGHTROPE

If, as Aristotle held, the two most choice-worthy callings are politics and philosophy, it must be acknowledged that there are few people for whom that really is a choice, and still fewer whose talents equip them well for either vocation. Edmund Burke, however, would surely deserve a place with Cicero in the Pantheon of those who have excelled in both domains.

Burke attracted favorable notice from such luminaries as Kant and Diderot for a little book on aesthetics published when he was only twenty-eight, but he never aspired to the life of a scholar. "He that lives in a college after his mind is sufficiently stocked with learning," he once said, "is like a man who having built and rigged and victualled a ship, should lock her up in dry dock."[1] Like Cicero who, not surprisingly, was the classical author he loved best, Burke was a "new man," a talented youth from the provincial gentry ambitious to succeed in the world of the forum.

Succeed he did, to the point where later generations would honor the Irish-born Burke not only as one of the greatest British statesmen, but as a major political philosopher.

The obstacles faced by an Irish outsider in eighteenth-century London were so formidable that Burke in his old age wrote, with a certain pride: "I was not . . . swaddled and rocked and dandled into a legislator. Nitor in adversum [I strive against adversity] is the motto for a man like me. . . . At every step of my progress in life (for in every step I was traversed and opposed), and at every turnpike I met, I was obliged to show my passport, and again and again to prove my sole title to the honour of being useful to my country."[2]

It was not until Conor Cruise O'Brien's masterful biography in 1992 that the full poignancy of that passage has become clear.[3] O'Brien, a scholar and statesman himself, had always sensed there was more to Burke's story than previous chroniclers had discovered. Thanks to O'Brien's research into Burke's Irish and Catholic connections, and his interpretation of how they affected his political life, a more interesting and complicated picture of the man has emerged. It is a picture of a man who, despite many successes, always remained a stranger in a strange land.

Burke was born in 1729 into a conquered country where most Catholic lands had been confiscated, and where the largely impoverished Catholic majority was ruled under the harsh system known as the Penal Laws. Catholics could neither vote nor hold public office, and were subject to severe restrictions on the ownership of property. Even the public practice of their religion was banned. The barriers to economic advancement were such that a Catholic man who wished to get ahead was under strong pressure to join the Protestant Church of Ireland (which required taking a public oath in which he repudiated the religion of his ancestors). There is evidence that Burke's father, Richard, registered as a convert in 1722, a year before he set up a legal practice in Dublin.

Although such conversions sufficed to open certain doors, converts remained suspect—often with good reason—of being crypto-Catholics. The Burke family was vulnerable in that respect, for Richard's wife, Mary Nagle, remained a practicing Catholic, and they raised their daughter as a Catholic, even though the law specifically forbade attorneys to educate their children in the Roman religion. The couple's three sons, however, were brought up in the Church of Ireland. To Edmund's lifelong friend, Richard Shackleton, a Quaker, it seemed that Richard Burke was more concerned to improve his sons' chances for success "than about controversial parts of religion, and therefore brought his sons up in the profession of that which he thought the public road to preferment, viz., the religion of the country, established by law."[4]

As a child, Edmund Burke was so frail that his parents placed him with his mother's relatives in County Cork, hoping that the boy's health would improve away from the fetid air of Dublin. There in Ballyduff, he received most of his early education in one of the little Catholic "hedge schools" that had sprung up all over Ireland in defiance of the law (so called because they were often held in the open air to enable teacher and students to quickly disperse). When Burke was twelve, his father moved him to a Quaker boarding school (run by Shackleton's father) to assure him a proper preparation for Trinity College, Dublin.

The parts of the Penal Laws banning the practice of Catholicism were spottily enforced, but they fostered watchfulness and secrecy among those affected. In some respects, the life of families like the Burkes was comparable to that of the Murano Jews in Spain, outwardly conforming but, to varying degrees, privately holding to their ancestral ways. O'Brien describes the relation of the Burke family to the Ireland of the Penal Laws as "tense, equivocal and secretive." They spent their lives in "a zone of insecurity, in which habitual reticence was the norm, and dissimulation an occasional resource."[5]

Children had to be taught caution at an early age. That Edmund Burke had learned his lessons well is apparent from a note he wrote at age sixteen to his friend Shackleton: "We live in a world where everyone is on the catch, and the only way to be safe is to be silent—silent in any affair of consequence; and I think it would not be a bad rule for every man to keep within what he thinks of others, of himself, and of his own affairs."[6]

After compiling a distinguished record at Trinity College, where he founded a debating club and a journal of opinion, Burke set out for

London. There, obedient to the paternal plan, he enrolled to read law at the Middle Temple. To Richard Burke's dismay, however, the twenty-one-year-old conceived an intense dislike for law studies. To make matters worse, rumors reached Dublin that he was becoming interested in Catholicism and might even have reverted to the faith of his mother and his forebears. He attended the Inns of Court sporadically over the next five years, but never followed his father into the practice of law.

It is not known whether Edmund Burke flirted with Catholicism in this period, for he later destroyed many of his personal papers. But it is certainly the case that he flirted with a young lady from a Catholic family, Jane Nugent, whom he married in 1757. His wife, like his mother, remained a practicing Catholic throughout what was, by all accounts, a very close and companionable marriage. Where Burke's own private beliefs are concerned, all the evidence indicates that he was a serious Christian who believed in the core doctrines shared by the Anglican Church to which he belonged and the Roman Catholic Church of his ancestors, paying little attention to the issues that divided them.[7]

Burke's aversion to the study of law is comprehensible. British legal education in his day was entirely organized by practitioners in their Inns located near the Royal Courts. English law was not taught in universities until 1758, when a special chair was established at Oxford for that purpose. The first occupant of that chair, the great jurist William Blackstone, explained in his inaugural lecture that the Inns of Court had little to attract a young man with a wide-ranging restless intellect:

> We may appeal to the experience of every sensible lawyer, whether any thing can be more hazardous or discouraging, than the usual entrance on the study of the law. A raw and inexperienced youth, in the most dangerous season of life, is transplanted on a sudden into the midst of allurements to pleasure, without any restraint or check but what his own prudence can suggest. . . . In this situation he is expected to sequester himself from the world and, by a tedious lonely

process, to extract the theory of the law from a mass of undigested learning. . . . How little, therefore, is it to be wondered at that we hear of so frequent miscarriages; that so many gentlemen of bright imaginations grow weary of so unpromising a search and addict themselves wholly to amusements, or other less innocent pursuits, and that so many persons of moderate capacity confuse themselves at first setting out, and continue ever dark and puzzled during the reminder of their lives.[8]

Far more interesting to Burke than the Inns of Court were London's famed coffee houses buzzing with ideas and argument, and its Houses of Parliament where one could hear debate on the great issues of the day. He also discovered to his delight that a good writer could make a decent living in London. His efforts were so successful that he soon became an established figure in that city's lively literary scene.

By his late twenties, he had published numerous articles and pamphlets, plus two well-received books. The first, A Vindication of Natural Society (1756), was a satirical work ridiculing the fashionable Deists of his day and the back-to-nature movement that had been inspired by Rousseau. His Philosophical Enquiry into the Origins of Our Ideas of the Sublime and Beautiful (1757) remains, according to Paul Johnson, "the most influential tract on aesthetics ever published in the Anglo-Saxon world."[9] Its admirers included Dr. Samuel Johnson, who was to become a good friend.

Burke also gained a reputation as a raconteur, possessed of a seemingly inexhaustible repertoire of well-told, pointed anecdotes. Describing the young man's acceptance into the circle of eminent Londoners that surrounded Johnson, the English essayist Thomas Babington Macaulay gave condescending credit to the newcomer's skill as a conversationalist:

A young Irishman had, some time before, come over to push his fortune in London. He had written much for the booksellers; but he was best known by a little treatise in which the style and reasoning of Bolingbroke were mimicked with exquisite skill and by a theory, of more ingenuity than soundness, touching the pleasures which we receive from the objects of taste. He had also attained a high reputation as a talker, and was regarded by the men of letters who supped together at the Turk's Head as the only match in conversation for Dr. Johnson.[10]

Johnson himself held the newcomer in something like awe. "Burke," he said, "is the only man whose common conversation corresponds with the general fame which he has in the world. Take up whatever topic you please, he is ready to meet you."[11] The story is told by Boswell that on one occasion when Johnson was ill, he refused a visit from Burke, saying, "That fellow calls forth all my powers. Were I to see Burke now, it would kill me."[12]

It was Burke's skill with a pen, however, rather than his rhetorical gifts that first caught the attention of politicians. At the age of thirty he was hired as the assistant to a member of Parliament who shortly thereafter became Britain's Chief Secretary for Ireland. As luck would have it, one of his first assignments—the preparation of a position paper on Ireland—brought him face to face with some of the most difficult dilemmas that principled men and women encounter in public life: How can I advance the causes I believe in—especially if they are unpopular—without rendering myself so marginal as to be politically ineffective? Can I achieve enough political influence to be an effective actor without betraying my principles in the process?

From that moment on, Burke found himself on a tightrope that he had to walk throughout the rest of his life in politics. At the beginning, he tiptoed cautiously—so cautiously that in later years some would criticize him for having written in his report on Ireland that the provisions of the Penal Laws excluding Catholics from public office were "just and necessary."[13] Certainly that concession was profoundly incompatible with everything that Burke was later to write about the subject. O'Brien pointed out, however, that the paper in question did criticize the Penal Laws, and that the statement in question was probably made to secure the agreement of Burke's boss to the other points in the paper. O'Brien added that, "While Burke generally argued from deep and strong conviction, he was not above the occasional tactical adjustment if it might serve to carry the rest of his argument."

How far was Burke prepared to go in making such "tactical adjustments"? We have his own interesting statement that, "Falsehood and delusion are allowed in no case whatever. But, as in the exercise of all the virtues, there is an economy of truth. It is a sort of temperance, by which a man speaks truth with measure that he may speak it the longer."[14]

The idea of an "economy of truth" did not sit well with Dr. Johnson, who often erred in the other direction, blurting out remarks that a more courteous or prudent person would have kept to himself. Political prudence, however, was a difficult concept for Johnson to appreciate. Despite his admiration for Burke, he once remarked to Boswell, "I do not say that he is not honest; but we have no reason to conclude from his political conduct that he is honest."[15]

Both Boswell and Johnson deplored Burke's option for politics as a great loss to the world of philosophy. In a famous passage from his life of Johnson, Boswell recounted a conversation about Berkeley's proposition that qualities of matter such as size and weight have no existence independent of the human mind. After listening to Boswell lament the difficulty of refuting such a notion, Johnson kicked a stone and said, "I refute it thus." That did not satisfy Boswell, whose thoughts turned to Burke:

> I know that the nice and difficult task was to have been undertaken by one of the most luminous minds of the present age, had not politicks 'turned him from philosophy aside.' What an admirable display of subtility, united with brilliance, might his contending with Berkeley have afforded us! How must we, when we reflect on the loss of such an intellectual feast, regret that he should be characterised as the man,
>
> Who born for the universe narrow'd his mind,
> And to party gave up what was meant for mankind?[16]

As Burke advanced up the political ladder, he was dogged by rumors concerning his Catholic affiliations. Cartoonists never failed to portray him in clerical garb, wearing a Roman collar, and with a whiskey bottle and a potato close at hand. Allegations of disloyalty, in fact, nearly cost him the position that launched him into Parliament. In 1765, Burke was hired as private secretary to the Marquess of Rockingham, the leader of a section of the Whig party that was opposed to King George III's encroachments on the constitutional order that had been established in the wake of the Revolution of 1688. The job was a giant step up, for Rockingham was then the head of a newly formed coalition government. But when the elderly Duke of Newcastle heard of the appointment, he urged Rockingham to drop his connection with Burke. The Irishman, he said, was a spy and adventurer whose real name was O'Bourke. He was not only a Roman Catholic, claimed the Duke, but—even worse—a concealed Jesuit![17]

Fortunately for Burke, Rockingham ignored the Duke's advice. But in the early days of his employment, Burke's position was precarious. That is evident from his response to an urgent message from an Irish relative about the plight of a cousin who had eloped with a Protestant heiress, a capital offense under the Penal Laws. Burke's letter explaining his inability to be of assistance is revealing:

> I am sincerely concerned for the match that Garrett was so unfortunate as to make, and did from the beginning expect no better issue from it, in a country circumstanced as ours is. Assure my uncle that there is no one step on earth in my power that I would not gladly take . . . but I believe when he reflects how newly and almost as a stranger I am come about these people, and knows the many industrious endeavors which malice and envy (very unprovoked indeed) have used to ruin me, he will see, that so early a request to suspend the operation of the Laws, upon my bare word, against the finding of a jury of the greatest County of the Kingdom, and that upon the most unpopular point in the world, could have no other effect than to do me infinite prejudice, without the least probability of succeeding in the object aimed at.[18]

Burke had good reason to be cautious, for the politics of personal destruction was zealously practiced in his day. Some of his enemies, seeking substantiation for their accusations of Papist sympathies, went so far as to induce an acquaintance of Burke's friend Shackleton to send Shackleton a seemingly innocent request for information about Burke's early life, religion, and family connections. Shackleton wrote a glowing reply, extolling Burke's gifts and virtues. Unaware of the writer's true purpose, Shackleton mentioned that Burke's mother "was of a Popish family" and that "she practiced the duties of the Romish religion with a decent privacy." He described Burke's wife as "a genteel, well-bred woman of the Roman faith whom he married neither for her religion, nor her money but from that natural impulse of youthful affection."[19]

When that letter was made public in 1770, Burke was furious at his friend's lack of discretion. "The more circumstances of all these which are brought out," he wrote to Shackleton, "the more materials are furnished for malice to work upon: and I assure you that it will manufacture them to the utmost."[20] It was only to be expected, he said, that a public figure such as himself should experience all sorts of buffeting, but it pained him to see his wife "the daily subject of Grub-street, and newspaper invectives."

Quite apart from the cruder forms of bigotry and the slanders of political opponents, Burke had to contend with assumptions about the Irish that were prevalent among the genteel Englishmen with whom he regularly associated. O'Brien compared Burke's position to that of "a Jewish person, brought up as a Christian, and having to listen, from time to time, to fellow Christians holding forth about 'the Jews' in hostile and contemptuous terms."[21]

It did not take long, however, for Burke to win the confidence of his new employer. Rockingham was so impressed with his secretary's skill as a writer and his prodigious capacity for hard work that, by the end of 1765, he had arranged for the younger man to be seated in the House of Commons as representative of the pocket borough of Wendover. As time went on, Rockingham came to depend ever more heavily on Burke, to the point where the former private secretary became the chief theoretician, strategist, and policy maker of the Rockingham Whigs.

From O'Brien's biography Burke emerges as a much lonelier figure in this period than had been previously supposed. He had to appear far more detached about the plight of Ireland than he felt, not only in the interest of his career, but for the sake of the Irish people whom he wished eventually to help. He was not yet strong enough to be of effective assistance, and to act prematurely might destroy his chances of being effective in the future. Yet there were times when the Rockingham Whigs were deeply involved in Irish affairs (about which they were often ill-informed). On such occasions, O'Brien speculates, Burke must have felt like "a tongue-tied and irritable passenger in a vehicle that was travelling in the wrong direction," and the artificiality of his public position "must have been a torment to him."[22]

In 1774, after a hard-fought campaign, Burke was elected to the most important political office he would ever achieve—Member of the House of Commons from Bristol, then the second-largest city in England. When one of Samuel Johnson's acquaintances expressed surprise at the Irishman's victory, Johnson predicted in reply that "We who know him, know that he will be one of the first men in the country."[23]

When Burke took his seat from Bristol, relations between Great Britain and her subjects in the American colonies were deteriorating, but he believed they were not beyond repair. He became a leading parliamentary proponent of conciliation, arguing that the colonists as Englishmen should enjoy the same benefits of citizenship as their compatriots in the mother country.[24] When those efforts failed, he and the other Rockingham Whigs became advocates for granting the colonies their independence rather than prolonging a costly war.

Some have found it puzzling that Burke supported independence for the Americans while opposing fellow Irishmen who were agitating for Irish independence. In the late eighteenth century, however, home rule for Ireland would almost certainly have meant increased oppression for the beleaguered Catholic population, for it would have freed the Irish Parliament, composed largely of Protestant landlords, from control by the British Privy Council. Burke's judgment was that the best chance of dismantling the system of Penal Laws was to work for reform within the British Parliament with the help of the Whigs—whom he considered the most enlightened and principled of English politicians. As he once said, "Everything in political conduct depends on occasions and opportunities."[25]

Burke was not willing to wait indefinitely, however, for the perfect occasion or the ideal opportunity. In his famous speech to the electors at Bristol, still a staple of college government courses, he announced the principle that eventually would cost him his seat. A representative, he said, should give great weight to the wishes of his constituents, but should not surrender his independent judgment:

> [H]is unbiased opinion, his mature judgement, his enlightened conscience, he ought not to sacrifice to you, to any man, or to any set of men living. These he does not derive from your pleasure,—no, nor from the law and the Constitution. They are a trust from Providence for the abuse of which he is deeply answerable. Your representative owes you, not his industry only, but his judgement; and he betrays, instead of serving you, if he sacrifices it to your pleasure.[26]

As representative of a great commercial center like Bristol, the expedient course for Burke would have been to support the protectionist trade measures favored by the city's leading merchants. Instead, he offended his constituents' economic interests by advocating free trade with Ireland, and aroused their prejudices by working to bring about reform of the Penal Laws.

It must have been disheartening to Burke that those politically costly efforts on behalf of the Irish Catholics brought him criticism from some of the very people whose lot he sought to improve. Some fellow Irishmen, failing to understand Burke's incremental approach, complained that he had only sought repeal of some laws while leaving other equally repressive measures on the books. But as Burke once explained in another context, "It is a settled rule with me to make the most of my actual situation, and not to refuse to do a proper thing because there is something else more proper, which I am not able to do."[27]

It was in fact a major accomplishment to achieve the passage of the controversial Catholic Relief Act of 1778, the first-ever reform of the Penal Laws. Though he had arranged to have the act presented by an English parliamentary colleague, Burke was the principal author of that path-breaking legislation. Word of his involvement soon got out, however, and when 60,000 rioters surrounded the House of Commons demanding repeal of the Act, there were many threats against his life. By 1780, his unpopularity with his Bristol constituents was so great that he withdrew his bid for reelection. He was able to keep a seat in the House of Commons only by securing election from the pocket borough of Malton, where he remained for the rest of his parliamentary life.

If Burke had been a different sort of person, he might simply have opted to blend into the dominant culture, and forget about Ireland. But he declined to take that route, and paid a price in the sense that his party never again considered him for high political office. Burke's nineteenth-century biographer, John Morley, deplored the ingratitude of the Whigs to the member to whom they owed so much:

> With the usual insolent thanklessness shown by patricians in every age and country towards the greater plebeians who supply them with ideas and a policy, the party never offered him a seat in their cabinets. But, for all that, he was their inspirer. To him they owed the whole vitality of their creed, the whole coherence of their principle, the whole of that enlightenment, that rational love of liberty, that antipathy to arbitrary ideas, on which rest their just claims to the gratitude of their descendants.[28]

Harvey Mansfield speculates that the party regulars distrusted their ablest member precisely "for the very energy he used in their behalf, for his eagerness to act against dangers of which only he could see and feel the full measure, and for the passion displayed in the gorgeous rhetoric they admired."[29]

Despite the fact that he never held high office, it is hard to imagine how Burke could have accomplished more in his remaining years of public service than he did as representative from Malton. By his own lights, his most important service in that period was his relentless crusade against the oppressive regime that the East India

Company had established with sovereign-like power in Bengal. During Burke's early years in the House of Commons, he had gone along with the policy of the Rockingham Whigs to support the East India Company in its efforts to resist parliamentary regulation. But gradually he became aware that the Company, headed by the Governor-General of Bengal, Warren Hastings, was presiding over a vast system of bribery, extortion, and other abuses, including torture. He persuaded the Rockinghams to change their position, and he himself became the most implacable enemy of the Company and its powerful leader.

Burke's efforts met with strong opposition, but he achieved a major success when the House of Commons voted in 1787 to bring Hastings before the House of Lords on a bill of impeachment, and designated Burke himself to present the case. As Cicero had done in the prosecution of Verres, the corrupt governor of Sicily, Burke painstakingly gathered evidence and prepared to give some of the best speeches of his life. He knew from the outset that the prospects of conviction were dim, for Hastings was well-connected, and it was nearly impossible to prove that he had personally committed crimes or even that he ordered others to do so. But the trial enabled Burke to place before the Lords and the public a detailed and shocking picture of large-scale corruption and abuse.

Hastings put on a vigorous defense, resting in part on the argument that his actions in India should not be judged by European standards, to which Burke issued a memorable reply in the language of universal moral law:

> This geographical morality we do protest against; Mr. Hastings shall not screen himself under it; and on this point I hope and trust many words will not be necessary to satisfy your Lordships. But we think it necessary, in justification of ourselves, to declare that the laws of morality are the same everywhere, and there is no action which would pass for an act of extortion, of peculation, of bribery, and of oppression in England that is not an act of extortion, of peculation, of bribery and oppression in Europe, Asia, Africa, and all the world over.[30]

In the end, Hastings was acquitted, after a trial that had dragged on with fits and starts for seven years in the House of Lords. But the prosecution was not in vain. By bringing the Company's practices out into the light of day, Burke had set in motion forces that would eventually put an end to the oppressive system that had prevailed under Hastings. Late in life, he wrote:

> If I were to call for a reward (which I have never done), it should be for those [services] in which for fourteen years, without intermission, I shewed the most industry, and had the least success; I mean in the affairs of India. They are those on which I value myself the most; the most for the importance; the most for the labour; most for the judgement; most for constancy and perseverance in the pursuit.[31]

Crowds had packed the galleries when the trial of Warren Hastings began in 1788. The Queen herself had attended on the first day, along with scores of celebrities. Burke's opening statements, where he portrayed what today would be called human rights violations in horrifying detail, were the talk of the town. But people soon wearied of the long, drawn-out legal proceeding, and public attention shifted to the exciting events that were taking place in France.

The early "constitutional" phase of the French Revolution had rendered many of Burke's political associates starry-eyed. To Charles James Fox, who became the leader of the Rockingham Whigs after Rockingham's death in 1782, the fall of the Bastille on July 14, 1789, was "the greatest event that ever happened in the world." Those were the heady days of which Wordsworth had written:

> Bliss was it in that dawn to be alive,
> But to be young was very heaven!—Oh! times,
> In which the meagre, stale, forbidding ways
> Of custom, law, and statute, took at once
> The attraction of a country in romance!
> When Reason seemed the most to assert her rights,
> When most intent on making of herself

A prime Enchantress—to assist the work,
Which then was going forward in her name![32]

To many English sympathizers, it seemed that the French were following the example set by the English themselves in 1688. They expected that the violent uprisings of 1789 would soon be followed by a benign and much-needed transition to constitutional monarchy.

Burke was much more wary of the motives of the French insurgents, noting that they had not hesitated to shed blood in July and October of that year while proclaiming the rights of man. In November 1789, while still on the fence, he advised a young French friend to consider not only the high-minded slogans of the revolution but the character of the people who were mouthing them:

> Never wholly separate in your mind the merits of any political question from the men who are concerned in it. You will be told that if a measure is good, what have you to do with the character and views of those who bring it forward? But designing men never separate their plans from their interests; and if you assist them in their schemes, you will find the pretended good in them thrown aside or perverted, and the interested object alone compassed, and that perhaps through your means. The power of bad men is no indifferent thing.[33]

By January 1790, Burke had made up his mind. He took a public stand after reading pamphlets suggesting that just as the French had been inspired by the English Revolution of 1688, the English could now learn from the French. Burke's vehement opposition, on the floor of the House of Commons, to English support for the French uprising brought him into open conflict with his longtime friend and party chieftain Fox. Within months, their disagreement over France had become so severe that Burke left the party that had been his political home since 1774. Up to that point, as Harvey Mansfield has shown, Burke had done more than any other man to revitalize English politics by promoting party government, often sacrificing personal interest to party loyalty.[34] He had helped to transform the Rockingham Whigs from a faction into a party that possessed and more or less consistently acted upon a set of known principles. Now he had reached a crossroads where personal friendship and party loyalty alike had to be sacrificed for the sake of defending what he called the country's "antient constitution."

Burke threw himself into working on his Reflections on the Revolution in France, the tract that was to become a best seller upon its publication later that year, and to remain a classic of Western political philosophy. He began by condemning the English pamphleteers and speakers who seemed to him to be promoting a monstrous distortion of the British Revolution of 1688:

> We ought not, on either side of the water, to suffer ourselves to be imposed upon by the counterfeit wares which some persons, by a double fraud, export to you in illicit bottoms, as raw commodities of British growth though wholly alien to our soil, in order afterwards to smuggle them back again into this country, manufactured after the newest Paris fashion of an improved liberty.[35]

What still astonishes readers of the Reflections is that Burke was able to forecast the horrors and totalitarian tendencies that were yet to come, and to do so at a time when many people assumed that the violent phase of the Revolution was over and that a new constitutional order was in the making. In 1790, with the Reign of Terror and the executions of the King and Queen still in the future, Burke seems to have been virtually alone in understanding that the Revolution had not run its course. He predicted not only its spiraling descent into terror ("In the groves of their academy, at the end of every visto, you see nothing but the gallows"),[36] but the likelihood that "some popular general" would take advantage of the chaotic situation and become "the master of your whole republic."[37] At the time, Napoleon Bonaparte was a twenty-one-year-old soldier.

At first glance, Burke's fierce opposition to the French Revolution might seem inconsistent with his sympathy for the cause of the American colonists and for the Revolution of 1688 that had given England a constitutional monarchy. But for Burke, it was a home truth that circumstances alter cases, and in his view, when all circumstances were considered, the French revolution was "the most astonishing that has hitherto happened in the world"—and far from the most admirable.[38] The English in 1688 did not destroy the whole fabric of their government; rather, they built upon the parts of their "antient constitution" that had served the country well. The Americans had fought against the arbitrary denial of the rights that belonged to them as Englishmen, and in establishing their own constitution they drew heavily on their British inheritance. The French revolutionaries, by contrast, were bent on tearing down an entire social order; theirs was not only a political revolution but a "revolution in sentiments, manners and moral opinions." "You began ill," Burke chided them, "because you began by despising everything that belonged to you. You set up your trade without a capital."[39]

He made clear that he was neither a blind worshipper of tradition nor a foe of political change. Indeed, he said, "A state without the means of some change is without the means of its conservation."[40] What he favored was the approach to change that had characterized the development of the English common law, building on and bringing forward what had proved its value in practice, while leaving behind what had proved harmful ("In what we improve, we are never wholly new; in what we retain, we are never wholly obsolete").[41] What he opposed above all were sudden, radical changes instigated by persons careless of the consequences. As for tradition, he held that there should be a presumption in favor of a governmental practice under which a people has flourished, but he well understood that presumptions can be rebutted.

Burke's Reflections were so dismissive of "theory," "metaphysics" and "speculation" that some have characterized him as a political theorist who mistrusted political theory.[42] Even the best of the French revolutionary leaders, he scoffed, were "only men of theory"— "professors of the rights of men" who were so busy teaching others that they never learned anything themselves about the practical arts of government.[43] Such passages, however, did not imply contempt for theory as such, but rather for abstract theory divorced from practical reason and experience.

Burke had an extraordinary ability to keep theory and practice working together. No one since Cicero had been at once so gifted in politics, and so grounded in philosophy. Morley's tribute to Burke captured that quality perfectly: "No one that ever lived used the general idea of the thinker more successfully to judge the particular problems of the statesman. No one has ever come so close to the details of practical politics, and at the same time remembered that these can only be understood and only dealt with by the aid of the broad conceptions of political philosophy."[44]

As with many thinkers whose works are too complex and nuanced to permit easy summary, Burke and his ideas have often been subject to oversimplification by critics and admirers alike. Most frequently, he is described as a leading "conservative." But even one of his severest critics had to admit that, "As an outsider who never got in, Burke often felt himself drawn to the oppressed, the wronged, the impotents of society: and alongside Burke the conservative there was also Burke the reformer who gets scant attention."[45] Perhaps Winston Churchill understood Burke's politics best when he observed:

> [A] charge of political inconsistency applied to this life appears a mean and petty thing. History easily discerns the reasons and forces which actuated him, and the immense changes in the problems he was facing which evoked from the same profound mind and sincere spirit these entirely contrary manifestations. His soul revolted against tyranny, whether it appeared in the aspect of a domineering Monarch and a corrupt Court and Parliamentary system, or whether, mouthing the watch-words of a non-existent liberty, it towered up against him in the dictation of a brutal mob and wicked sect. No one can read the Burke of Liberty and the Burke of Authority without feeling that here was the same man pursuing the same ends, seeking the same ideals of society and Government, and defending them from assaults, now from one extreme, now from the other.[46]

When the Reflections were published in 1790, Burke was nearing the end of his parliamentary career. For twenty-five years, he had championed five causes linked by a single theme. His efforts on behalf of the American colonists, the Catholics in Ireland, and the peoples of India, together with his condemnation of the French Revolution and his defense of the British constitutional system against royal encroachment, were all part of what W. B. Yeats in his poem "The Seven Sages" called "Burke's great melody," a lifelong struggle against the abuse of power.[47]

Four years later, by arrangement with the nobleman who controlled the pocket borough of Malton, Burke stepped down so that the seat could be taken by his only son Richard. Richard Burke seems to have had little inclination or ability to live up to his father's expectations. Nevertheless, Burke doted upon him and expended a great deal of political capital in promoting his career. He was filled with paternal pride when Richard was elected to succeed him, and devastated when the young man died of a sudden illness only weeks later. The acquittal of Warren Hastings the following year, though expected, only served to deepen Burke's increasingly melancholy mood. Not long before he died in 1797 at the age of sixty-eight, Burke wrote:

> Had it pleased God to continue to me the hopes of succession, I should have been according to my mediocrity and the mediocrity of the land I live in, a sort of founder of a family. . . . But a Disposer whose power we are little able to resist, and whose wisdom it behooves us not at all to dispute, has ordained it in another manner. . . . The storm has gone over me; and I lie like one of those old oaks which the late hurricane has scattered about me. I am stripped of all my honours, I am torn up by the roots, and lie prostrate on the earth. . . . They who ought to have succeeded me have gone before me. They who should have been to me as posterity are in the place of my ancestors.[48]

If judged only by the results visible in his lifetime, Burke's labors as a parliamentarian could be said to have been largely unsuccessful. America was lost. The Irish Catholics and the peoples of India remained oppressed. France had been convulsed with terror and was headed for tyranny. Burke's "great melody," however, continues to resonate with those who have ears to hear it.

NINE

TOCQUEVILLE THE POLITICIAN

$\mathbf{A}$ modern vocational counselor consulted by someone with Alexis de Tocqueville's talents would be hard put to encourage his ambitions for a political career. To be sure, the young aristocrat's brilliance, literary flair, and distinguished family background assured that a variety of vocational paths would be open to him. But his unprepossessing appearance, chronic ill health, weak voice, and proneness to stage fright did not augur well for a life in the public arena. The philosopher-statesman Pierre Royer-Collard, a family friend, gently but frankly advised Tocqueville to choose some other line of work, telling him that he would not get far in politics without the gift of oratory. Tocqueville himself was conscious of his drawbacks, but filled with yearnings that were too powerful to be denied. He confided to his future wife Mary Mottley that, "With limited abilities, I yet feel vast desires; with delicate health, an inexpressible need for action and emotion."[1]

For most of his life, the man who would be remembered as one of the greatest social theorists of all time persisted in believing that he was destined for statesmanship rather than scholarship. Even after the first edition of *Democracy in America* had become a runaway best seller, he rejected the idea of a literary career, telling Eugène Stoeffels, his boyhood friend and lifelong correspondent, "Do not believe that I have a blind enthusiasm, or indeed any kind of enthusiasm for the intellectual life. I have always placed the life of action above everything else."[2]

His political ambition was not strong enough, however, to subdue the fiercely independent temperament that put him at odds with all the established parties of his day. Though he lacked leadership qualities, he could not tolerate being a follower, or even bring himself to be a team player. He was thus doomed to a relatively marginal role during his public life. It was only toward the end of his days that he came to see his writings as his most important legacy, and to realize that his lasting contribution to politics would be in the realm of theory rather than practice.

Tocqueville was raised in a household where memories were vivid of the old regime and of the sufferings that family members had endured in the bloody Revolution that ended their former way of life. The most renowned of his forebears was his great-grandfather, Chrétien de Malesherbes, who had been a minister of state in the reign of Louis XVI. A man of the Enlightenment and an early advocate for the civil rights of Protestants and Jews, Malesherbes had resigned from the King's service in 1787 on principle in disappointment over the monarchy's failure to make what he regarded as necessary liberalizing reforms. In 1792, again on principle, he came out of retirement to defend the King against the charge of treason. The following year, when the Reign of Terror was in full swing, Malesherbes paid dearly for being a man of integrity. He himself ended up on the guillotine, along with several of his relatives.

Among those imprisoned and slated for execution were Tocqueville's parents, then newlyweds in their twenties. They were saved by the fall of Robespierre in July 1794, but Madame de Tocqueville never fully recovered physically or emotionally from their harrowing experience. She went on, however, to bear three sons, the third and youngest of whom, Alexis, was born in 1805, the year that Napoleon

Bonaparte had himself crowned Emperor. Tocqueville's father, Hervé de Tocqueville, occupied himself with local and familial affairs until the fall of the Napoleonic regime. Then, with the restoration of the Bourbon monarchy, he offered his time and talents to the State, serving with distinction as a public official under King Louis XVIII and his successor, Charles X.

As Tocqueville biographer André Jardin has explained, a civil service career in that period was regarded by many of the nobility as both a privilege and a duty. Count Hervé "saw his bond as vassal to the Bourbons strengthened by the sacrifice of the Malesherbes."[3]

> And this gentle, courteous man claimed for himself and his family the right to serve the State in his proper position in the hierarchy of public office. Ambitious and ostentatious, he freely spent his fortune in the service of the king. . . . These prefects of the early years of the Restoration kept alive the spirit of independence of the intendants of the Ancien Regime. . . . Around 1820 they would be replaced by docile civil servants in the modern style.

The family tradition of public service was so strong, according to Jardin, that Alexis "could not conceive of fulfilling his personal destiny in any other way than by active participation in political life."[4] Ill-suited by temperament or constitution for a military career like that of his older brothers, he opted for the public square. Like many an aspiring politician before and since, he enrolled in law school. And like many others, including Cicero and Burke, he found the study of law rather boring.

Upon completing his legal education in 1826, Tocqueville did not have to pound the cobblestones in search of a job. He stepped right into a patronage appointment as a junior magistrate. All it took was a letter from an official of the Court of Louis XVIII to the Minister of Justice recommending that a position be found for the youngest son of the Prefect of Versailles. The letter suggested that it would be "extremely suitable to do his father a favor that would amount to creating a veritable bond in Versailles between the administration and the judicial system."[5] In due course, the twenty-two-year-old novice was given a post created especially for him at the Versailles law courts. (In France, unlike in the Anglo-American systems, the ordinary judiciary is a branch of the civil service where candidates can be accepted for entry-level positions as soon as they have completed the required course of studies.)

To his relief, Tocqueville found his duties at the court more interesting than law school. To a boyhood friend he wrote that, "Law, which disgusted me in theory, doesn't produce the same effect in practice. All my abilities come together to find a solution or method; I feel that my mind is active, and developing in every way."[6] Though plagued by gastrointestinal difficulties that often prostrated him for days, he enjoyed his work. It irked him, however, that colleagues to whom he felt intellectually superior were better at it than he was: "I find it hard to get used to speaking in public: I grope for words and cut my arguments too short. Beside me are men who reason ill and speak well. That puts me in a continual rage. It seems to me that I am their superior, but when I come to make an effect, I know I am inferior."[7] In this peculiar frustration, he resembled his renowned predecessor Montesquieu, who once confessed that at the outset of his legal career, "I understood the questions in themselves well enough, but nothing of the procedure. I applied myself; but what disgusted me the most is that I saw in some idiots the very ability that escaped me."[8]

Among Tocqueville's co-workers at Versailles was another young aristocrat who was similarly ambitious to enter public life. Gustave de Beaumont and Alexis de Tocqueville became fast friends. Since legislation then in force required members of the Chamber of Deputies to be at least forty years old, the two junior magistrates began developing a long-range plan. At Tocqueville's suggestion, they embarked on a reading and study program that he described as aimed at "fashioning in ourselves the political man."[9]

Casting a shadow over that plan, however, was their uneasiness about the political situation in France. The late 1820s were marked by intense struggles among ultra-royalists who clung to the hope of turning back the clock; moderate royalists who favored a move toward constitutional monarchy; and republicans who were aiming for some form of representative government. Early in 1830, faced with rising social discontent, King Charles X tried to put a lid on the situation by issuing peremptory decrees abolishing freedom of the press and dissolving the newly elected Chamber of Deputies. When Tocqueville heard of those extraordinary measures, he publicly denounced them as illegal.

That rash outburst alarmed Tocqueville *père*, who fired off a note instructing his youngest son on the importance of prudence in politics: "Whatever you may think of the measures taken, I engage you to express yourself with restraint and moderation. You will easily realize that both sides will be much exasperated, and that the government, having taken such a decision, will have to break all opposition. Young people above all must be prudent so as not to compromise their position, especially those who having most talent can excite most envy."[10]

As it turned out, Tocqueville had nothing to fear from King Charles and his allies, for the days of their rule were numbered. In July 1830, a violent uprising forced Charles to abdicate in favor of a constitutional monarchy headed by the Duke of Orléans, who became King Louis-Philippe.

Civil servants who wanted to retain their positions were allowed to do so, but only if they would swear an oath of loyalty to the new King. That created a dilemma for Tocqueville. Most of his family and friends despised the nobles of the House of Orléans because the latter had openly sympathized with the French Revolution. Tocqueville, however, had come to believe that the Bourbons, with their arbitrariness and resistance to reasonable reforms, did not deserve the sacrifices that others had made on their behalf. It seemed to him that constitutional monarchy now offered the best prospect for the future of France. But the choice was not an easy one. "Right up to the end," he later recalled, "I had felt some remnants of hereditary affection for Charles X, but that king fell because he had violated rights that were dear to me, and I was able to hope that my country's freedom would be revived rather than extinguished by his fall."[11]

Tocqueville was painfully aware that his decision to take the oath would be regarded by many in his own circle as a repudiation of everything he had been brought up to believe. He also knew that some would see it as the kind of opportunism that was all too characteristic of members of his chosen profession. As historian Donald Kelley recounts, French jurists had proved remarkably adept at adjusting to sudden regime changes:

> In 1815, the law faculty shouted "Vive l'Empereur!" but welcomed his successor Louis XVIII in the "nineteenth year of his reign" even more enthusiastically with cries of "Vive le Roi!" "Vivent les Bourbons!" In fact, lawyers seemed to be instinctive Talleyrands. . . . Their sense of history allowed them, in other words, to move with the currents of change. It was not the king or the republic that "never dies," to paraphrase the old maxim; it was the legal profession.[12]

Fortunately for Tocqueville, his decision was eased by his under-standing father. Hervé de Tocqueville assured his sons that he would support them whatever they decided to do.[13] But Tocqueville remained troubled about the effect upon others in his circle, confiding his dis-comfort to Mary Mottley:

> My conscience is absolutely clear, but nonetheless I am deeply upset, and I count this day as among the unluckiest of my life. Marie, this is the first time since I entered society that I have had to avoid the company of people I admire while disapproving of them. . . . I have not failed in my duty, rather I have done what I should for my country which can find salvation only in the dominion now arising to save us from anarchy. But have I done my duty to myself, to my family, to those who once died for the cause which I am ceasing to serve just as everything turns against it?[14]

Beaumont, having taken the oath, was in a similar position. As Tocqueville had feared, many supporters of the old monarchy did regard them as traitors. Moreover, men like Tocqueville and Beau-mont did not gain many points with supporters of Louis-Philippe simply by virtue of having made a public profession of loyalty. They had too many ties through friends and family with the old regime. The new King had come to power with the backing of France's commercial and entrepreneurial classes. The rising bourgeoisie, now in political ascendancy, viewed with suspicion anyone who had royalist connections.

All things considered, it was a good time for Tocqueville and Beaumont to keep a low profile. "Truly," Tocqueville complained to his friend, "the world of politics is a foul pit."[15] But their determination to make their mark in that world remained as strong as ever. The best course of action, they decided, would be to get away from France for a while, particularly if that could be arranged in such a way as to further their eventual political prospects.

They settled on the idea of a trip to study conditions in the United States. A visit to the new republic would provide them with firsthand knowledge that would set them apart from the crowd; it would give them the opportunity to learn how a democratic experiment really works; and the experience would, as they say today, look good on their résumés. To make the most of the venture, Tocqueville suggested that they should aim at producing "some sort of publication" upon their return that would "alert the public to one's existence and turn the attention of the parties to one."[16] Accordingly, the two friends sought a commission from the Ministry of the Interior to travel to the United States. They proposed to study the new nation's prison system, then supposed to be the most enlightened in the world. Permission granted, they set sail from Le Havre on April 2, 1831, on the journey that would make one of them very famous.

Upon their homecoming nine months later, they found the political situation unimproved. The collapse of the Bourbon Monarchy had initiated a long-lasting era of chronic political instability characterized by struggles among Orléanists (bourgeois supporters of Louis-Philippe), royalists (now known as legitimists), Bonapartists nostalgic for the idea of France as a world power, Republicans, and, eventually, socialists.

Shortly after their return, both left their posts at the court. Beaumont was dismissed for refusing to act as prosecutor in what he regarded as a politically motivated case. Tocqueville, regarding his friend's dismissal as unfair, took the occasion to resign and to devote all his energies to his book about the democratic experiment that was underway in the United States.

He proceeded by supplementing notes based on his firsthand observations with a program of reading, research, and interviews so extensive that he referred to it as a "second trip."[17] In the actual writing process, Tocqueville had the enthusiastic support of his family. According to Jardin, "The father and brothers of the young writer weighed every turn of phrase, down to individual words, and all three required the sort of exactness that gives Alexis's style, in places, a crystalline purity."[18] *Democracy in America* also shows how deeply Tocqueville's thought was influenced by the three authors with whom Tocqueville said he "lived a little every day"—Montesquieu, Rousseau, and Pascal.[19]

Though it had always been part of his plan to enhance his political credentials by writing about America, no one was more surprised than Tocqueville when *Democracy in America* became an instant best seller upon its publication in 1835. "I am amazed at its success," he told Stoeffels. "I feared, if not failure, at least a chilly reception, owing to the care its author took to distance himself from all the parties."[20]

His emphatic message to the French was that the advance of democracy was irresistible, and that the only question was how to maximize its benefits while steering clear of the perils of despotism on the one hand and anarchy on the other. The American example was encouraging in his view because it showed that a free, egalitarian republic was possible. But he was careful to insist that it was not a model that could be copied by any other nation. The French would have to chart their own course, drawing such lessons as they could from the experiences of a people with very different history and circumstances.

At age thirty, Tocqueville unexpectedly found himself a celebrity, and at last within sight of realizing his most cherished goals. The legal age for membership in the Chamber of Deputies had been lowered to thirty, and the success of *Democracy in America* had paved the way for the political career that he so ardently wished to pursue. Brooking a certain amount of family disapproval, he also proposed to his long-time confidante Miss Mottley, an Englishwoman of respectable though not aristocratic family who was somewhat older than he. Her willingness to become a Catholic helped to assuage the family's reservations, and the couple was married the following year.

When Tocqueville announced his intention to run for the legislature in 1837, the circumstances seemed relatively favorable. For one thing, the financial considerations that deter so many aspiring politicians today did not weigh heavily on him. While he did not possess a great fortune, his independent income was sufficient for his purposes. He was offered powerful support, moreover, from King Louis-Philippe's Prime Minister, who, as it happened, was a distant Tocqueville relative, Count Louis Mathieu Molé. Molé must have been astonished when Tocqueville asked him not to interfere, insisting that he did not wish to owe any political favors. "You are well aware," he wrote in declining, "that I am not an enemy of the government in general, and particularly not of those who govern at this moment. But I wish to be able to support it intelligently and freely, which I could not do if I let myself be brought in by the government. I am well aware that some men forget, on entering the Chamber, how they got there; but I am not of that sort. I wish to enter as I mean to go on, in an independent position."[21] Not surprisingly, Tocqueville failed in his first bid for public office.

Two years later, however, he ran successfully—still on an independent platform, but this time with the help of a skillful campaign manager. They made a list of electors in Tocqueville's home district in Normandy, and went door to door, getting to know the residents and listening to their concerns. In his campaign literature, the candidate emphasized his independence both from the government and the parties: "I am a new man who brings to the new circumstances that now exist nothing but a free mind and an ardent and sincere love of representative government and the dignity of our country. . . . I am not tied to a party. I am even more firmly independent where the government is concerned; I am not a government candidate and I do not in the least want to be one."[22]

At the age of thirty-three, Alexis de Tocqueville finally achieved his goal of membership in France's unicameral legislature, the Chamber of Deputies. Having run as an independent, he was immediately faced with the problem of where to sit, since seating in the Chamber was arranged by affiliation, ranging from ultra-Royalists on the right to radicals on the far left. He wrote to Royer-Collard that he did not feel an affinity with any of them, and that he had "an almost invincible repugnance to associating myself in a permanent manner with any of the political men of our times, and among all the parties that divide our country, I do not see a single one to which I would want to be tied."[23] Obliged to decide, he took a place in the center-left among supporters of King Louis-Philippe and members of various small parties.

There he confronted the problem facing any politician who refuses to accept party discipline or follow a party line: How could he maintain his independence without rendering himself isolated and ineffective? Sadly, Tocqueville was never able to solve that problem, and thus never achieved the political influence he so desperately desired. As summed up by one biographer, "his years in the Chamber of Deputies were passed in helpless frustration. He failed to become a real leader in the Chamber. All his major programs or recommendations were defeated or stymied."[24]

By his own lights, Tocqueville acquitted himself honorably during his twelve years of parliamentary service, devoting most of his energies to extending the right to vote, abolishing slavery in the colonies, and improving the condition of the working classes and the poor. Neither his concern for social justice nor his travels to Algeria, however, ever led him to reject French colonialism, which he viewed as essential to the country's national interests. His most famous parliamentary speech is remembered for the uncanny prescience with which he forecast the Revolution of 1848. In January of that year, he warned his colleagues that "we are sleeping on a volcano":

> People say that there is no danger because there are no riots; they say that since there is no significant disorder on the surface of society, revolution is far from us. Gentlemen, let me say that I think you are deceiving yourselves. . . . For the first time in, perhaps, sixteen years there is a feeling, a consciousness of instability, and that is a feeling which goes before revolutions, often announcing them and sometimes bringing them about, and that feeling is there to a very serious extent across the country.[25]

Just one month later, Tocqueville's prediction came true. King Louis-Philippe abdicated and fled, the Chamber of Deputies was dissolved, and elections were scheduled for a more representative assembly.

Tocqueville seized the occasion to prepare a new preface for the 1848 edition of *Democracy in America*, emphasizing the relevance of his study to the volatile French situation. "However sudden and momentous be the events which have just taken place so swiftly," he wrote, "the author of this book can claim that they have not taken him by surprise. This work was written fifteen years ago with a mind constantly preoccupied by a single thought: the thought of the approaching irresistible and universal spread of democracy through-out the world."[26] With an eye toward his own and the nation's future, he went on to affirm his own republican sympathies, and to empha-size the fateful significance of the choices that the French would soon be making:

> It is not a question now of finding out whether we are to have monarchy or republic in France; but we still want to know whether it is to be an agitated or a tranquil republic, an orderly or a disorderly republic, pacific or warlike, liberal or oppressive, a republic which threatens the sacred rights of property and the family, or one which recognizes and honors them. It is a fearful problem concerning not France alone, but the whole civilized world. . . . According as we establish either democratic liberty or democratic tyranny, the fate of the world will be different.

The election that followed the February 1848 revolution was France's first experience with universal male suffrage. Tocqueville ran for the new assembly, as always without governmental or party sup-port. Of his frame of mind in those turbulent days, he later wrote:

> I felt that I was still in my prime; I had no children and few needs, and above all I had at home the support, so rare and precious in a time of revolution, of a devoted wife with an acute, steadfast mind and a naturally lofty soul that would

be equal to any turn of events, and could rise above any misfortunes. So I decided to throw myself into the arena and commit myself to the defense, not of such and such a government, but of the laws of society itself, not sparing my fortune, my peace of mind or my person.[27]

He did not lament the demise of the regime of Louis-Philippe. In fact, he later gave full expression in his memoir to the contempt he had felt for the July Monarchy. Under Louis-Philippe, he wrote, "the bourgeoisie had settled into every office, prodigiously increased the number of offices, and made a habit of living off the public treasury almost as much as from its own industry. They treated government like a private business, each member thinking of public affairs only insofar as they could be turned to his private profit, and in his petty prosperity easily forgetting the people."[28]

In his 1848 election circular, Tocqueville declared his opposition to socialism and to all forms of tyranny, whether of the monarchical or military-Napoleonic variety. Monarchy, he said, was no longer a viable institution in France. He now described himself as a republican, which meant, he said, that he favored "true, sincere, real liberty for everyone, within the limits of the law; the government of the country by the country's free majority."[29] A republic was "above all the reign of the rights of each man, guaranteed by the will of all; it is profound respect for all types of legitimate property."

Tocqueville, secure in his Norman base, succeeded in his bid for election to the newly formed constituent assembly. There, his literary prestige earned him a place on the committee preparing a constitution for what was to become the Second Republic. In the spring of 1848, as that work got underway, the economy was deteriorating, and the political situation remained highly unstable. Violent social disorder broke out again in May and June. Still hoping to be able to influence the course of events, Tocqueville was determined to ride out the storm. He wrote to Beaumont, "Politics has become our career. Perhaps we were wrong to take it up, but take it up we did. It would grieve me to abandon it just when such great events are occurring."[30]

The most fateful of those developments was the election in December of that turbulent year of the nephew of Napoleon Bonaparte as President of the new republic. Louis Napoleon, who had been living abroad in exile, was swept into office with 74 percent of the popular vote. Tocqueville attributed the landslide in part to a longing for stability and in part to nostalgia for the glory days of Napoleon I. But he was dismayed at what he regarded, correctly, as a setback for democracy.

Though Tocqueville had supported Louis Napoleon's opponent in the election, the new President asked him to take the position of Minister for Foreign Affairs, apparently believing that it would bolster the government's standing to have a minister with a reputation for being above party politics. Tocqueville accepted the portfolio, stipulating—less than tactfully—that he would never participate in overthrowing the republic.[31] He need not have worried that he would be ousted just five months later, when the President disbanded the cabinet and began extending his powers. That turn of events came as a shock to some of the political figures who had supported Louis Napoleon. Tocqueville would later castigate such persons in his memoirs, claiming that "they had chosen him, not for his worth, but for his presumed mediocrity. They thought he would be a tool for them to use at will and break any time they wanted. In this they were mightily deceived."[32] It had been, he wrote, "a sorry plight to be minister of foreign affairs at such a time."[33]

For Tocqueville, it was a time for reflection on, and reassessment of, his chosen path. His physical condition, never robust, had begun to decline seriously, as he experienced the first symptoms of the pulmonary tuberculosis that would cause his death a decade later at the age of only fifty-three. Increasingly disillusioned with politics, he was beginning to realize that his real title to fame would lie elsewhere. He wrote a friend that, "It seems to me that my true worth is above all in works of the mind; that I am worth more in my thoughts than in my actions; and that, if I am ever to leave some trace of myself in the world, it will be much more the trace of what I have written than in the memory of what I have done."[34] The man who once valued his writing chiefly as a means to advance his political career, now began to see his political experience, including his failures, as lending depth to his writing: "The last ten years which have been so sterile for me in so many ways, have nevertheless given me a truer understanding of human affairs and practical matters, so I think I am better suited than I was when I wrote the *Democracy* to tackle successfully some great topic of political literature."

Tocqueville's reference to the sterility of the preceding decade reflected a personal as well as a political sorrow. His marriage to Mary Mottley had been childless. Although he once remarked that he had "no very keen desire to draw from the great lottery of paternity,"[35] his failure to have an heir must have been a particular source of regret to a man who felt as deeply as he about family name and lineage. A passage on the aristocratic family in *Democracy in America* is evocative of the attitudes that were deeply ingrained in the Tocqueville clan:

> There is a sense in which all the generations are contemporaneous. A man almost always knows about his ancestors and respects them; his imagination extends to his great-grandchildren, and he loves them. He freely does his duty by both ancestors and descendants and often sacrifices personal pleasures for the sake of beings who are no longer alive or are not yet born.[36]

Tocqueville's memoirs also reveal his keen personal sense of the tie between a noble family and its land. In the turbulent days that followed the Revolution of 1848, Tocqueville visited his ancestral estate in Normandy. There, he was overcome with emotion at the thought of the way of life that had come to an end. Recalling the scene, he wrote:

> I had just seen the Monarchy fall; since then I have witnessed the most terrible scenes of bloodshed. All the same I declare that neither at the time nor now in recollection do I feel such deep and poignant emotion about any of those disasters as I felt that day at the sight of the ancient home of my ancestors and at the memory of the quiet happy days I passed there without realizing how precious they were. Believe me, it was

then and there that I most fully understood the utter bitterness of revolutions.[37]

After his dismissal from the cabinet, Tocqueville watched with dismay as the democratically elected Louis Napoleon arrogated ever more power to himself. Under the Constitution that Tocqueville had helped to draft, the President was limited to a single four-year term. But as the expiration of Louis Napoleon's term approached, it became apparent that he had no intention of returning to private life. In July 1851, Tocqueville wrote in discouragement to Stoeffels: "I don't believe in the future. . . . No longer do I hope to see the establishment in our country of a government that is at once lawful, strong, and liberal. That ideal was the dream of my whole youth, as you know, and also of the days of my prime, which have already gone by."[38]

Tocqueville's forebodings proved well-founded, for, later that year, Louis Napoleon announced the dissolution of the assembly and the formation of a new government. Tocqueville, along with some 230 other deputies who had denounced the President's actions as illegal, was arrested and briefly imprisoned. Shortly thereafter, Louis Napoleon proclaimed himself emperor of France, taking the title of Napoleon III. That coup by the nephew of Napoleon Bonaparte provided the occasion for Karl Marx's famous remark that history repeats itself, first as tragedy, then as farce.[39]

Replying to a letter from a local official in Normandy who had asked for news of the events in the nation's capital, Tocqueville revealed the depth of his disappointment, not only with politics, but with what French society had become. "What has just happened in Paris," he wrote, "is abominable. The nation, at this moment, is mad with fear of the socialists and a passionate desire to regain its well-being. It is incapable and, though I say it with much regret, unworthy, of being free. This nation which has forgotten what bureaucratic and military despotism is like is getting a taste of it once again, and this time without the seasoning of greatness and glory."[40]

Louis Napoleon's coup d'état marked the end of Tocqueville's political career. After having devoted most of his adult life to the cause of a free French republic, he retired to the work that had first brought him into the public eye. Addressing the French Academy of Moral and Political Sciences in 1852, he reflected on the relation between theory and practice in politics. In his youth, he said, he had regarded political science as the road to governing, but now, after twelve years in the legislature, he realized that the practice of politics requires different qualities from those needed for its study. Yet he had come to appreciate the role of ideas as a powerful political force. "Who produced the French Revolution, in short, the greatest event in history? Men of theory, who sowed in the minds of our fathers all the seeds of novelty from which suddenly sprouted so many political institutions and civil laws unknown to former times."[41]

With hindsight, it is easy to see that in Tocqueville's day, as in Cicero's, there was little opportunity for any individual, no matter how gifted, to advance ideas of limited government. In his *Recollections*, Tocqueville reflected ruefully, "I had spent the best years of my youth in a society that seemed to be regaining prosperity and grandeur as it regained freedom; I had conceived the idea of a regulated and orderly freedom, restrained by religion, manners, and law; I was touched by the joys of such a freedom, and it had become my whole life's passion; I had felt that I could never be consoled for its loss, and now I saw clearly that I must give it up forever."[42]

There is no denying, however, that some of the reasons for Tocqueville's ineffectiveness in his chosen career lay not in his stars but in himself. There is a fine line between the spiritedness that a great statesman must possess and more venal forms of ambition. It seemed to Royer-Collard, who had advised Tocqueville against going into politics, that his young friend was at times susceptible to the latter, while lacking the qualities that should accompany the former. Early in his legislative career, Tocqueville reported to his wife that Royer-Collard "told me that I was too concerned with myself. I admitted that this was true to a certain extent, but I said that if an occasion occurred where I might forget myself in order to throw myself into something large, he would see that I was capable of doing so."[43] Royer-Collard apparently was not convinced. After the exchange, he told Molé that he was disappointed in Tocqueville's unseemly "need for success," adding, "he lacks a certain elevation of soul that makes for perfect rectitude."[44]

Another impediment, in the estimation of biographer Hugh Brogan, was a certain aristocratic aloofness that hampered him when he had to deal with people "whose good will he needed but whom he regarded as coarse and vulgar."[45] To many people, he seemed remote and disdainful. Tocqueville himself understood that he was woefully deficient in the qualities that had enabled his more sociable friend Beaumont to become a popular figure in the Chamber of Deputies. At the most basic level, it is said that he had trouble remembering names or recognizing people, often mistaking one person for another.[46] Looking back over his years in the Chamber of Deputies, Tocqueville himself admitted in his *Recollections* that he "completely lacked the art of holding men together and leading them as a body. It is only in *tête-à-tête* that I show any dexterity, whereas in a crowd I am constrained and dumb."[47] Nor did he have patience for the "constant repetition" that characterized so much of political speech-making.[48] On the other hand, he managed to unbend and socialize easily with the residents of his home district, winning their confidence and overcoming their residual mistrust of the nobility. After his first successful election, his Norman neighbors returned him to office with large majorities until he retired.

Despite increasingly severe bouts of illness, Tocqueville produced works in his final years that gained him far more recognition than he had ever achieved in the political sphere. His personal memoir, *Recollections,* is still regarded by many as the best book ever written about the Revolution of 1848. Although he died before he could complete what was to be a major study of the French Revolution, he lived to see its first volume—*The Old Regime and the French Revolution*—become a commercial and critical success.

In that book, he gave memorable expression to the themes that were always at the heart of his political faith. Though stoutly rejecting nostalgia for the old regime, he refused to discount what had been lost when aristocratic civilization gave way to democratic habits and attitudes. He warned against excessive centralization of power, pointing out that it is only in society's little "schools for citizenship" where citizens can develop the skills of self-government. He called attention to the political importance of women and the family, insisting that the habits and attitudes of each nation's citizens would be decisive in determining the fate of their democratic experiments. He embraced the equality principle that was transforming the world, but he admitted that liberty was always his overriding passion: "Freedom is the strongest of my passions. Voilà, this is the truth."[49] "I love liberty by inclination," he told John Stuart Mill, "and equality by instinct and reason."[50] Of his love of freedom, he wrote in *The Old Regime*, "Do not ask me to analyze this sublime yearning; for it is something one must feel, and logic has no part in it. It is a privilege of noble minds which God has fitted to receive it, and it inspires them with a generous fervor. But to meaner souls, untouched by the sacred flame, it may well seem incomprehensible."[51]

The very independence of mind that proved such an obstacle to Tocqueville's political career lends an enduring quality to his political writings. Politically homeless during his lifetime, he remains difficult to classify as liberal or conservative. He is claimed as a kindred spirit today by men and women across the political spectrum. Far-sighted as he was, however, he did not foresee how deeply the political, economic and philosophical movements just taking rise would affect the habits and beliefs that he considered to be essential for the maintenance of free democratic societies. It would fall to Max Weber, born in 1864, to grapple with the challenges to politics and philosophy in the post-Marxian, post-Nietszchean world where all that was once considered solid now seemed "to melt into air."[52]

TEN

Max Weber

SCHOLARSHIP AND POLITICS IN THE DISENCHANTED WORLD

In November 1917, with war raging in Europe, the most famous public intellectual in Germany accepted an invitation from a Munich University student group to speak about "Science as a Vocation."[1] Fourteen months later, with Germany in defeat, Max Weber returned to a Munich roiled by civil unrest, to deliver a lecture on "Politics as a Vocation."[2] The two lectures were the distillation of his life's experience as a scholar and political activist. Their messages, however, were as dark and puzzling as the times in which they were delivered.

Any aspiring scholar who was hoping for words of encouragement from the speech on the academic calling must have gone away troubled. Weber began by painting a bleak picture of the hurdles along the path to a post in a German university. After studying for years, completing a doctoral thesis, and surviving a rigorous interviewing process, one might be invited to give a course as an instructor while working on one's *Habilitationschrift* (the second thesis required of candidates for teaching positions). But it could still be several years before one would be paid enough to be self-supporting. Whether one eventually succeeded in becoming a full professor or the head of a research institute, he said, is determined "to an unusually high degree by chance."[3]

Faculty discussions of appointments are seldom agreeable, he revealed. Established professors tend to favor their own disciples, and the lucky person who emerges from the push-and-pull of academic politics is often a second- or third-rate scholar rather than the best qualified. (The same holds true, he remarked, for papal conclaves and for presidential nominations in the United States where "only exceptionally does the first-rate and most prominent man get the nomination of the convention.")[4]

An additional hurdle is the need to demonstrate one's qualifications as a teacher as well as one's scholarly accomplishments and potential. Giving voice to what all students know, he observed that pedagogical skills and excellence in research do not necessarily coincide. To illustrate the point, he named a couple of eminent professors (then deceased) who had been abysmal teachers. Conceding that good teaching is hard to evaluate, he deplored that people tend to rely on enrollment figures. High or low enrollments, he said, may well be due to factors other than the competence of the professor.

The proper test of a good teacher, Weber insisted, ought to be whether he aids his students to think for themselves and to reach a stage at which, in terms of their own ideals, they can form a judgment and take a stand. He had nothing but scorn for professors who advance their own political views in the classroom, condemning them for shortchanging their students, and deriding them for posing as courageous in settings where they encounter little opposition. Weber acknowledged that teachers are not always able to master, or even be conscious of, their biases, just as they may make errors of fact. But he insisted that they should at least have the intellectual integrity to see that it is one thing to state facts while it is another to offer judgments of value and prescriptions for action.[5]

Mere chance, he said, plays such a role in academic progress that, when young scholars had sought his advice, he sometimes found the responsibility of encouraging them almost unbearable. "If he is a Jew, of course one says *lasciate ogni speranza*," (a curious remark since

Weber himself had fought prejudice by mentoring several Jewish students over the years).[6] The question for any aspiring academic, he told his audience, is: "Do you in all conscience believe that you can stand seeing mediocrity after mediocrity, year after year, climb beyond you, without becoming embittered and without coming to grief?"[7]

Those of his listeners who were hoping to hear the great scholar affirm that the quest for knowledge was so rewarding in itself as to compensate for the risks and difficulties he had just outlined were in for a further dash of discouragement. Turning to the satisfactions one might expect from a life devoted to *Wissenschaft* ("science" in its broadest sense), Weber said that most scholars today could expect to spend their entire academic lives working within rather narrow confines. The natural and human sciences alike, he said, had "entered a phase of specialization previously unknown and this will forever remain the case."[8] Science could not advance without rigorous specialized knowledge, yet the need for specialization would increasingly diminish the satisfactions of the scholar.

True, he said, one could hope to make a discovery that advances knowledge in one's field. But no one can count on it. If one is to accomplish anything worthwhile, one has to have ideas and they have to be correct, but "such intuition cannot be forced"—"a man may be an excellent worker and yet never have had a valuable idea of his own."[9]

Even someone who is fortunate enough to push forward the frontiers of knowledge in his specialty has to accept that whatever he has accomplished is destined to be surpassed, for every advance raises new questions. "Each of us knows that what he has accomplished will be antiquated in ten, twenty, fifty years."[10]

Why then, he asked, would anyone "engage in doing something that in reality never comes, and never can come, to an end?"[11] Do not look to science, as the classical philosophers did, for answers to the great questions of the meaning of life and how one should live. "Only a prophet or a savior," he said, can answer such questions, and, "If there is no such man, or if his message is no longer believed, then you will certainly not compel him to appear on this earth by having thousands of professors . . . attempt as petty prophets in their lecture-rooms to take over his role."[12]

By now, many in the audience must have been wondering how a man who had devoted so much of his own life to teaching and research would justify his own choice. What would impel someone like Max Weber to stay the course? Weber answered in terms of the quest for self-knowledge: "Science today is a 'vocation' organized in special disciplines in the service of self-clarification and knowledge of interrelated facts."[13] If one is competent in that vocation, he said, "we can help the individual to give himself an *account of the ultimate meaning of his own conduct.* This appears to me as not so trifling a thing to do even for one's own personal life."[14] A scholar who succeeds in that endeavor "stands in the service of 'moral' forces; he fulfils the duty of bringing about self-clarification and a sense of responsibility."

To those who might have expected a lecture on the academic calling to end on a loftier note, Weber had only this to say: "The fate of our times is characterized by rationalization and intellectualization and, above, all by the 'disenchantment of the world.'"[15] To those who cannot bear that fate, he remarked disdainfully, the "old churches" are still there to receive you. To those who are ready to take up the vocation of science in the post-religious, disenchanted world, his parting words were: Bear it "like a man;" set to work, and meet the demands of the day. That will be simple, he said, "if each finds and obeys the demon who holds the fibers of his very life."[16] With that peculiar flourish, he left the podium.

Strangely, the great man uttered not one word about the *eros* of the mind, the excitement of insight, the joys and necessity of teamwork, or the sense of playing one's role in the unending drama of the quest for knowledge.

One person who was dissatisfied with that lecture and dared to say so was Weber's longtime friend and admirer, the philosopher Karl Jaspers. Later, when Jaspers and Weber were sitting in the garden of Weber's Heidelberg home with Richard Thoma, a constitutional lawyer, Jaspers asked Weber the question that must have been on the minds of many in the lecture hall: Why did he occupy himself with scholarship if "science" was only as he had described it?[17] Did not science, as Kant suggested, point beyond itself? When Weber did not respond, Jaspers prodded him again, remarking to Thoma, "He,

himself, does not know what meaning science has and why he is pursuing it." According to Jaspers, Weber then "winced visibly" and said,
"Well, to see what we can withstand, but we'd better not talk about it."

No doubt, Jasper's provocative question had stirred memories of
missed opportunities and disappointed hopes. For Max Weber from
his earliest years had longed for a life in politics, and had never completely renounced his youthful dreams. Born in 1864, Weber grew up
in the age of Bismarck, the period that saw the birth of the German
empire after Prussian armies had vanquished Denmark in 1864,
Austria in 1866, and France in 1870. Under Kaiser Wilhelm I and his
Iron Chancellor, Bismarck, a strong and unified Germany had become
a major industrial nation and had embarked on colonial expansion in
Africa and the East Indies.

All through those heady years, the Weber household had been
close to the center of power. Max Weber Sr. was a wealthy and
prominent Berliner who held high office in the city government, and
who had also served in the *Reichstag* and the Prussian Chamber of
Deputies. The family home was a gathering place for some of the most
influential politicians and intellectuals of the day.

As sociologists Hans Gerth and C. Wright Mills have pointed out,
the conditions under which Weber was raised were unusually favorable for the kind of work he would later produce: "The intellectual
traditions and the accumulated scholarship of Germany, especially in
history, the classics, psychology, theology, comparative literature,
philology, and philosophy, gave the late nineteenth century German
scholar a pre-eminent base upon which to build his work."[18] Weber's
secondary education "equipped him in such a way that the Indo-
Germanic languages were but so many dialects of one linguistic
medium"; his family background gave him a head-start on economics,
law, history, philosophy and theology; and his financial circumstances
gave him opportunities for "fruitful leisure."

Coming of age in such an environment, at a time when his country was taking its place on the world stage as a great economic and
military power, the Webers' gifted eldest son felt certain that the future
held an important role for him. As a teenager, he was a voracious
reader—of novels, the Greek and Latin classics, and especially of

history. Never burdened with excessive modesty, Weber wrote in later years that the concept of "vocation" in the sense of a particular calling had little meaning for him in his youth, for he sensed that many paths would be open to him.[19]

Where the academic world was concerned, his self-confidence was fully justified. In fact, he breezed through all the hurdles that he would later portray as so forbidding in the lecture on "Science as a Vocation." At Heidelberg University, where his major area of study was law, his professors made it clear to him that an academic career was his for the asking. After Weber's defense, in Latin, of his doctoral thesis on the history of trading companies in the Middle Ages, the great Roman law scholar Theodor Mommsen paid an astonishing tribute to the candidate: "When I have to go to my grave someday, there is no one to whom I would rather say: 'Son, here is my spear; it is getting too heavy for my arm,' than the highly esteemed Max Weber."[20]

The twenty-four-year-old Weber, however, was more attracted to the practice of law as a pathway to public life. While working on his *Habilitationschrift*, he wrote to his favorite uncle that, "purely scientific work has lost all its excitement, because I live under the impression that practical interests, the regulation of which is the basic task of law, offer combinations which are not to be grasped by means of science."[21] He was chagrined when his application for a job as an attorney for the municipal government in Bremen was turned down. It was for want of a better opportunity that he continued preparing for an academic post, completing his habilitation thesis on the agricultural history of Rome at the age of twenty-seven. Once again, he succeeded so brilliantly that he moved rapidly along the path that was not his first choice.

The following year, he was invited to give courses at the University of Berlin. At the same time, he became engaged to a distant cousin, Marianne Schnitger, a woman who shared his intellectual and political interests, and who would go on to become a prominent writer and speaker on women's issues. In a biography written after her husband's death, Marianne Weber wrote that he was not only regarded in those days as a rising academic star, but was also being eyed in political circles as a promising future candidate. In her view, he was "a born fighter and ruler even more than a born thinker. The question was whether the right form for it would be found, whether his time offered the appropriate material for the crystallization of these forces."[22] He was intensely interested, she said, in political and social questions, and "as a strong-willed person he longed for great responsibilities."[23] Weber himself confided to a friend at the time:

> I simply am not . . . a real scholar. For me, scholarly activity is too much bound up with the idea of filling my leisure hours, even though I realize that due to the division of labor scholarly activity can be carried on successfully only if one devotes one's entire personality to it. I hope that the *pedagogic* side of my university post, the indispensable feeling of *practical* activity will give me satisfaction, but as yet I cannot tell whether I have any talent for this aspect of it.[24]

Despite his ambivalence, Weber kept advancing in the academic world. Immensely energetic, he remained active in political circles, giving talks and writing newspaper articles on the issues of the day. In the fall of 1894, he was called to Freiburg as a professor of economics, and two years later, at thirty-two, he was invited to assume a prestigious chair in political economy at Heidelberg. The Heidelberg invitation was a tremendous honor for such a young man, but the responsibilities of a chair meant curtailing his political activities. Weber wavered before accepting it. He wrote to an older relative about his concerns, "I am confronted with the following choice: to remain here [at Freiburg] and to continue my political activities as long as there is opportunity and stimulus, or to take an important position and with it the obligation to give up all other effectiveness."[25] He realized that it was advisable to take the chair, but added, "I know not whether I might regret this in the future."

No sooner was Weber installed in Heidelberg, than he was approached by the Liberal Party about whether he would be interested in running for the Reichstag. He declined on grounds that he had just accepted the Heidelberg appointment, but Marianne Weber notes that there was an additional reason: he admired the individualism and democratic ideals of the Liberals, but could not accept their views on two of the great issues of the late nineteenth century.[26] The Liberals were suspicious of social legislation, whereas Weber was a strong supporter of factory laws and other protective measures. Moreover, as a staunch nationalist, he did not share the Liberals' relative lack of enthusiasm for Germany's destiny as a great world power. It was already becoming apparent that Weber's political aspirations, like Tocqueville's, would be hampered by his difficulty in fitting into the existing political parties.

Weber remained conflicted about his career path. From Heidelberg he wrote to a friend, "If I have achieved personally unsought and un-demanded successes in my academic career, I must say that these successes leave me rather cold because they do not answer my question whether I am in my right place."[27] Now that he was free to choose topics for study without casting an eye toward thesis directors or appointments committees, Weber's research began to reflect his political interests. Marianne Weber wrote that the principles guiding his selection of material "were first and foremost political passion, then a sense of justice for workers, and further the conviction that freedom and human dignity ought to be made possible for everyone."[28] He worked along those lines, she said, in the belief that he would one day be called to assume high political responsibility.

He did not, however, neglect his academic duties. Indeed, by all accounts, Weber was an extraordinarily inspiring teacher. Long after his death, many of his students from the Heidelberg years regarded him as the most important intellectual influence in their lives. Unusually for his time, he took an interest in and encouraged the careers of Jewish students and women.

In 1898, however, Weber's meteoric rise was interrupted by the catastrophic onset of what was then called a nervous breakdown. At age thirty-four, he was laid low by an affliction so severe that he was unable to work, and often unable even to read, for almost four years. Ordered to rest, and blessed with sufficient private means to maintain himself and his wife, he devoted himself entirely to travel and study. According to his friend Jaspers, it was during a visit to Rome that Weber felt the first signs of recovery from his illness while looking at

Michelangelo's ceiling in the Sistine Chapel.[29] As he gradually regained his health, he did not feel able to return to his university position, but he resumed writing. The years that followed were a period of prodigious scholarly creativity.

The first fruit of Weber's recovery was his most famous work, *The Protestant Ethic and the Spirit of Capitalism*, published in 1904. As often happens with works possessing any degree of subtlety, the thesis of that book has been frequently misstated. Weber never asserted, as many would later claim, that Protestantism "caused" capitalism. His thesis was rather that Protestantism had fostered habits and attitudes—thrift, delayed gratification—that were important factors in creating conditions that were favorable to the development of capitalism. Though Weber agreed with Marx's stress on the importance of economic factors as determinants of human behavior, he criticized those who, like Marx, were "unable to give religious ideas a significance for culture and national character which they deserve."[30] He made clear that he was not proposing a mono-causal explanation: "[I]t is, of course, not my aim to substitute for a one-sided materialistic an equally one-sided spiritualistic causal interpretation of culture and history." To Weber, rationalization and bureaucratization, along with religious ideas and economic factors, were prominent among the factors that were shaping the modern age.

Much of Weber's work was influenced by his appreciation for Marx's historical and economic approach, but Marxism in his view was simply inadequate as an approach to the study of complex, mutually conditioning social systems. As Gerth and Mills put it, "He felt that Marx, as an economist had made the same mistake that, during Weber's days, anthropology was making: raising a segmental perspective to paramount importance and reducing the multiplicity of causal forces to a single-factor theorem."[31]

As time passed, the intense preoccupation with politics that had characterized Weber's writing before his illness gave way to more theoretical concerns. He began to focus on methods in the social sciences, the relationship between what can be verified and what represents a value judgment, and the far-reaching effects of bureaucratization and rationalization in modern society. From this period came the body of work that would prompt Raymond Aron to write, "To me, Max Weber is the greatest of the sociologists; I would even say that he is *the* sociologist."[32] Aron explained, "He combined a vast and profound knowledge of history with a curiosity about what is essential," and "he asked the most important questions: What is the meaning men have given their existence? What is the relation between the meaning men have given to their existence and the way they have organized their societies? What is the relation of men's attitudes toward profane activities and their conception of the sacred life?"[33]

Though Weber's recovery from his illness was marked by ups and downs, he also resumed some political activities, but on a more limited basis than previously. By the time World War I began in 1914, he was eager to offer his services to the nation. Too old for the army at age fifty, he was put in charge of nine military hospitals in Heidelberg. There, he carried out his duties conscientiously, but it pained him that he could not serve in the field as his three younger brothers were doing. In a letter to his mother, he expressed his regret that so much of life had passed him by. "I may be the most martially disposed of your sons. That fate and the experience of this—despite everything— great and wonderful war finds me here in the office and passes me by like this, I shall add to many other things. . . . Unfortunately, I cannot march and thus cannot be used at the front and this is really very hard for me."[34]

With energy returning, yet with the active life for which he had longed now out of reach, Weber turned to political journalism. As the war dragged on, he worked himself into a fury over what he regarded as the incompetence of German leadership. He laid much of the blame for a missing generation of capable leaders on Bismarck. Though Weber admired Bismarck for leading Germany to unity and greatness, he faulted him for leaving the country politically handicapped. By smashing strong political parties, Bismarck had prevented the rise of political talent, saddled the country with a powerless parliament filled with mediocre personalities, and empowered a massive civil service establishment whose members possessed integrity but not political vision. The result, Weber thought, was a nation without political education or political will, whose citizens were accustomed to having a great statesman take care of all aspects of public affairs.[35]

As for the current emperor, Kaiser Wilhelm II, Weber could hardly contain his contempt for his erratic personal style of governing, and his arrogant conduct of foreign policy. As early as 1906, Weber had advised a leader of the Progressive People's Party to distance himself from the Kaiser, warning that Germany was becoming isolated "because this man rules us in this way and because we tolerate it and make excuses for it."[36]

Toward the end of 1915, after German forces had compiled a series of military victories, Weber believed that the time had come to seek peace, and that such a move would be successful if Germany would renounce any territorial annexation.[37] When it became apparent that the war effort would continue, he argued in vain against pressure from the military for stepped-up submarine warfare, predicting, correctly, that such a move would bring the United States into the war and that German defeat would surely follow.[38]

Increasingly pessimistic about the outcome of the war, Weber next turned his efforts toward making the case that the best path for Germany in the future would be through some form of parliamentary government. His proposals for constitutional changes to increase the power of parliament attracted a good deal of public attention and became planks in the platforms of the leftist parties. After Germany's surrender on November 11, 1918, he continued to write on constitutional reform and was invited to participate in the drafting of the constitution of the Weimar Republic, where his ideas had considerable influence.

For a time, it seemed as though Weber might at last become a major player in the political arena. He traveled from city to city, giving well-received speeches on behalf of the German Democratic Party. After a rousing speech in Frankfurt, local party members put him at the top of their list of proposed candidates for the Reichstag. Weber made it clear that he was willing to serve, but only if "called," and that he would not to take the initiative on his own behalf, or make the usual efforts to cultivate support.[39] John Stuart Mill had managed to get away with taking such a position and to be elected to a brief term in Parliament in 1865.[40] But it is hardly surprising that Weber's conditions were rejected by party leaders in Berlin who decided to stick with insiders rather than the unpredictable professor.

Years later, the political scientist Karl Loewenstein, a disciple of Weber's who emigrated to the United States after Hitler's rise to power, commented that he and others among Weber's friends at the time "believed that his exclusion from active politics was the greatest mischance that could have befallen Germany."[41] Eventually, however, Professor Loewenstein came to see the matter differently: "Given his temperament and his knowledge, he would probably have cut a great figure in political life, but he would have offended so many people that he would have created hosts of enemies. And as for the course of affairs under Weimar, the tragic course of affairs, he would probably have been unable to check it in any way." As Weber himself had acknowledged in "Science as a Vocation," [T]he qualities that make a man an excellent scholar and academic teacher are not the qualities that make him a leader to give directions in practical life or, more specifically, in politics."[42] To Karl Jaspers, it seemed in retrospect that Weber's failure was due to his lack of the all-consuming "will for power that made great statesmen—Caesar and Napoleon, Cromwell and Bismarck—admirable, but also made them intolerable as human beings."[43]

Weber continued to be sought out as a political advisor, however, and was called in by the German government to assist with preparations for peace negotiations with the Allies.[44] In "Politics as a Vocation," Weber had presented his thoughts on how that process ought to proceed.

> [I]nstead of searching like old women for the "guilty one" after the war—in a situation in which the structure of society produced the war—everyone with a manly and controlled attitude would tell the enemy, "We lost the war. You have won it. That is now all over. Now let us discuss what conclusions must be drawn according to the objective interests that came into play and what is the main thing in view of the responsibility towards the future which above all burdens the victor."

Anything else is undignified and will become a boomerang. A nation forgives if its interests have been damaged, but no nation forgives if its honor has been offended, especially by a bigoted self-righteousness.[45]

By the time Weber joined the committee that was to meet with the Allies, that strategy was a non-starter. England, France, and the United States had indicated that they were determined not only to affix blame, but to exact enormous reparations. When the time came for the German delegation to go to Versailles, Weber accompanied them with foreboding. The experience was a painful one for him and provoked a bitter reflection on academics in politics. "It is the peculiar fate of the world," he wrote, "that the first real ruler of the world should be a professor [Woodrow Wilson]. How much of a professor he is may be seen from the great folly that he has committed: his terms for an armistice."[46]

In the end, the only choice given Germany was either to accept or reject the harsh terms proposed by the Allies. Weber was among the minority who opposed acceptance, foreseeing "nothing but a long series of humiliations and torments, because the conditions cannot be fulfilled."[47] Nevertheless, the majority asked him to lend his pen to their decision. Describing the experience to Marianne, he said, "It was horrible in Versailles. I was not consulted on *anything*, that is, *authoritatively* consulted, and in the end they did make this unreasonable demand of me: Now *you* write the introduction to this draft. I did it in such way I knew they would not accept."[48]

It is no wonder that, three months earlier, with his hopes fading for an "honorable peace," Weber had tried to cancel his scheduled lecture in Munich on "Politics as a Vocation." He began the speech by saying, "This lecture, which I give at your request, will necessarily disappoint you in a number of ways."[49]

Politics, he said, is about power—"striving to share power or striving to influence the distribution of power, either among states or among groups within a state."[50] Many men are politicians by avocation, taking part in political activities to varying degrees (as Weber himself did), without making politics "their life." As for those who make politics their vocation, Weber pointed out that very few individuals in modern times can live *for* politics without also making a living *from* politics. Thus, the leadership class in a modern state will be primarily composed of men who may or may not live "for" politics, but definitely live "off" it.[51]

After an extensive discussion of governments and political parties in the United States and Europe, Weber asserted that the development of political leaders with skills suited for a modern democratic state had been impeded in Germany by the fact that so much of the business of government under Bismarck and Kaiser Wilhelm I had been placed in the hands of career civil servants. The German system of civil-service rule—he called it *Beamtenherrschaft*—had created a cadre of outstanding administrators, famed for their integrity and conscientiousness, but who, by the nature of their role, were apolitical. As a result, Germany lagged behind other Western countries in developing a real political class: its legislature was "impotent," and thus "no man with the qualities of a leader would enter Parliament permanently."[52]

Perhaps, Weber speculated, the "enormous collapse" brought on by the war and the civil unrest that followed would open the way to a transformation. But he said that he could not see clearly how Germany would move from the rule of administrators "without a calling, without the inner charismatic qualities that make a leader," to a regime with effective parties and politicians like those who had emerged in countries where parliamentary democracy was well in place.[53] It was difficult to imagine how Germany would make the transition from bureaucrats who follow prescribed impersonal procedures to political leaders who take stands and take personal responsibility for their actions.

Weber then turned to consider what "politics as a vocation" could mean under existing circumstances. What qualities must someone possess if he is to wield power responsibly? "What kind of man must one be if he is to be allowed to put his hand on the wheel of history?"[54] The most important qualities, according to Weber, are passion for a cause (as distinct from love of power for power's sake), a strong sense of responsibility, and—most important of all in Weber's view—an ability to face reality with "detachment," by which he said he meant the strength to carry on while bearing "the knowledge of tragedy with which all action, but especially political action, is truly interwoven."[55]

Whoever wants to engage in politics as a vocation, he went on, has to be able to deal with the world as it is, taking human frailty into account and even using it for his purposes. He must be able to bear the irrationality of the world in which evil sometimes comes from good and good sometimes comes from evil. He has to understand that the attainment of good ends may even require using morally dubious or at least dangerous means, and that if one chases after the ultimate good, then the good he seeks may be damaged or discredited for generations. He must realize that the choice of one value may slight another, and be ready to accept responsibility for the consequences. What is decisive, said Weber, "is the trained relentlessness in viewing the realities of life and the ability to face such realities and to measure up to them inwardly."[56]

Warming up to his conclusion, Weber told his listeners that he wished he could return in ten years' time to "see what has become of those of you who now feel yourselves to be genuinely 'principled' politicians."[57] Striving to end on a positive note, he added, "Certainly all historical experience confirms the truth—that man would not have attained the possible unless time and again he had reached out for the impossible. But to do that a man must be a leader, and not only a leader but a hero as well in a very sober sense of the word."[58]

A few months later, after returning in discouragement from Versailles, Weber told a friend that he was finished with politics. "I am now a man of the pen, not of the rostrum. But what must be, must be."[59] Yet, not long afterward, when Marianne Weber suggested to her husband that perhaps he would be called after all to help with the reconstruction of Germany, he replied, "Yes, I have the feeling that life is still keeping something in reserve for me."[60] But that was not to be.

Weber, who died of pneumonia on June 14, 1920, at the age of fifty-six, would not live to see what became of his young listeners, nor how his hopes for a heroic leader would be realized. Tragically, for Germany and the world, the charismatic figure who emerged from the economic and social turmoil of the postwar years was a case of powerful ambition gone wildly, spectacularly wrong. "Not for nothing," as Henry Kissinger once wrote, "is history associated with the figure of Nemesis, which defeats man by fulfilling his wishes in a different form or by answering his prayers too completely."[61]

In testimony to the enduring quality of Weber's thought, over a thousand persons attended a 1964 conference in Heidelberg to mark the hundredth anniversary of his birth. For three days, scholars as diverse as Talcott Parsons, Jürgen Habermas, Raymond Aron, Max Horkheimer, and Herbert Marcuse argued heatedly over the Weberian legacy.[62]

To Aron, Weber was not only the greatest of sociologists, but a proto-existentialist philosopher:

> a man who was constantly asking himself the ultimate questions—the relation between knowledge and faith, science and action, the Church and prophecy, bureaucracy and the charismatic leader, rationalization and personal freedom—and who, thanks to an almost monstrous historic erudition, searched all civilizations for the answers to his own questions, at the risk of finding himself, at the end of his necessarily inconclusive explorations, alone and lacerated in the choice of his own destiny.[63]

Other participants criticized Weber's insistence that the social scientist must not project his value judgments or political preferences into his research. Weber had held that even though one's choice of subjects can be, and often is, inspired by one's passionate interests, one must put one's personal concerns aside in order to arrive at conclusions that are verifiable by others. That view was contested by some who argued that objectivity in social science was impossible and others who claimed that it was undesirable. Still others charged that Weber had not lived up to his own standards of objectivity.

Weber's political legacy was also the subject of controversy, with Habermas taking Weber to task for his militant nationalism and for advocating "Caesar-like leader-democracy on the contemporary basis of a national state imperialism."[64] Karl Loewenstein, who had fled Germany during the National Socialist era, suggested that his former teacher's national pride should be seen in historical perspective. In his centennial lecture on Weber, delivered in Munich in 1964, he said:

> He was a German patriot. What else could he be? Today he is criticized for his attachment to the *Machststaat*, the power state. He was indeed attached to it. At the time he saw no other choice. In the years before 1914 and until after the end of the First World War, there were no effective idealistic pacifists or internationalists in Germany or elsewhere in Europe. Max Weber was committed to the idea of the *Machtstaat* because he believed that the German people and German civilization were worth preserving against the rising Slavic tide. . . . Germany as a whole represented a real value to him. To charge him with believing in power for its own sake or with being a forerunner of the horrors of the recent past is to misunderstand him completely.[65]

Today, Max Weber remains a towering figure in social thought, even though scholarship and politics alike have moved beyond the horizons within which he worked. In the wake of National Socialism and the horrors of World War II, questions of truth and universal values came back into prominence, while the absoluteness of national sovereignty came into question. As we shall see, nothing illustrated that double movement away from Weberian premises more dramatically than the collaboration among statespersons and philosophers that produced the Universal Declaration of Human Rights in 1948. First, however, we will meet Weber's American contemporary, Oliver Wendell Holmes, Jr., a scholar and statesman who sought a way to live those vocations in the midst of the social and economic changes that were transforming both of them.

ELEVEN

OLIVER WENDELL HOLMES

THE TRADITION-HAUNTED ICONOCLAST

$\mathbf{B}$y the close of the nineteenth century, changes in the political and economic landscapes of Europe and the United States were altering the vocations of statesmen and scholars alike. For a young man like Oliver Wendell Holmes, Jr., born in 1841 with talents and advantages to match his vaulting ambitions, it was not easy to discern a path toward fulfilling the desire for recognition that he felt so strongly.

Only a few years before Holmes's birth, Tocqueville had posed the question of whether the advance of democracy would summon men of character, intelligence, and vision to the direction of public affairs. Some of the most extraordinary statesmen who ever lived had presided over the American Founding. Yet, as Tocqueville traveled around the United States in 1831, it seemed to him that statesmanship was in short supply. "Among the immense thrusting crowd of American aspirants to public office, I saw very few men who showed that virile candor and manly independence of thought which often marked the Americans of an earlier generation and which, wherever found, is the most salient feature in men of great character."[1]

The French visitor was particularly struck by the contrast between the "vulgar" atmosphere of the House of Representatives, where one "can often look in vain for a single famous man," and the Senate, where, a few paces away, he saw "eloquent advocates, distinguished generals, wise magistrates, and noted statesmen."[2] Noting that election to the House was by direct popular vote, while Senators at the time were chosen by state legislatures, he speculated that universal suffrage might bring many advantages, but that improvement in the quality of political leadership might not be one of them.

Among Americans of his own class, he found that many were disinclined to enter politics because it would be "so difficult for them to remain completely themselves and to advance without debasing themselves."[3] Ambitious men tended to be drawn to trade and industry "not only for the sake of promised gain, but also because they love the emotions it provides." It seemed to him that in the new society that was emerging, "nothing has brighter luster than commerce; it attracts the attention of the public and fills the imagination of the crowd; all passionate energies are directed that way."[4] Jacksonian America was teeming with energetic and spirited men, but to Tocqueville, with his aristocratic sensibilities, they appeared devoid of lofty ambitions. American men, he wrote, were "less concerned than those in any other lands for the interests and judgment of posterity. The actual moment completely occupies and absorbs them. . . . They are much more in love with success than with glory."[5]

Nor was he sanguine about the prospects for high culture in the new nation. "Up to the present," he noted, "America has had only a few remarkable writers; it has had no great historians and does not count one poet."[6] There were many people making use of scientific innovations, but he saw little evidence of the disinterested passion for knowledge that had so consumed a man like Pascal that "he died of old age before he was forty."[7] The future, he said, would "show whether such rare, creative passions come to birth and grow in democracies as in aristocratic communities. For myself, I confess that I can hardly believe it."

What sort of men, he wondered, would come to the fore in the democratic era?

If Tocqueville, who died in 1859, had lived to witness Abraham Lincoln's leadership during the Civil War years and to read Lincoln's speeches, he might well have relaxed his anxiety about whether statesmanship and "remarkable writers" could flourish under democratic conditions in a large commercial republic.

The question would soon resurface, however. As we have seen, Max Weber suggested that it was rationalization and bureaucratization, rather than democracy and wider suffrage, that were transforming science and politics. In Germany, the power of the professional civil service had rendered the legislature so ineffective that "no man with the qualities of a leader" would be attracted to a permanent parliamentary career.[8] In the United States, political parties were "purely organizations of job hunters drafting their changing platforms according to the chances of vote-grabbing."[9] Neither system, in Weber's view, was conducive to statesmanship.

When Oliver Wendell Holmes, Jr., came home to Boston after heroic service in the battles of Balls Bluff, Fredericksburg, and Antietam, he was determined to achieve something great before he was forty. But in 1864, the spirited twenty-four-year-old was far from seeing a clear route to that end.

Like Tocqueville, Holmes was the gifted scion of a distinguished family. He was raised in a social milieu that had enchanted Tocqueville and Beaumont on their visit to Boston. The two French aristocrats had been pleasantly surprised by the culture of that city's elite, the refinement of its ladies, and the contrast with New York. Tocqueville wrote that they felt almost at home in this outpost of civility: "Society, at least that to which we have been introduced, and I think it is the best, is almost exactly like that of the upper classes in Europe. . . . Almost all the women speak French well, and all the men we have met up to now have been in Europe. Their manners are distinguished and their conversation turns on intellectual subjects; one feels one has escaped from those commercial habits and money-conscious spirit which makes New York society so vulgar."[10] There were even, he noted, "some people who write." Among the luminaries of literary Boston, none was more celebrated in his day than the eminent physician, poet, and novelist Oliver Wendell Holmes, Sr. The elder Holmes was the acknowledged leader of a circle that included Ralph Waldo Emerson, Henry Wadsworth Longfellow, Nathaniel Hawthorne, and James Russell Lowell.

Like Max Weber, the younger Holmes had grown up with the awareness that many paths were potentially open to him, and with the knowledge that much was expected of him. Like many young people today, he decided to study law as a way of keeping a number of options open before definitely settling on a career. By the time he graduated from Harvard Law School in 1866, Holmes seems to have decided to try to make his mark through writing. He joined a Boston law firm, but began devoting nearly all of his free time to preparing articles and presenting lectures on legal subjects. His boyhood friends William and Henry James were taken aback at what they considered to be his unseemly degree of ambition. "The noble qualities of Wendell Holmes," William told his brother, were becoming "poisoned" by a "cold-blooded, conscious egotism and conceit."[11] Marriage to Fannie Dixwell in 1872 did not cause the young lawyer to swerve from his self-imposed regimen. "For at least the first ten years of their marriage," according to biographer Mark De Wolfe Howe, "the story of their life was, in its essentials, the story of his striving for and achievement of intellectual eminence."[12]

Around 1875, Holmes plunged into deep seclusion. While keeping up his law practice, he shunned all social engagements in order to work on the lectures and essays that were to become his book, *The Common Law*. William James reported to Henry that their friend had become "a powerful battery, formed like a planing machine to gouge a deep self-beneficial groove through life."[13] A cousin who was also a fellow lawyer was more sympathetic. He recalled conversations from that period in which Holmes had spoken of his aims:

> In our conversations he told me he had a theory that anyone could accomplish anything he wished, if he only wished it hard enough, continuously, morning, noon, and night, and perhaps subconsciously while sleeping. Expressing my interest in this theory, I asked what he wished most to do. He replied that he was trying to write a book on the common

law which he hoped would supplant Blackstone and Kent's Commentaries.[14]

Holmes's years of relentless effort bore fruit when *The Common Law,* published in 1881, was instantly acclaimed as an intellectual tour de force. He later confided to one of his correspondents: "I remember that I hurried to get it out before March 8 because then I should be 40 and it was said that if a man was to do anything he must do it before 40."[15]

The American legal stage was ready for someone with Holmes's talents and interests. A generation earlier, Tocqueville had pronounced it "strange" that the United States, though one of the most legalistic societies the world had ever seen, had not yet produced any "great writers inquiring into the general principles of the laws."[16] As if in response to Tocqueville, Holmes proclaimed in the book's first sentence that, "The object of this book is to present a general view of the Common Law."[17] The view was to be a realistic one, forged in the crucible of experience by a man who had been immersed in the gritty details of law practice at every stage of its writing. "The life of the law," he famously wrote, "has not been logic: it has been experience."[18] The book was also notable for its emphasis on the creative lawmaking function of the judge in situations where a decision is required but where the law is silent, obscure, or incomplete. In a passage meant to shock, Holmes offered his theory of what judges were making law from. Expediency, opinion, and even prejudice "avowed or unconscious," he said, had all played a greater role "than the syllogism in determining the rules by which men should be governed."[19] Holmes was far ahead of most of his contemporaries in his perception that the time was overdue for the legal system to adapt to the novel problems generated by industrialization and urbanization, and the concomitant increase in statutory regulation.

The book had its desired effect. Shortly after its publication, Holmes was offered a professorship at Harvard Law School, which he accepted, stipulating, however, that he might resign if he were offered a judgeship. To the shock of the law faculty, Holmes left only three months later to accept an appointment to the Massachusetts Supreme

Judicial Court. Explaining his reasons for such an abrupt career change to an English friend, he wrote of his desire to be engaged "in the practical struggle of life":

> My motives so far as I could disentangle them in half an hour, which is all the time I had to decide the momentous question, were, in a word, that I thought the chance to gain an all round experience of the law not to be neglected, and especially that I did not think one could without moral loss decline any share in the practical struggle of life which naturally offered itself and for which he believed himself fitted. . . . I felt that if I declined the struggle offered me I should never be so happy again—I should feel that I had chosen the less manly course.[20]

Years later, in a letter to Felix Frankfurter, Holmes again reflected on why he had turned away from the life of a professor, saying:

> Academic life is but half life—it is withdrawal from the fight in order to utter smart things that cost you nothing except the thinking them from a cloister. My wife thinks I unconsciously began to grow sober with an inarticulate sense of limitation in the few months of my stay at Cambridge. . . . Business in the world is unhappy, often seems mean, and always challenges your power to idealize the brute fact—but it hardens the fibre and I think is more likely to make more of a man of one who turns it to success.[21]

Another reason, as he told the English political scientist Harold Laski, was that he had realized that he would not be satisfied with doing conventional legal scholarship: "The law *stricto sensu* is a limited subject—and the choice seemed to be between applying one's theories to practice and details or going into another field—and apart from natural fear and the need of making a living I reasoned (at 40) that it would take another ten years to master a new subject and that I couldn't bargain that my mind should remain suggestive at that age. . . . I am glad on the whole that I stuck to actualities against philosophy (the interest of all actualities.)"[22]

Holmes was in fact pursuing what Weber would identify a few years later as an important but little acknowledged sort of political vocation, one that was becoming more attractive to spirited individuals than the life of a professional politician. Writing on political subjects for an educated general audience, if done well, Weber said, "requires at least as much 'genius' as any scholarly accomplishment."[23] Though he chose the judiciary over a professorship, Holmes had no intention to give up the kind of writing that Weber called high journalism. Freed from the constraints of conventional scholarship, he continued to write and lecture throughout his long tenure on the bench, and kept up a voluminous correspondence with Laski, the English jurist Sir Frederick Pollock, and the Chinese scholar and diplomat John C. H. Wu, among many others. On one occasion, when Laski wrote to say that he had turned down an invitation to run for Parliament, Holmes applauded his decision, telling Laski that his political writings were "better both as a contribution to the world and as a form of self-expression."[24]

From a speech that Holmes gave to Harvard undergraduates early in his judicial career, it is clear that he had no more intention of being merely a judge than he had in the past to be merely a professor or legal practitioner. Revealingly, he spoke to the students of "the secret isolated joy of the thinker, who knows that, a hundred years after he is dead and forgotten, men who never heard of him will be moving to the measure of his thought, the subtle rapture of a postponed power, which the world knows not because it has no external trappings, but which to his prophetic vision is more real than that which commands an army."[25]

As it happened, Holmes's influence, both as a judge and as a writer, was such that countless American lawyers would be moving to the measure of his thought throughout the twentieth century. By the time Holmes stepped down from the bench in 1932 at the age of ninety-one, his legacy included several landmark decisions and dissents, notable as much for their literary style as their substance. His writings, studded with quotable aphorisms, set the agenda of legal scholarship for the next several decades. Legal realism, pragmatism, sociological jurisprudence, the law-and-economics movement, and the various schools of critical legal theory are all little more than elaborations of themes memorably articulated by Holmes.

After Holmes had spent twenty years on the Massachusetts Court (three of them as Chief Justice), President Theodore Roosevelt named him, at age sixty-one, to the Supreme Court of the United States. In communicating the news to various friends, he made no effort to conceal his pride and pleasure at the appointment. The Court, he said, was a "center of great forces" to which came a "mighty panorama of cases from every part of our great empire," briefed and argued by "the strongest men in the country."[26]

It was a sign of the times that a man as ambitious as Holmes was drawn to the life of a judge and public intellectual rather than to electoral politics. As Tocqueville had already observed, the power of the judiciary in the United States had no counterpart anywhere else in the world. John Marshall, as Chief Justice of the Supreme Court from 1801 to 1835, had helped to shape the course of the young nation in decisive respects. The American judge's influence, Tocqueville noted, "extends far beyond the precincts of the courts; [he] is constantly surrounded by men accustomed to respect his intelligence as superior to their own, whether he is at some private entertainment or in the turmoil of politics, in the marketplace, or in one of the legislatures, and apart from its use in deciding cases, his authority influences the habits of mind and even the very soul of all who have cooperated with him judging them."[27] No other country at the time permitted its judges to rule on the constitutionality of the actions of the legislature or the executive.

It was not until the late nineteenth century, however, that the United States Supreme Court began actively to exercise the power of judicial review that Marshall had asserted in the 1803 case of *Marbury v. Madison*.[28] By the time of Holmes's appointment in 1902, the Court's first sustained adventure with judicial review was in full swing. Invoking the Due Process clauses of the Fifth and Fourteenth Amendments, the justices struck down the precursor of the federal income tax as well as a host of state and federal statutes designed to improve conditions for the nation's workers.

Although Holmes, upon his appointment, had proudly likened the justices interpreting the laws to "statesmen governing an empire,"[29] he quickly established himself as the Court's leading exponent of judicial self-restraint. Throughout his long judicial career, he steadfastly insisted that the Court must not sit as a super-legislature substituting its views on economic and social policy for those of the people's elected representatives.[30] With rare exceptions, he voted to uphold legislation with which he strongly disagreed, because, as he remarked late in life, "About seventy-five years ago, I learned that I was not God. And, so when the people . . . want to do something I can't find anything in the Constitution expressly forbidding them to do, I say, whether I like it or not, 'God-damit, let 'em do it.'"[31] A regular dissenter from the Court's decisions striking down early social legislation, Holmes lived long enough to see his position prevail. A changing Court began to uphold regulatory legislation—tentatively in the 1920s, and regularly during the New Deal era.

Holmes's explanations of his reasons for deferring to the judgments of the elected branches on divisive social and economic issues remain canonical. The best-known appeared in his dissent in the 1905 case of *Lochner v. New York*, in which the majority had struck down—as a violation of freedom of contract—a New York State law establishing a maximum sixty hour work week for bakery employees.[32] In refusing to join the decision, Holmes wrote:

> This case is decided upon an economic theory which a large part of the country does not entertain. If it were a question of whether I agreed with that theory, I should desire to study it further and long before making up my mind. But I do not conceive that to be my duty, because I strongly believe that my agreement or disagreement has nothing to do with the right of a majority to embody their opinions in law. . . . I think that the word liberty in the Fourteenth Amendment is perverted when it is held to prevent the natural outcome of a dominant opinion, unless it can be said that a rational and fair man necessarily would admit that the statute proposed would infringe fundamental principles as they have been understood by the traditions of our people and our laws.[33]

Holmes's frequent deference to the more representative branches was no blind adherence to a mechanical formula; it was guided, rather, by his sense of the Court's place in a constitutional design that both distributes and limits governmental powers, simultaneously promoting and checking popular rule. Neither a "liberal" nor a "conservative" as those terms are now used, he could be as vehement in defending the political and civil rights of individuals against majoritarian infringement as in protecting the freedom of electoral majorities to act within the limits imposed by "fundamental principles." He adhered to the view of judging set forth in his *Lochner* dissent with impressive consistency throughout his long career. His occasional lapses (commentators still argue about what counts as a lapse) are less remarkable than his overall obedience to a principled, restrained approach to adjudication.

Legal and political theorists will long debate whether it is cause for regret or rejoicing that the most brilliant and influential figure in twentieth-century American law was also an energetic debunker of the role of tradition, reason, and even of morality in the law. In an 1897 lecture that remains the most widely quoted law review article ever published, Holmes adopted the posture that Thomas Hobbes had taken vis-à-vis Lord Edward Coke. "You will find some text writers telling you," he said to an audience at Boston University Law School, that law "is a system of reason."[34] One should not be misled by such statements, he said. Law is nothing more or less than "command," expressed in cases and statutes and backed up by the armed might of the state. The aim of legal study, he went on, is simply the science of prediction, prediction of "where the axe will fall." In words that nearly every American law student still knows by heart, he said that if you want to know the law, "you must look at it as a bad man does," a man "who cares only for the material consequences which such knowledge enables him to predict."[35] He exhorted his listeners to use "cynical acid" to wash away all the moralizing language of right and wrong so that they could see the law as it truly is. "For my own part," he opined, "I often doubt whether it would not be a gain if every word of moral significance could be banished from the law altogether."

Then Holmes explained his "ideal" for law in the future. He began by deploring that "wherever one looks in the law," one finds "tradition" getting in the way of "rational policy." What was needed, he said, was to put the legal system on a more modern and "scientific" basis through clear thinking about means and ends, costs and benefits. To meet the needs of the day, every lawyer should acquire a knowledge of economics, for the "man of the future is the man of statistics and the master of economics."

Like Weber, Holmes had no use for ideas of human rights. In 1918, the same year that Weber held forth in Munich on "Politics as a Vocation," Holmes argued in a short article titled "Natural Law" that the "search for criteria of universal validity" was bound to be futile.[36] People who believe in natural law were simply mistaking their own beliefs for universal principles. "Not that one's belief or love does not remain. Not that we would not fight and die for it if important," said the Civil War hero, but "we have learned to recognize that others will fight and die to make a different world, with equal sincerity or belief." A dog, he said, "will fight for its bone."

There was something disingenuous, however, about Holmes's relentless trashing of reason, tradition, and morality. For he himself drew deeply from the springs of the very heritage he regularly disparaged. The same Holmes who set his face against tradition could in another mood liken the law to a "magic mirror" in which the trained observer could see a mighty princess eternally weaving into her tapestry dim and distant figures of the ever-lengthening past.[37] The same man who proposed to erase all moral language from the law could observe that legal history is a panorama of the moral development of the human race: "The law is the witness and external deposit of our moral life. . . . The practice of it, in spite of popular jests, tends to make good citizens and good men."[38]

The same judge who urged law students to wash the law with "cynical acid" hastened to assure them that he did not mean any disrespect for their common calling. "I venerate the law," he solemnly avowed.[39]

In his complex relation to the law, Holmes bears a striking resemblance to those of his contemporaries whom Hilton Kramer has called the great "tradition-haunted" artists—Picasso and Matisse, Schönberg and Stravinsky. With his vision of the mighty princess, with his mastery of his craft, and with his relentless ambition, Holmes was a Picasso-like figure—larger than life, boldly iconoclastic, yet deeply indebted to his predecessors. And like Picasso, he probably handicapped many of his successors by teaching them to ignore the springs that had nourished him.

Like Machiavelli, however, Holmes continued to be drawn to the classical thinkers whose ideas he had rejected. In 1933, when the newly inaugurated President Franklin D. Roosevelt paid a courtesy call to the famous Justice, he found Holmes reading Plato.[40] "Why do you read Plato, Mr. Justice?" he asked. "To improve my mind, Mr. President," was the answer. At the close of the visit, Roosevelt posed another question to the old man. With the nation in the depths of the Depression, he said, "You have lived through half our country's history; you have seen its great men. This is a dark hour. Justice Holmes, what is your advice to me?" Holmes replied, "You are in a war, Mr. President. I was in a war, too. And in a war there is only one rule: Form your battalions and fight."

Two years later, Oliver Wendell Holmes died at the age of ninety-three. His reaction to the carnage of the Civil War had been to adopt an existential stance similar to Weber's. He committed himself to soldiering on in a world he had come to see as devoid of any meaning other than what the individual creates for himself. By the time World War II came to a close, however, many statespersons and scholars had come to fear the political consequences of thoroughgoing relativism. Eleanor Roosevelt was among those who were ready to entertain the view of classical and Judeo-Christian thinkers that persons and polities are more likely to flourish if human beings are encouraged to raise rather than lower their sights. In the age of specialization and bureaucratization, she not only grasped the necessity for teamwork, but developed her own distinctive mode of leadership as she presided over a historic collaboration between statespersons and scholars.

TWELVE

THE FIRST LADY AND THE PHILOSOPHER

ELEANOR ROOSEVELT, CHARLES MALIK, AND THE HUMAN RIGHTS PROJECT

In the spring of 1945, as World War II was coming to an end, Franklin and Eleanor Roosevelt made plans to travel to San Francisco for the founding conference of the organization that would be known as the United Nations. The American President had been a strong supporter of proposals for a new peace and security organization, and he was looking forward to being present at its creation. On April 12, however, just two weeks before the conference opened, Mrs. Roosevelt received the news that her husband had succumbed to a heart attack in Warm Springs, Georgia, in the company of a woman he had sworn never to see again after an affair that had nearly ended their marriage years before. Stunned by the double shock, she canceled all previous plans and began preparing to move out of the White House. The furthest thing from her mind must have been that the events in California would lead to the most important achievement of her long and active public life.

Meanwhile, among the delegates arriving in San Francisco was a young Lebanese philosopher who had, with great reluctance, agreed to serve as his newly independent country's first Ambassador to the United States. Only a few months earlier, Charles Malik was happily settled in what he believed to be his life's work, teaching at the American University of Beirut. He and his wife Eva had been surprised to receive an invitation to a party at the home of Lebanon's President, Bechara El-Khoury, a gala affair attended by a hundred or more of the new nation's political and economic leaders. An inveterate diarist, he wrote later that night that it had been a "terrible, awful, horrible evening."[1] He was repelled by the atmosphere of "snobbishness, ruthlessness, commercialism, and sensuality." Of one thing he was quite certain: "I do not belong in this crowd of unreality and untruth." He had no idea that he was being given the once-over.

To Lebanon's leaders, the Harvard-educated professor, with his fluency in languages and his popularity among both Muslim and Christian students, must have seemed like just the man they needed for an important diplomatic post. They appealed to Malik's patriotism and, by Christmas Eve 1944, he confessed ruefully to his diary that he had "fallen to political, worldly seduction." He told himself that the ambassadorship to the United States was "only a temporary job."

As the San Francisco conference got underway, Malik discovered that many delegates from the smaller countries were disappointed with the conference agenda that had been prepared by representatives of the major powers. As envisioned by the "Big Three" (Great Britain, the Soviet Union, and the United States), the chief purpose of the new organization was to provide mechanisms for settling disputes between nations and forestalling future aggression. The representatives of several other countries, however, had come with more ambitious goals. In fact, the Latin American delegates—the largest single group at the conference—had met earlier that spring and voted to seek inclusion of a transnational declaration of rights in the UN Charter.[2]

Malik shared the view that the agenda was too limited. When his first turn came to speak, he used it to criticize the conference plan. He questioned whether one could devise measures for the maintenance of peace and security without addressing the underlying causes of conflict and aggression. That night, he agonized in his diary: "I could have done better. I missed many chances. . . . This is not where I ought to be."

Eventually, he joined forces with the Latin Americans and others in a successful effort to include the protection of human rights among the purposes of the UN, and to require the UN to establish a Human Rights Commission. But when the conference came to a close, Malik remained deeply discontented. He wrote in his diary: "Intrigue, lobbying, secret arrangements, blocs, etc. It's terrible. Power politics and bargaining nauseate me. There is so much unreality and play and sham that I can't swing myself into this atmosphere and act." He sent a note to his old Harvard professor, Alfred North Whitehead, saying, "My interest in politics and diplomacy is only temporary. My heart lies definitely in teaching and speculation to which I shall return as soon as I find my mission reasonably fulfilled."[3]

No one knew what, if anything, would become of the human rights language in the UN Charter. In the planning process that preceded the San Francisco conference, Franklin Roosevelt had been the only Allied leader to favor even mentioning human rights. Eleanor Roosevelt, who had followed the conference proceedings from a distance, wrote to a friend, "One feels in the San Francisco conference that a strong hand is missing."[4] Neither she nor Charles Malik could have imagined that the seeds Malik had helped to plant in the Charter would sprout into a project that would occupy them both for the next several years—a project aimed at nothing less than changing the moral terrain of international relations.

Mrs. Roosevelt was still at loose ends later that summer when President Harry Truman asked her to be a member of the U.S. delegation to the first meeting of the UN General Assembly to be held in London in October. The new President was eager to associate the Roosevelt name with his administration, and he knew that the former First Lady had been pondering how best to continue her public service activities. She initially hesitated to accept the appointment, due to her lack of experience in international affairs. But in talking it over with family and friends she came to believe that the UN work could be a good solution to the problem of how to make a new life for herself.

With diligent preparation, plus political skills honed over years of involvement in domestic politics, Mrs. Roosevelt quickly established herself as an effective actor in the new setting. (It did not hurt her progress that public opinion polls regularly named her "the most admired woman in the world.") Shortly after the UN's London meeting, the Economic and Social Council tapped her to chair a small ad hoc committee charged with making recommendations concerning the structure and functions of the Commission on Human Rights.[5]

The most important recommendation to emerge from the ad hoc committee was that the Human Rights Commission's first project should be the preparation of "an international bill of rights." As Mrs. Roosevelt explained in *Foreign Affairs*, "Many of us thought that lack of standards for human rights the world over was one of the greatest causes of friction among the nations, and that recognition of human rights might become one of the cornerstones upon which peace could eventually be based."[6] The idea was to produce a document that could serve as a moral yardstick by which the nations could measure their own and each other's progress in protecting human dignity.

In January 1947, when the eighteen-member Human Rights Commission assembled for the first time, Eleanor Roosevelt was unanimously elected its Chair. The Nationalist Chinese delegate, Peng-chun Chang, was chosen as Vice President, and Charles Malik became the Rapporteur, responsible for preparing official reports on the group's work and its conclusions. This triumvirate, symbolically representing West, East, and, in the case of Malik, a crossroads of many cultures, constituted the leadership of the Human Rights Commission throughout the entire period of the preparation of the document that became the Universal Declaration of Human Rights.

From the beginning, the problem of universality loomed large. Was it really possible to produce a declaration of principles that could win acceptance from representatives of countries containing four-fifths of the world's population? Six of the fifty original U.N. members were within the emerging Soviet bloc; in eleven, Islamic culture was strong; four countries had a large Buddhist population; and thirty-seven were more or less marked by Judeo-Christian traditions and Enlightenment thought. As soon as the ambitious plan was announced, the leaders of the American Anthropological Association warned that such a document could not be "conceived only in terms of the values prevalent in the countries of Western Europe and America."[7]

When Julian Huxley, the director of the United Nations Educational, Social and Cultural Organization (UNESCO) got news of the project, he created a committee to investigate whether there were areas of potential agreement among the world's varied cultural, religious, and philosophical traditions. That blue-ribbon commission was chaired by the English diplomat and historian E. H. Carr, with University of Chicago philosopher Richard McKeon as Rapporteur. French philosopher Jacques Maritain, then serving as his country's Ambassador to the Holy See, was one of the committee's most active members.

The group began its work by sending an elaborate questionnaire to statesmen and scholars in every part of the world. Replies flooded in, reflecting on human rights from Chinese, Islamic, Hindu, and customary law perspectives, as well as from the United States, Europe, and the countries of the Soviet bloc. The respondents included such notables as Mahatma Gandhi, Benedetto Croce, Pierre Teilhard de Chardin, and Aldous Huxley.

Somewhat to the committee's surprise, the lists of basic rights and values they received from their far-flung sources were roughly similar. McKeon's final report recorded their conclusion that it was indeed *possible* to achieve agreement across cultures concerning certain rights that "may be viewed as implicit in man's nature as an individual and as a member of society."[8] The philosophers were well aware that such an agreement did not go very deep. Maritain related the story of how a visitor to one meeting had expressed surprise that partisans of violently opposed ideologies had been able to agree on a list of fundamental rights. The man was told, "Yes, we agree about the rights, but on condition no one asks us why."[9]

Maritain and his colleagues did not regard the lack of consensus on foundations as fatal. The fact that an agreement could be achieved across cultures on several practical concepts was "enough," he wrote, "to enable a great task to be undertaken."[10] Such an agreement, McKeon optimistically added, would at least provide a "framework within which divergent philosophical, religious, and even economic, social and political theories might be entertained and developed."[11]

More serious than divergence on the "why" of each right, the philosophers surmised, would be the problems of arriving at a common understanding of what the principles meant in practice, of reconciling tensions among the various rights, of integrating new rights, and of incorporating new applications. As McKeon pointed out: "Different understandings of the meanings of rights usually reflect divergent concepts of man and of society." He correctly foresaw that "difficulties will be discovered in the suspicions, suggested by these differences, concerning the tangential uses that might be made of a declaration of human rights for the purpose of advancing special interests."[12]

While the UNESCO philosophers were pondering the challenges to universal rights posed by cultural and philosophical differences, it was becoming apparent to Eleanor Roosevelt that the project assigned to her Commission would have to be steered through four political minefields: the drafting process in the Human Rights Commission; approval by the Commission's parent body, the Economic and Social Council; approval by the large UN Committee on Social, Humanitarian and Cultural Affairs; and final approval by the General Assembly. Although she had long been one of the most powerful figures in the Democratic Party, her political skills were about to be tested to the utmost in this new situation.

Five of the eighteen seats on the Human Rights Commission had been allocated to the representatives of the "great powers"—China, France, the Soviet Union, the United Kingdom, and the United States. The remaining thirteen seats were assigned on a rotating basis in order to assure representation of the major regions of the world. It was only to be expected that there would be all sorts of competing and conflicting interests among the members.

The Cold War, moreover, was deepening, which meant that Roosevelt would find herself opposed at nearly every juncture by four hard-nosed, hostile, and often rude colleagues—the Soviet representative and three members from Soviet-bloc states. On another front, the Palestine crisis was erupting. The Arab League had turned to Charles Malik as one of its chief spokesmen, while another Commissioner, René Cassin, was an ardent Zionist. To make matters worse, conflict was breaking out in China and Korea, and the Berlin blockade was threatening to plunge the world into yet another hot war. The Commission's task—to prepare a human rights declaration and to get it approved by a succession of UN bodies before the window of opportunity closed—was close to a mission impossible.

The Commission got off to a rocky start at its very first meeting when Malik precipitated the group's first big argument. The erstwhile philosophy professor began somewhat pompously, lecturing his colleagues about the deeper implications of their project. "When we speak of human rights," he said, "we are raising the fundamental question, what is man?" When we disagree about human rights, he went on, we are really disagreeing about the nature of the person: "Is man merely a social being, like a bee or an ant? Is he merely an animal with biology governing his destiny? Is he just an economic being, a rational calculator of self-interest?"[13]

In the heated discussion that followed, the Yugoslavian member asserted that liberty consists in "perfect harmony between the individual and the community," and that the common interest, as embodied in the State, takes priority over individual claims.[14] "The psychology of individualism," he opined, "has been used by the ruling class in most countries to preserve its own privileges. A modern declaration of rights should not only consider the rights favored by the ruling classes."[15]

Malik retorted that, "The deepest danger of the age is posed by a collectivism which demands the extinction of the human person as such in his own individuality and ultimate inviolability."[16] He then proposed four principles to guide the work of the Commission: First, the human person is more important than any national or cultural group to which he may belong. Second, a person's mind and conscience are his most sacred and inviolable possessions. Third, any pressure from the state, church, or any other group aimed at coercing consent is unacceptable. Fourth, since groups, as well as individuals, may be right or wrong, each person's freedom of conscience must be supreme.[17]

The Soviet representative then chimed in, dismissing Malik's four principles as completely unsuitable. An individual's rights, he insisted, must be seen in relation to his obligations to the community which is "the main body which provides for his existence, and the enjoyment of the human rights which belong to him."[18]

The more pragmatic members of the group, meanwhile, were becoming annoyed with the direction that the discussion was taking. Impatient to get on with the work at hand, India's Hansa Mehta intervened to say: "We are here to affirm faith in fundamental human rights. Whether the human person comes first or the society, I do not think we should discuss that problem now. The Commission should not enter into this maze of ideology."[19]

Malik, still far from developing the suave diplomatic manner for which he would later become famous, rebuked Mrs. Mehta for suggesting that the Commission could avoid "ideological" disputes. "Whatever you may say, Madam, must have ideological presuppositions," he observed, "and no matter how much you may fight shy of them, they are there, and you either hide them or you are brave enough to bring them out in the open and see them and criticize them."[20]

Mrs. Roosevelt let the discussion go on for some time before weighing in. Then, she observed, "It seems to me that in much that is before us, the rights of the individual are extremely important. It is not exactly that you set the individual apart from his society, but you recognize that within any society the individual must have rights that are guarded."[21] The Commission, she said, might not have to decide with absolute certainty whether government exists for the good of the individual or the group, but "I think we do have to make sure, in writing a bill of rights, that we safeguard the fundamental freedoms of the individual."

Though welcoming Mrs. Roosevelt's support, Malik took pains to differentiate his own nuanced view of personhood from "individualism." The person, as Malik used that term, was neither Marx's "species being" nor the lone rights-bearer imagined by many Anglo-American thinkers. Without derogating from the unique value of each human being, Malik saw the human person as constituted in important ways by and through his relationships—with his family, his community, his nation, and his God. Malik's anthropology thus challenged not only members of the Soviet bloc who wanted to subordinate the person to the state, but also the more individualistic

Westerners on the Commission. In the end, it was Malik's view, endorsed by Chang, the Latin Americans, and most other delegates, that helped to bolster the Declaration's claim to universality, by assuring that the document would be neither collectivist nor radically individualist.

The exchanges provoked by Malik marked a defining moment. Not only did fundamental disagreements become more clear, but the arguments concerning "man" and "society" foreshadowed divisions over what was to prove the most contentious and time-consuming subject during the entire drafting process: the formulation of social and economic rights. The controversy over social and economic rights was not, as many people later assumed, over whether such rights should be included in the document. There was broad consensus on that issue. The flash points concerned the emphasis that such rights should receive in relation to traditional political and civil rights, whether they should be specifically enumerated, how they should be phrased, and, above all, how and by whom they should be implemented.[22]

By the end of the first meeting, it was apparent that there were going to be serious divisions, not only between the Soviet bloc representatives and members from the West, but between the more philosophically inclined and the more practical-minded members. It also became evident that a discussion document could not be produced by the full eighteen-member Commission. The members thus unanimously agreed that a "preliminary draft" of an international bill of rights should be prepared by the three officers of the Commission (Roosevelt, Chang, and Malik) with the assistance of the UN Human Rights Division, headed by Canadian lawyer John Humphrey.[23]

Eager to get started, Mrs. Roosevelt invited Chang, Malik, and Humphrey for tea at her Washington Square apartment. A longtime believer in the benefits of enabling people to get to know one another on a personal level, she had invited Chang and Malik in the hope, as she put it, "that our work might be advanced by an informal atmosphere."[24] The scholarly Chinese diplomat and the Lebanese philosopher had already emerged as the Commission's two leading intellectuals, but they were very different in temperament and outlook.

As Roosevelt described the conversation in her 1958 memoir, the differences between the two learned Commissioners pointed up the challenge of finding a set of principles that could be defended as universal.

> They arrived in the middle of a Sunday afternoon, so we would have plenty of time to work. It was decided that Dr. Humphrey would prepare the preliminary draft, and as we settled down over the teacups, one of them made a remark with philosophical implications, and a heated discussion ensued. Dr. Chang was a pluralist and held forth in charming fashion on the proposition that there is more than one kind of ultimate reality. The Declaration, he said, should reflect more than simply Western ideas and Dr. Humphrey would have to be eclectic in his approach. His remark, though addressed to Dr. Humphrey, was really directed at Dr. Malik, from whom it drew a prompt retort as he expounded at some length the philosophy of Thomas Aquinas. Dr. Humphrey joined enthusiastically in the discussion, and I remember that at one point Dr. Chang suggested that the Secretariat might well spend a few months studying the fundamentals of Confucianism! But by that time I could not follow them, so lofty had the conversation become, so I simply filled the teacups again and sat back to be entertained by the talk of these learned gentlemen.[25]

Chang, the head of Nationalist China's UN delegation, was a Chinese version of the Renaissance man. He was a playwright, an accomplished musician, an experienced diplomat, and an educator who had studied with John Dewey at Columbia University in the 1920s. He was devoted to traditional Chinese culture, but conversant with Islamic and Western societies, having served as his country's Ambassador to Chile and Turkey before being posted to the UN.[26] Humphrey described him as a "master of the art of compromise," and a pragmatic thinker who, under cover of a quotation from Confucius, "would often provide the formula which made it possible for the Commission to escape from some impasse."[27]

Though Malik, at forty-one, was the youngest Commissioner, he cut such an imposing figure that few would have suspected how ill at ease he felt in his role. His striking looks made him a favorite of political cartoonists, one of whom described him as "a tall, broad-shouldered giant, with a formidable nose that would make Durante, Fields, and Cyrano tremble together. His curly hair is as untamable as his passion for debate. When he talks, his strong body waves like a palm tree in a storm, and his voice is thunder."[28]

A Greek Orthodox Arab, Malik grew up in a small Lebanese village where his father was the local doctor. The Lebanon of his youth was a unique blend of Islamic, Christian, Arabic, and French cultures, its population about equally divided between Christians and Moslems. As a university student in Beirut, Malik had developed a passionate interest in the philosophy of science, which led him to write Harvard's Alfred North Whitehead inquiring about scholarship opportunities for an impecunious foreigner.[29] The famous professor responded encouragingly, and Malik enrolled as a doctoral candidate at Harvard where, in 1935, he was awarded one of the university's coveted traveling fellowships. He had planned to use the grant to study with Martin Heidegger, but abandoned that idea after being beaten up in a Freiburg street on account of his Semitic looks. He beat a hasty retreat to Harvard, where he completed his doctoral thesis on "The Metaphysics of Time in the Philosophies of Whitehead and Heidegger." Malik then headed home to begin teaching philosophy in Lebanon.

Full of hopes for the future, he began meeting with a group of idealistic young professors of diverse backgrounds—Christian, Islamic, Jewish, Marxist, radical secularists—to discuss "building bridges between Middle Eastern and Western cultures." He was well embarked on his dream of "mediating the things of the mind and spirit to the youth of the Arab world" when he was dragooned into what he thought would be a short stint in politics.[30]

Mrs. Roosevelt must have been pleased that her tea party resulted in a plan of action according to which John Humphrey would prepare a preliminary draft. But some members of the Human Rights Commission were beginning to have second thoughts about the composition of the small drafting group. Accepting their complaints that the group was "insufficiently representative," Mrs. Roosevelt expanded its membership to include the delegates from Australia, Chile, England, France, and the Soviet Union. That potentially unwieldy assemblage had the good sense, however, to appoint a four-person "working" group (composed of Roosevelt, Malik, France's René Cassin, and Geoffrey Wilson of the British Foreign Office). The working group, in turn, chose to put Cassin, the only lawyer in their midst, in charge of the actual drafting process.

It was a felicitous choice. Cassin was one of the most distinguished jurists of the twentieth century. During World War II, he had been General Charles de Gaulle's principal legal adviser, and at the end of the war De Gaulle entrusted him with the formidable task of rehabilitating the compromised French administrative system. In later years he would go on to hold high legal positions in France, to serve as one of the first judges of the European Court of Human Rights, and to win the Nobel Peace Prize in 1968.

Thanks to Cassin's technical expertise, the document that emerged from the working group was, in form and style, an exemplary product of continental European methods of legislative drafting. The Preamble and the Proclamation, as well as Articles 1 and 2 of the thirty-article Declaration, constituted its "general part," setting forth the premises, purposes, and principles that were to guide the interpretation of the specifically enumerated rights that followed. The final three articles also contain interpretive guides, contextualizing rights in relation to limits, duties, and the social and political order in which they are to be realized. Since the civil law tradition is the most widely distributed legal tradition in the world, the draft—in form—was widely recognizable as belonging to a legal family that includes not only the rights declarations in continental European constitutions, but the constitutions and charters that had appeared or were soon to appear in many Latin American, African, and Asian countries. So far as content was concerned, however, Cassin had relied chiefly on the preliminary draft prepared by Humphrey on the basis of what the UN proudly proclaimed as "the most extensive documentation on the subject of human rights ever assembled."[31]

Meanwhile, another dispute had erupted within the Commission between those members who wanted the document to be a covenant legally binding on signatory nations and those who preferred a non-binding declaration of principles. Unable to come to agreement, the group decided to proceed on both fronts. Mrs. Roosevelt favored a declaration, telling State Department officials that "the essential in present day consideration of human rights is to secure publicity" in cases of serious violations.[32] She continued to chair the group working on the declaration with Cassin, while Malik and Chang moved over to the group working on a covenant.

After undergoing several revisions in the light of the Commission's discussions and suggestions received from member states, the draft declaration was ready in May 1948 for final approval by the full Commission. Festering disagreements over economic and social rights now came to a head.

Mrs. Roosevelt opened the May meeting with a strong endorsement of the "second generation" rights, saying that no personal liberty could exist without economic security and independence.[33] However, she added, the declaration should not try to specify methods for ensuring the realization of those rights, because methods "would necessarily vary from one country to another." The Soviet bloc representatives, for their part, were adamant that the declaration should emphasize the role of the state as guarantor of social and economic rights. Representatives of developing nations were unwilling to endorse rights to things their governments could not possibly deliver in the near future, while the communists made it clear they would oppose any language that put social and economic rights on an inferior footing to political and civil rights.

The stalemate was finally resolved when the Commission approved the idea of a mini-preamble to emphasize the importance of this group of rights, and accepted a proposal to specify that the rights in question would be implemented "in accordance with the organization and resources of each State."[34] The majority of the Commissioners, with the Soviet-bloc representatives abstaining, then voted to approve the draft. The proposed declaration was now ready to be sent to the Commission's parent body, the UN's Economic and Social Council (ECOSOC), for the next stage of approval.

It was a stroke of good fortune for those who had worked so hard on the declaration that the man chosen earlier that year to head the Economic and Social Council was none other than a rising young diplomat named Charles Malik. "The year 1948," Malik later recalled, "witnessed the oddest coincidence of my life at the United Nations."[35] His election as president of ECOSOC in February was followed by his election that fall to the chairmanship of the UN's Social, Humanitarian and Cultural Affairs Committee, the body that had to present the declaration for approval by the General Assembly at its December meeting in Paris. Thus, Malik said, he found himself as Rapporteur of the Human Rights Commission submitting to himself, as President of ECOSOC, the draft of the declaration prepared by the Commission. Then, as President of ECOSOC, he had to present the draft to himself as Chair of the committee that would present it to the General Assembly!

How can one explain the meteoric rise of a man who considered himself so ill-suited for public life? How did the awkward professor become the polished diplomat elected by secret ballot to so many key UN positions? How had he come so far in a mere three years? When Lebanon was first given a seat on ECOSOC, Malik was not at all pleased with the assignment. In notes scribbled to himself one evening, he wrote:

> I went to the Council room this morning in the car alone. I sat there at the Council table alone. I almost sat at lunch alone, but for the kindness of the Yugoslav delegate who asked me to sit with him. Last evening I was all alone back at the hotel. When I returned this afternoon I returned in the car alone. I am now all alone eating at the restaurant of the hotel. A feeling of void and blankness overtakes me. I must bear my loneliness. Drink and sex can never relieve it. On the contrary, they cover it up, for a time only. Then it comes back with added force. It cannot be evaded, it must be faced.

At some point, however, Malik's loneliness seems to have become for him a source of strength. He gained a reputation for independence, for which he was respected even by those who opposed his positions.

The *New York Herald Tribune*, in reporting that Malik was the leading candidate for the presidency of ECOSOC, said that his popularity was "based on his personal UN record and is maintained despite criticism from some sources that Lebanon, as a member of the Arab bloc defying the UN decision to partition Palestine, should not be singled out at this time for one of the UN's highest honors."[36] Humphrey would later say of Malik: "He was one of the most independent people ever to sit on the Human Rights Commission and he was dedicated to human rights."[37]

Discovering by trial and error what Mrs. Roosevelt knew in her bones about the political importance of personal relationships, Malik began to invite others to join him for meals instead of waiting to be asked, or dining alone. He became sought after by journalists, perhaps because he never lost his professorial love for explaining, arguing, and analyzing.

As for how Malik was thinking about his own transition from philosopher to diplomat, his diary reveals that as soon as he ceased agonizing over his lack of political skills, he began berating himself for playing the game. A diary entry from this period can be read as a metaphor for his conflicted feelings about having capitulated to politics. He had just eaten a meal in a filthy restaurant and upon returning to his hotel wrote: "The whole place was disgustingly dirty. The cook in front of us touching everything with his hands—the meat, the potatoes, the bread, the waffle, the pieces of butter, the dollars and silver change, and finally with his dirty hands wiping his face. I ate the waffle."

To the extent that Malik eventually came to peace with his new role, he seems to have done so only by accepting it as an onerous duty. At the height of his influence in the UN, he wrote: "Politics is by nature the sphere of compromise and calculation. A certain degree of untruth and impurity and insincerity must needs cling to the politician. He must carry it as a chastening cross." Malik finally reached the same conclusion as Plato and Cicero, but with far more reluctance. If decent people do not go into politics, he wrote, "then in a world desperately hungry for truth and conviction leadership must pass to others, no matter how perverted and false those others may be."

When ECOSOC convened in July 1948, the declaration was but one of many items on a crowded agenda that had to be covered in six weeks. The members of that body were mainly hard-nosed politicians who were not particularly sympathetic toward the UN's human rights program, and John Humphrey became increasingly nervous as time passed with no action on the item he deemed most important. Like Malik, Humphrey was a diligent diarist, and he used his journal to let off steam about what he saw as "utterly inept" leadership on Malik's part. He noted that Malik had sent the declaration to a subcommittee that he chaired himself and where, Humphrey complained, "he invites debate, does little to direct the discussion, and tries to be everybody's friend."[38] To Humphrey it seemed that Malik was allowing the delegates to "ride off furiously in every direction." He could not understand why Malik had allowed precious days to be taken up with trivial issues, or why he permitted the Soviet representative to talk "ten times at least as much as any other delegate."

Malik, however, seems to have taken a page from Mrs. Roosevelt's book, letting discussion meander while he studied how best to get to the desired result. As the days passed, and it became clear that there would not be time for ECOSOC to discuss the draft declaration at length, the Council simply approved a routine motion to transmit the draft to the General Assembly's Committee on Social, Humanitarian and Cultural Affairs (known as the Third Committee) for the next round of scrutiny. Malik was starting to master his new métier.

That September, when the Third Committee met in Paris to begin its deliberations, the international scene was extremely tense. Relations were worsening between the Soviet Union and the West, while smaller nations were becoming resentful of the influence of the great powers and suspicious of their motives. Cynicism and power politics had taken a heavy toll on the mood of hopefulness in which the human rights project had been launched. Given the deterioration of the international situation, most observers believed that if the declaration was not approved by the time the General Assembly's fall meeting adjourned, it would be tabled indefinitely.

A decade later, Eleanor Roosevelt told an interviewer, "We thought we were presenting such a good draft that there would be very little discussion. We found we were mistaken. In the [Third] committee they argued every word. And so we had some terrible times in Paris."[39]

With Malik in the Chair, the Third Committee discussed, debated, and revised the draft declaration during more than eighty stormy meetings. Malik's fluency in Arabic, French, German, and English enabled him to move easily between East and West, and between large and small nations. He made the most of the fact that the document reflected input from diverse sources, and he took pains to point the delegates to the places in the Declaration where they could either find their own country's contributions, or the influence of the culture to which they belonged. Throughout the process, Mrs. Roosevelt, Cassin, and Chang worked assiduously to marshal support among the members of a UN that had expanded from fifty to fifty-eight members.

Later, viewing that tense time through the soft lenses of memory, Malik wrote, "Those were great days twenty years ago when we were in the throes of elaborating for final submission to the General Assembly of the United Nations the draft Universal Declaration of Human Rights. Mrs. Roosevelt, M. Cassin, Mr. Chang, Mr. Santa Cruz [of Chile] and I, together with our respective advisors and assistants, soon achieved a fairly close identity of views on aims and objectives. We worked more or less as a team."[40]

Putting aside their disagreements over philosophy and religion, Malik and Chang made a formidable duo. And nothing is more indicative of the extraordinary personal qualities of Malik and Cassin than their close collaboration on the declaration throughout the Palestine crisis of 1947 and 1948. Malik during all this period was a prominent spokesman for the Arab League, while Cassin, who had lost twenty-nine relatives in concentration camps, was deeply committed to the establishment of a Jewish homeland. Yet they did not permit their political differences to get in the way of their collaboration in a common cause.

The Soviet-bloc representatives made repeated efforts to stall and drag out the process. With each delay, the prospects for success grew dimmer, to the point where Humphrey and Cassin began to fear that all the the work they had done might go for naught. But Malik was up to the challenge. John Humphrey greatly upgraded his estimate of Malik's political skills: "We were fortunate in having Charles Malik in the chair," he conceded in his memoirs. "Presiding over a much more turbulent body [than ECOSOC]—perhaps the most turbulent in the United Nations, he conducted the proceedings with a firmness that first surprised me. There were indeed times when he approached arrogance, even losing his temper, and with a bang of the gavel refusing the floor to delegations. But my respect for him grew as the session progressed, and he got the Declaration through the Committee."[41] One of Roosevelt's State Department advisers remarked with awe that Malik was "the only person I ever knew who succeeded in holding a stopwatch to Pavlov [the most voluble of the Soviet delegates]."[42] The debates wore on for two months, often lasting late into the night, until December 4, when the Third Committee voted to send the draft to the General Assembly for final approval, with no nays and seven abstentions.

On December 9, when Malik rose to present the draft to the General Assembly, he directed his words to the public and posterity as well as to his fellow delegates. Unlike previous rights declarations that had sprung from particular cultures, he said, the Universal Declaration was "a composite synthesis of all these outlooks and movements and of much Oriental and Latin American wisdom. Such a synthesis has never occurred before in history."[43] The Latin American countries, he specified, had brought to the process the ideas and experience gained in preparing the 1948 Pan-American Declaration on the Rights and Duties of Man; India had played a key role in advancing the non-discrimination principle, especially with respect to women; the United Kingdom and the United States had shared the wisdom acquired in their long experience with traditional political and civil liberties; the Soviet Union had championed the cause of improving the living conditions of the broad mass of people; the importance of including duties had been emphasized by participants from China, Latin America, the Soviet Union, and France; many smaller countries contributed to the articles on freedom of religion and the rights of the family; the social, economic, and cultural rights had numerous fathers and mothers.

When Mrs. Roosevelt spoke, she told the General Assembly that the Universal Declaration might well become a landmark in the history of human freedom:

> We stand today at the threshold of a great event both in the life of the United Nations and in the life of mankind, that is the approval by the General Assembly of the Universal Declaration of Human Rights recommended by the Third Committee. This declaration may well become the international Magna Carta of all men everywhere. We hope its proclamation by the General Assembly will be an event comparable to the proclamation of the Declaration of the Rights of Man by the French people in 1789, the adoption of the Bill of Rights by the people of the United States, and the adoption of comparable declarations at different times in other countries.[44]

In the wee morning hours of December 10, the Declaration was approved. Though eight countries abstained (Byelorussia, Czechoslovakia, Poland, Saudi Arabia, South Africa, the Soviet Union, Ukraine, and Yugoslavia), there were no dissenting votes. Eleanor Roosevelt received a standing ovation.

No American woman has been so admired at home and abroad as was Eleanor Roosevelt in her lifetime, and none has left behind such a distinguished record of public service. At her death in 1962, the *New York Times* described her as "more involved in the minds and hearts and aspirations of people than any other First Lady in history" and as "one of the most esteemed women in the world."[45] It is illustrative, however, of the difficulties women have faced in politics, that historians and writers on foreign affairs have underrated Eleanor Roosevelt's role in the process that led to the approval of the Universal Declaration. Most have tended to portray her as merely having chaired the UN's Human Rights Commission while Malik, Humphrey, Cassin, and others did the heavy lifting.

No doubt Eleanor Roosevelt herself contributed to the tendency to underestimate her achievements. She had been raised in an ethos in which women were schooled to be self-effacing, and she was not above feigning naïveté when it suited her purposes. Early in life, she had learned how to work within the parameters of what society expected of a "lady." As time went on, she became adept at simultaneously exploiting and expanding those parameters. According to her close friend Joseph Lash, she was particularly fond of a passage from a poem by Stephen Vincent Benet in which he described a woman who was able "To take the burden and have the power/And seem like the well-protected flower."[46] By the time she assumed the chair of the Human Rights Commission, she had perfected a personal, low-key, but very effective mode of leadership that served her causes well.

In view of the enormous obstacles Eleanor Roosevelt had to overcome in shepherding the Universal Declaration from the drafting process through final approval, to say she "merely" presided is to miss the magnitude of her achievement. George Washington, too, "merely" presided over the Constitutional Convention, but historians agree that without the force of his personality and the great respect in which he was held, there would have been no Constitution.

As in the case of the U.S. Constitution, however, full credit for the Universal Declaration belongs not to any one person but to an extraordinary collaboration. Roosevelt, Malik, Maritain, McKeon, Cassin, Chang, and their colleagues were justly proud of their accomplishment. At the same time they were well aware of its fragility. In fact, they foresaw nearly every problem that the postwar human rights project would encounter—its buffeting from power politics, its dependence on common understandings that would prove elusive, its embodiment of ideas of freedom and solidarity that would be difficult to harmonize, and its vulnerability to politicization and misunderstanding. But subsequent events also provided grounds for encouragement. The Universal Declaration became the model for most post–World War II rights declarations; it was the polestar for the movements that brought about the relatively peaceful collapse of totalitarian governments in Eastern Europe; and it remains the single most important reference point for cross-national discussions of how to order our lives together on an increasingly interdependent planet.

The Universal Declaration of Human Rights—like the Justinian *Corpus Juris Civilis*, the Code Napoleon, and the United States Constitution—stands as a monument to what can be achieved through creative collaboration between statespersons and scholars, collaboration that in some cases extends not only across disciplines but over generations. Given the increased specialization that Weber saw as a hallmark of the modern age, it is likely that teamwork will be as indispensable in the future to the human sciences as it has become in the natural sciences where, more often than not, it is a diverse community of knowers, rather than any one individual that accomplishes significant advances.[47]

Such collaborative enterprises require participants with a somewhat different set of qualities from those possessed by persons like Tocqueville who could not bring himself to be a team player or Weber whose desire for recognition caused him to lament that one's best work is sure to be superseded in the future. Eleanor Roosevelt, Charles Malik and their colleagues not only looked forward to the day when others would improve upon their work, but they took deep satisfaction in being part of the great conversation that has continued through the ages between the forum and the tower.

Epilogue

That kings should philosophize or philosophers become kings is not to be expected. Nor is it to be wished, since the possession of power inevitably corrupts the untrammeled judgment of reason. But kings or kinglike peoples which rule themselves under laws of equality should not suffer the class of philosophers to disappear or to be silent, but should let them speak openly. This is indispensable to the enlightenment of the business of government.

Immanuel Kant, *Perpetual Peace* (1795)

$\mathbf{N}$o matter which vocational path claimed their primary allegiance, all the scholars and political actors profiled here shared the belief that statespersons should keep in touch with the world of ideas and that political theorists should attend to what is going on in the life of the polity. Even Hobbes and Rousseau gave nods to that idea in theory if not in practice.

Plato, torn between the forum and the tower for most of his life, ridiculed both the man of action who never looks beyond his immediate concerns and the scholar who keeps his head in the clouds. The man who has "knocked about from youth in the law courts," says Socrates in the *Theaetetus*, "acquires a tense and bitter shrewdness, but his mind is narrow and crooked. . . . He passes from youth to manhood with no soundness in him and turns out, in the end, a man of formidable intellect—in his own imagination."[1] The old philosopher is equally dismissive of the sort of thinker who "cannot even find his way to the marketplace or the forum," who has "never looked at the text of a law," and to whom it has never occurred "even in dreams to take an interest in the rivalries of political cliques, in meetings, dinners, and merrymakings."[2] Such a man "is unaware what his neighbor is doing, hardly knows indeed whether the creature is a man at all; he spends all his pains on the question, what man is. . . . Only his body sojourns in his city, while his thought, disdaining all such things as worthless, takes wings . . . seeking the true nature of everything as a whole, never sinking to what lies close at hand."

Cicero followed Plato in regarding the ideal statesman as one whose actions are illuminated by philosophy. "[W]hat can be more glorious," he asked, "than the conjunction of practical experience in great affairs of state with the knowledge of these arts acquired through study and learning?"[3] Recalling great Romans who had done so in the past, he said, "The person who has had the will and the capacity to acquire both—that is, ancestral institutions and philosophical learning—is the one who I think has done everything deserving of praise." Cicero's advice to philosophers was that they should attend to public affairs not only out of civic duty, and not only to stay grounded in reality, but also—and just as importantly—to assure the maintenance of conditions under which intellectual life can flourish.

Locke, with a foot in both camps, agreed. Both the man of action and the man of contemplation are diminished, he wrote, if they remain shut up in their own worlds: "They have a petty traffic with known correspondents in some little creek . . . but will not venture out into the great ocean of knowledge, to survey the riches that nature hath stored other parts with, no less genuine, no less solid, no less useful."[4]

Even the ancients realized, however, that no one person can master everything. Already in the first century BC, Cicero fretted that the various academic disciplines were becoming so divided into parts that people were losing sight of "the alliance and affinity that connects all the liberal arts and sciences, and even the virtues themselves."[5] As we have seen, political actors long ago learned to make use of expert advisers. Today, as the fields of knowledge become increasingly fragmented and experts increasingly specialized, teamwork among statespersons and scholars is more essential than ever if practice is to remain in touch with theory and vice versa.

The world of politics, no less than the world of scholarship, has undergone momentous transformations over the years. That is why James Madison, convinced that democratic government required special kinds of excellence on the part of citizens and statesmen alike, declined to speculate on what might become of the American experiment with changes of circumstances and the passage of time. That, he said in *Federalist No. 55*, "requires a prophetic spirit to declare, and that makes no part of my pretensions."[6]

By 1831, when Tocqueville visited Jacksonian America, it seemed to the French observer that spirited men were more attracted to business than to public service, and he worried about whether government would continue to attract leaders with the exceptional qualities of character and competence that had characterized the founding generation.[7] Max Weber, a generation later, thought that the rise of bureaucracy had stepped up the challenges for the future of statesmanship in continental Europe.[8] Nor did he view with envy the political landscape in the United States. There, it seemed to him, the political parties had become "purely organizations of job hunters drafting their changing platforms according to the chances of vote-grabbing."[9]

In recent years, political theorist Francis Fukuyama has again raised the question whether, under current conditions, talented men and women are deterred from choosing careers in the public sector and private citizens discouraged from making time for community service.[10] To Fukuyama, contemporary preoccupation with private satisfactions evokes the specter of Nietzsche's "last men," "men without chests" who are ingenious at finding ways to satisfy their mundane desires through calculation of self-interest, but who lack the desire to rise above those wants. He asks whether future generations of Americans, "throwing themselves into essentially unpleasant or stultifying work with a view to the accumulation of greater material satisfactions and petty signs of prestige, [will] lead increasingly fragmented and purposeless existences in a world of unprecedented materialism, desperate personal isolation, and inner psychological weakness verging on collapse."[11]

But as the stories collected here have shown, life and history are full of surprises. *Thymos* and the *eros* of the mind are not easily suppressed, and can appear in unexpected places. The same social upheavals that awaken concern about the future of statesmanship and scholarship can also create new opportunities. Often it has been talented outsiders—"new men" like Cicero and Burke—who have infused the public square with fresh ideas and energy.

With the advance of liberal democracy, more and more persons who would once have been excluded or marginalized have brought their talents and perspectives to bear on new challenges. At a time when women's access to public roles was severely limited, for example, Eleanor Roosevelt pioneered a mode of leadership that was highly effective in a multicultural and multidisciplinary setting. She managed to keep a diverse collection of strong personalities working together, despite tensions and conflicts that constantly threatened to derail their progress on the Universal Declaration of Human Rights.

Today, among our contemporaries and near-contemporaries, there are many persons of great capacity and accomplishment who have bridged the worlds of statesmanship and scholarship under challenging new circumstances. One thinks, for example, of extraordinary intellectuals like Vaclav Havel and Karol Wojtyla who were at the forefront of the movements that brought a nonviolent end to totalitarian regimes in Eastern Europe; of scholars like George Shultz and Henry Kissinger who served as advisors to latter-day princes; of learned diplomats like George Kennan and Abba Eban; of distinguished professors like Francis Fukuyama and James Q. Wilson who combine occasional public service with high political journalism of the sort that Weber recognized as a new type of political vocation; of the senatorial careers of sociologist

Patrick Moynihan in the United States and philosophers Marcello Pera and Rocco Buttiglione in Europe.

The vocational journeys of such persons will one day be fascinating and instructive to explore. As the essays in this volume illustrate, however, the full significance of the life of a statesperson or philosopher tends not to emerge until some time after he or she has passed from the scene. If one message emerges from the stories collected here, it is that just because one does not see the results of one's best efforts in one's own lifetime does not mean those efforts were in vain.

NOTES

PREFACE

1. Carnes Lord translation (University of Chicago Press, 1984), 199.
2. Henry A. Kissinger, "Current International Trends and World Peace," in *Charity and Justice in the Relations among Persons and Nations, Proceedings of the XIIIth Plenary Session of the Pontifical Academy of Social Science* (Libreria Editrice Vaticana, 2007), 233.
3. Max Weber, "Politics as a Vocation" in *From Max Weber: Essays in Sociology*, Hans Gerth and C. Wright Mills eds. (London: Routledge, 1991), 117.
4. Kissinger, "Current International Trends," 233.
5. Cicero, "The Laws," in Marcus Tullius Cicero, *The Republic and The Laws*, Niall Rudd translation (Oxford: Oxford University Press, 1998), 118.
6. Cicero, "The Republic," in *The Republic and The Laws*, 7.
7. Max Weber, "Science as a Vocation," in Gerth and Mills, 150.
8. Plato, "Seventh Letter," in *The Platonic Epistles*, J. Harward translation (New York: Arno Press, 1976), 331c-d.

INTRODUCTION

1. *Federalist* No. 72 (Hamilton).
2. Plato, "Seventh Letter," in *The Platonic Epistles*, J. Harward translation (New York: Arno Press, 1976), 328 b, c.
3. Hugh Brogan, *Alexis de Tocqueville: A Life* (New Haven: Yale, 2006), 279.
4. Max Weber, "Science as a Vocation," in *From Max Weber: Essays in Sociology*, Hans Gerth and C. Wright Mills eds. (London: Routledge, 1991), 150.
5. Letter from Charles Malik to Alfred North Whitehead, June 27, 1945 (Malik Papers, Library of Congress, Manuscript Division).
6. "The Republic," in Marcus Tullius Cicero, *The Republic and The Laws*, Niall Rudd transl. (Oxford: Oxford University Press, 1998), 4.
7. Cicero, "The Republic," 6–7.
8. Anthony Everitt, *Cicero: The Life and Times of Rome's Greatest Politician* (New York: Random House, 2001), 259.
9. A Letter to a Noble Lord, in *Edmund Burke: Selected Writings and Speeches*, Peter Stanlis ed. (Gloucester, MA: Peter Smith, 1968), 563.

CHAPTER 1

1. Diogenes Laertius, "Life of Plato," in *Lives of Eminent Philosophers*, R. D. Hicks transl. (Cambridge, MA: Harvard University Press, 1959), Book III, Ch. 4.

2. Plato, "Seventh Letter," in *The Platonic Epistles*, J. Harward transl. (New York: Arno Press, 1976), 324d.
3. *Gorgias*, in Collected Dialogues of Plato, Edith Hamilton and Huntington Cairns eds., W.D. Woodhead translation (Princeton: Princeton University Press, 1971), 229.
4. "Seventh Letter," 325a.
5. Ibid.
6. "Seventh Letter," 324c.
7. "Seventh Letter," 327a.
8. The incident is recounted in "The Life of Dionysius," in Plutarch's *Lives*, Thomas North transl., Vol. 8 (New York: Limited Editions Club, 1941), 267, 303–305, and in "The Life of Dion," Plutarch's *Lives*, Thomas North transl., Vol. 7 (New York: Limited Editions Club, 1941), 240–241.
9. Glenn R. Morrow, *Plato's Cretan City* (Princeton: Princeton University Press, 1993), 6.
10. "Life of Diogn," 249.
11. Plato, "Seventh Letter," 328 b, c.
12. Ibid.
13. "Life of Dion," 250.
14. "Seventh Letter," 330 a–c.
15. "Life of Dion," 255.
16. Ibid.
17. "Seventh Letter," 350d.
18. The Republic, I, 347c.
19. Id. at 331 c–d.
20. Alfred North Whitehead, *Process and Reality* (New York: Free Press, 1979), 39.
21. Glenn R. Morrow, *Plato's Cretan City* (Princeton: Princeton University Press, 1993), 19, 51.
22. See W. K. C. Guthrie, *A History of Greek Philosophy*, Vol. 4 (Cambridge: Cambridge University Press, 1987), 322.
23. *The Laws*, 624a. In this chapter, I rely primarily on Thomas Pangle's translation in *The Laws of Plato* (New York: Basic Books, 1980). I have also used the Benjamin Jowett translation in *The Dialogues of Plato* (Chicago: Encyclopedia Britannica, 1990) and Trevor Saunders's translation in *Plato: The Laws* (London: Penguin Classics, 1975).
24. *The Laws*, 691d.
25. *The Laws*, 853c.
26. *The Laws*, 714a.
27. *The Laws*, 957c.s
28. *The Laws*, 714b ff.
29. *The Laws*, 644e.
30. *The Laws*, 702d.
31. *Plato's Cretan City*, 3–4.
32. *The Laws*, 746b.
33. *The Laws*, 739a.
34. *The Laws*, 704a ff.
35. *The Laws*, 747d.
36. *The Laws*, 709a.

37. *The Laws*, 720e ff.
38. *The Laws*, 765d.
39. *The Laws*, 804–805.
40. *The Laws*, 802, 805.
41. *The Laws*, 793b.
42. See John Cleary, *"Paideia* in Plato's Laws," in *Plato's Laws: From Theory into Practice*, S. Scolnicov and L. Brisson eds. (Sankt Augustin: Academia Verlag, 2003), 166–174.
43. *The Laws*, 719–720.
44. *The Laws*, 701e, 711e–712a.
45. *The Laws*, 715d.
46. *The Laws*, 769d.
47. *The Laws*, 701d.
48. *The Laws*, 641d.
49. Plato's *Phaedo*, Eva Brann transl. (Newburyport: Focus Publishing, 1998), 78a.

CHAPTER 2

1. "The Republic," in Marcus Tullius Cicero, *The Republic and The Laws*, Niall Rudd transl. (Oxford: Oxford University Press, 1998), 4.
2. "The Republic," 4.
3. "The Republic," 61.
4. Ibid.
5. Cicero's message to his son in "On Duties," in *Selected Works*, Michael Grant transl. (London: Penguin Books, 1971), 161.
6. Marcus Tullius Cicero, *Selected Letters*, P. G. Walsh transl. (Oxford: Oxford University Press, 2008), 49, 50.
7. "The Republic," 92.
8. "The Republic," 33.
9. For the account of Cicero's life and career in this chapter, I have relied on two excellent biographies: Anthony Everitt, *Cicero: The Life and Times of Rome's Greatest Politician* (New York: Random House, 2001) and Elizabeth Rawson, *Cicero: A Portrait* (London: Bristol Classical Press, 2001).
10. Plutarch's *Lives*, Volume II, Dryden transl. (New York: Modern Library, 2001), 409.
11. Rawson, *Cicero*, 20.
12. Plutarch, 442.
13. Quoted in Rawson, *Cicero*, 25–26.
14. Rawson, *Cicero*, 28.
15. *Tusculan Disputations*, J. E. King transl. (Cambridge: Harvard University Press, 1960), 491.
16. Quoted in Rawson, 35–36.
17. Plutarch, 415.
18. "The Republic," 35.
19. "The Republic," 81.
20. "The Republic," 88–89.
21. Dante, *Paradiso* XXII, lines 133–138.
22. "On Duties," in *Selected Works*, Michael Grant transl. (London: Penguin Books, 1971), 160.

23. Rawson, *Cicero*, 135.
24. Cicero, *Selected Letters*, 254, 262.
25. Plutarch, 439.
26. Plutarch, 441.
27. Plutarch, 409.
28. "The Republic," 6–7.
29. Rawson, *Cicero*, 149.
30. "The Republic," 6–7.
31. Rawson, 119.
32. Cicero, *Selected Letters*, P. G. Walsh transl. (Oxford: Oxford World's Classics, 2008), 33.
33. "On Duties," in Marcus Tullius Cicero, *Selected Works*, Michael Grant transl. (London: Penguin Books, 1971), 165.
34. "On Duties," 166.
35. Quoted in Everitt, *Cicero*, 163.
36. Cicero, *Selected Letters*, 196, 197.
37. Cicero, *Selected Letters*, 250.
38. Augustine, *Confessions*, Henry Chadwick transl. (Oxford: Oxford University Press, 1991), 38.
39. Rawson, *Cicero*, 232.
40. Rawson, *Cicero*, 254.
41. "The Republic," 19.
42. "On Duties," 184–185.

CHAPTER 3

1. See, generally, Mary Ann Glendon, Paolo G. Carozza, and Colin B. Picker, *Comparative Legal Traditions*, 3rd ed. (St. Paul, MN: Thompson/ West, 2007), 52–72.
2. Quoted in Edward Gibbon, *The Decline and Fall of the Roman Empire*, Vol. II (Chicago: Encyclopaedia Britannica, 1952), 72.
3. Cicero, The Laws, in Marcus Tullius Cicero, *The Republic and The Laws*, Niall Rudd transl. (Oxford: Oxford University Press, 1998), 167.
4. Edward Gibbon, 72–73.
5. Quoted in Elizabeth Rawson, *Cicero: A Portrait* (London: Bristol Classical Portraits, 2001), 45.
6. Edward Gibbon, 76.
7. John Henry Wigmore, *A Panorama of the World's Legal Systems* (Washington, DC: Washington Law Book Co., 1928), 398.
8. Edward Gibbon, 76.
9. Edward Gibbon, 80.
10. Edward Gibbon, Chapter 6.
11. Wigmore, 443.
12. Edward Gibbon, *The Decline and Fall of the Roman Empire*, Vol. I, 245.
13. Wigmore, 439.
14. Edward Gibbon, Vol. II, 78.
15. Edward Gibbon, 78.
16. Edward Gibbon, 78–79.

17. See James Allan Evans, *The Emperor Justinian and the Byzantine Empire* (Westport, CT: Greenwood Press, 2005), 23.
18. "The Composition of the *Digest*," in *Digest of Justinian*, Alan Watson transl., Vol. I (Philadelphia: University of Pennsylvania Press, 2008) (pages un-numbered).
19. Evans, 26–29.
20. H. F. Jolowicz, *Historical Introduction to the Study of Roman Law* (Cambridge: Cambridge University Press, 1965), 520–521.
21. H. F. Jolowicz and Barry Nicholas, *Historical Introduction to the Study of Roman Law*, 3rd ed. (Cambridge: Cambridge University Press, 1972), 507–508.
22. The *Digest* is available in English in four volumes edited and translated by legal historian Alan Watson, *The Digest of Justinian* (Philadelphia: University of Pennsylvania Press, 2008).
23. Digest of Justinian, vol. I, p. 1.
24. Id. at 2.
25. Edward Gibbon, *The Decline and Fall of the Roman Empire*, Vol. II (Chicago: Encyclopaedia Britannica, 1952), 71.
26. Edward Gibbon, 80.
27. Franz Wieacker, "The Importance of Roman Law for Western Civilization and Western Legal Thought," 4 *Boston College Law Review* 257, 270 (1981).
28. Alan Watson, "The Importance of 'Nutshells,'" 42 *American Journal of Comparative Law* 1, 9 (1994).
29. Jean-Luc Chartier, *Portalis: Père du code civil* (Paris: Fayard, 2004), 143–206.
30. Alain Levasseur, "Code Napoleon or Code Portalis?" 43 *Tulane Law Review* 762, 765 (1968–1969).
31. French Civil Code, Articles 4 and 5.
32. Quoted in Edouard Leduc, *Portalis* (Paris: Panthéon, 1990), 176.
33. Wigmore, 1031.
34. Alan Watson, "Preface" to *Digest of Justinian*, Vol. I (pages un-numbered).

CHAPTER 4

1. The research assistance of Christina Hoffman on this chapter is gratefully acknowledged. Pasquale Villari, *The Life and Times of Niccolò Machiavelli*, Vol. 1, Linda Villari transl. (London: T. Fisher Unwin, 1898), 15.
2. Roberto Ridolfi, *The Life of Niccolò Machiavelli*, Cecil Grayson transl. (Chicago: University of Chicago Press, 1963), 15.
3. Quentin Skinner, *Machiavelli* (Oxford: Oxford University Press, 1981), 9.
4. Maurizio Viroli, *Niccolò's Smile: A Biography of Machiavelli* (New York: Farrar, Straus & Giroux, 2000), 53–54.
5. Ridolfi, 68.
6. Ridolfi, 70.
7. Skinner, 11.
8. *The Prince*, Harvey Mansfield transl. (Chicago: University of Chicago Press, 1998), 27.

9. *The Prince*, 65–66.
10. *The Prince*, 33.
11. Villari, Vol. 1, 385.
12. Ibid.
13. Niccolò Machiavelli, *The Florentine Histories*, G. B. Niccolini transl. (New York: Paine and Burgess, 1845), 204.
14. *Discourses on Livy*, Harvey Mansfield and Nathan Tarcov transl. (Chicago: University of Chicago Press, 1996), 6.
15. *Discourses on Livy*, 214–215.
16. Described in Viroli, 136.
17. Ridolfi, 175.
18. Machiavelli, "Letter to Francesco Vettori," in *The Prince*, Appendix, 108–109.
19. *The Prince*, Dedication, 4.
20. Ridolfi, 189.
21. *Discourses on Livy*, 5.
22. *The Prince*, Chapter 61.
23. Plato, "Seventh Letter," in *The Platonic Epistles*, J. Harward transl. (New York: Arno Press, 1976), 351 d–e.
24. *The Prince*, 61.
25. Aristotle, *Politics*, Carnes Lord transl. (Chicago: University of Chicago Press, 1984), 1253a31–32.
26. *The Prince*, 66–67.
27. Ibid.
28. Ernest L. Fortin, "In the Shadow of the Gallows," in *Human Rights, Virtue and the Common Good*, Brian J. Benestad ed. (Lanham, MD: Rowman & Littlefield, 1996), 73, 80.
29. *The Prince*, 61.
30. *The Prince*, 101.
31. *Discourses on Livy*, 131.
32. *The Prince*, 70.
33. Skinner, 38.
34. *Mandragola*, Mera J. Flaumenhaft transl. (Prospect Heights, IL: Waveland Press, 1981), 39.
35. Viroli, Vol. 1, 258.
36. Skinner, 87.
37. Machiavelli, "Letter to Francesco Vettori," in *The Prince*, Appendix, 109–110.
38. See, especially, Viroli, *Niccolò's Smile*, and Villari, *The Life and Times of Niccolò Machiavelli*.
39. "Translating Politics: A Conversation with Harvey Mansfield," Humanities May/June 2007, 9.
40. Villari, Vol. 2, 517.
41. Villari, Vol. 2, 515.
42. Villari, Vol. 2, 517.
43. Villari, Vol. 2, 515.
44. Harvey C. Mansfield, *Machiavelli's Virtue* (Chicago: University of Chicago Press, 1996), ix. (Emphasis in original.)

45. *The Prince*, 6.
46. Viroli, 222.
47. Plato, "Seventh Letter," 331 c–d.
48. Plato, "Seventh Letter," 330 e–331 a.

CHAPTER 5

1. The account that follows is based on Edward Coke's own report, "On the Conference between King James I and the Judges of England in 1612," 6 Coke's Reports 63 (1612). See also, Catherine Drinker Bowen's biography of Coke, *The Lion and the Throne* (Boston: Little Brown, 1956), 302–306.
2. J. H. Baker, *An Introduction to English Legal History*, 2nd ed. (London: Butterworths, 1979), 144.
3. Id. 93, 145.
4. Bowen, *Lion and the Throne*, 453.
5. Id., 457.
6. Id., x.
7. Id., 457.
8. Theodore Plucknett, *A Concise History of the Common Law*, 5th ed. (Boston: Little Brown, 1956), 244.
9. Id., 243.
10. Bowen, *Lion and the Throne*, 82.
11. Id., 258–259.
12. Id., x.
13. Id., 293.
14. A. P. Martinich, *Hobbes: A Biography* (Cambridge University Press, 1999), 2.
15. Id. at 162.
16. *Leviathan*, Ch. 13.
17. Ibid.
18. Id., Ch. 15, 20.
19. Id., Ch. 13.
20. Id., Ch. 13, 14.
21. Ibid.
22. Id., Ch. 14.
23. Id., Ch. 8.
24. Id., Ch. 6.
25. Id., Ch. 11.
26. Id., Ch. 17.
27. Id., Ch. 21.
28. Id., Ch. 18.
29. Id., Ch. 21, Ch. 30.
30. Plucknett, 62.
31. *Leviathan*, Ch. 22.
32. Id., Ch. 29.
33. Id., Ch. 26.
34. Id., Ch. 21.
35. Ibid.

36. Id., Ch. 18.
37. Id., Ch. 21.
38. Id., Ch. 11.
39. Id., Ch. 26.
40. Id., Ch. 11.
41. Edward Coke, *The First Part of the Institutes of the Laws of England*, p. 97b, s. 138.
42. Ibid.
43. *Leviathan*, Ch. 26.
44. Laurence Berns, "Thomas Hobbes," in *History of Political Philosophy*, Strauss and Cropsey eds., 3rd ed. (Chicago: University of Chicago Press, 1987), 397.
45. Aristotle, *Ethics*, Book I, Ch. 3.
46. Thomas Hobbes, *Writings on Common Law and Hereditary Right, consisting of a Dialogue between a Philosopher and a Student of the Common Laws of England and Questions Relative to Hereditary Right*, Alan Cromartie and Quentin Skinner eds. (Oxford: Oxford University Press, 2005).
47. Berns, "Thomas Hobbes," at 397.
48. *Leviathan*, Ch. 26.
49. Id., Ch. 6.
50. See J. G. A. Pocock, *The Machiavellian Moment: Florentine Political Thought and the Atlantic Republican Tradition* (Princeton: Princeton University Press, 2003), 158–161.
51. The Prince, Ch. II.
52. *Leviathan*, Ch. 29.
53. Peter Laslett, "Introduction," in *John Locke: Two Treatises on Government* (Cambridge: Cambridge University Press, 1963), 103–104.
54. See J. H. Hexter, "Thomas Hobbes and the Law," 65 *Cornell Law Review* 471, 489–490 (1980).
55. Edward Coke, *Commentaries on Littleton*, 142a.
56. William Blackstone, *Commentaries on the Laws of England*, Vol, 1, *17.

CHAPTER 6

1. The research assistance of Adam Lebovitz on this chapter is gratefully acknowledged. Peter Laslett, "Introduction," in *John Locke: Two Treatises of Government*, Peter Laslett ed. (Cambridge: Cambridge University Press, 1963), 29.
2. Roger Woolhouse, *Locke: A Biography* (Cambridge: Cambridge University Press, 2007), 37.
3. Woolhouse, 60, 66.
4. Woolhouse, 86.
5. Woolhouse, 90–91.
6. Maurice Cranston, *John Locke: A Biography* (London: Longmans, Green, 1957), 159.
7. Cranston, 130.
8. Cranston, x.
9. Laslett, 77–78. Scholars agree that the *Two Treatises* were largely written between 1679 and 1683, but there is much disagreement about the precise dates. See Woolhouse, 181–182.

10. Woolhouse, 265.
11. Mark Goldie, "Introduction" to *John Locke, Political Essays* (Cambridge: Cambridge University Press, 1997), xv.
12. Cranston, 324.
13. Woolhouse, 218–219.
14. Woolhouse, 265.
15. The *Letter* and the *Treatises* were post-dated 1690 by the publishers.
16. Laslett, 50.
17. Goldie, xiv–xv.
18. Cranston, 329.
19. Cranston, 325.
20. Woolhouse, 267, 355–357, 400–401.
21. Woolhouse, 401.
22. Laslett, 325–326.
23. Woolhouse, 187.
24. Thomas L. Pangle, *The Spirit of Modern Republicanism: The Moral Vision of the American Founders and the Philosophy of John Locke* (Chicago: University of Chicago Press, 1988), 126.
25. *Second Treatise on Civil Government*, par. 1.
26. Id., par. 6.
27. Id., par. 8.
28. Id., par. 13.
29. Id., par. 77.
30. Id., par. 13.
31. Id., par. 123.
32. Id., par. 25.
33. Id., par. 27.
34. Id., par. 26.
35. Id., par. 27.
36. Id., par. 33, 34.
37. Palazzolo v. Rhode Island, 533 U.S. 606, 627 (2001), (Kennedy, J.).
38. *Second Treatise on Civil Government*, par. 38.
39. Id., par. 50.
40. Id., Ch. 16.
41. Id., par. 34.
42. Id., par. 37.
43. Ernest Fortin, "Human Rights and the Common Good," in *Human Rights, Virtue, and the Common Good*, J. Brian Benestad ed. (Lanham, MD: Rowman & Littlefield, 1996), 19, 23.
44. Pangle, 161.
45. *Second Treatise*, par. 123, 127.
46. Marie-Thérèse Meulders-Klein, "The Right over One's Own Body: Its Scope and Limits in Comparative Law," 6 *Boston College International and Comparative Law Review* 29 (1978).
47. *Second Treatise*, par. 23.
48. Hobbes, *Leviathan*, Ch. 21.
49. Laslett, 91.
50. Quoted in Laslett at 100.

51. John Locke, *Posthumous Works of Mr. John Locke* (London: W. B. for A. and B. Churchill, 1706), 9–10.

CHAPTER 7

1. Quoted in *The Mind of Napoleon*, J. Christopher Herold ed. (New York: Columbia University Press, 1955), 67.
2. Quoted in Donald Kelley, *Historians and the Law in Postrevolutionary France* (Princeton: Princeton University Press, 1984), 53.
3. Jacques Mallet Du Pan, quoted in Will and Ariel Durant, *Rousseau and Revolution* (New York: Simon & Schuster, 1967), 891.
4. Paul Johnson, *Intellectuals* (New York: Harper & Row, 1988), 1–2.
5. Rousseau, "First Discourse," in *The Social Contract and Discourses*, G. D. H. Cole transl. (New York: Dutton, 1973), 16.
6. I Corinthians 20; cf. Thomas à Kempis, *Imitation of Christ*, ch. 3: "Where are all those masters and doctors who while they lived flourished greatly in their learning? Truly he is great that hath great charity."
7. John Stuart Mill, *On Liberty* (Indianapolis: Bobbs-Merrill, 1956), 57.
8. Rousseau, *The Confessions*, J. M. Cohen transl. (New York: Penguin Classics, 1985), 322, 332–334.
9. Confessions, 334.
10. James Miller, *Rousseau: Dreamer of Democracy* (New Haven: Yale University Press, 1984), 136, 143.
11. Alexis de Tocqueville, *The Old Regime and the French Revolution*, Stuart Gilbert transl. (Garden City: Doubleday Anchor, 1955), 147.
12. "Second Discourse," in *The Social Contract and Discourses*, 45.
13. Montesquieu, *The Spirit of the Laws*, Thomas Nugent transl. (New York: Hafner Press, 1949), 4.
14. "Second Discourse," 46.
15. "Second Discourse," 56.
16. Here, Rousseau parted company with Montesquieu, who held that man was "a sociable animal," "formed to live in society," and led into society by his natural inclinations. *Spirit of the Laws*, 4–5, 30.
17. "Second Discourse," 54.
18. "Second Discourse," 103. Here, Rousseau seems to have a debt to Montesquieu who wrote: "Man, that flexible being, conforming in society to the thoughts and impressions of others, is equally capable of knowing his own nature, whenever it is laid open to his view, and of losing the very sense of it, when this idea is banished from his mind." *Spirit of the Laws*, Preface, xxxvii.
19. "Second Discourse," 83.
20. "Second Discourse," 83.
21. "Second Discourse," 76.
22. "Second Discourse," 89.
23. "Second Discourse," 105.
24. "Second Discourse," 104.
25. Ibid.
26. "Second Discourse," 105.

27. *Social Contract,* in *The Social Contract and Discourses,* 165.
28. *Social Contract,* 165.
29. *Social Contract,* 194.
30. *Social Contract,* 206.
31. *Social Contract,* 207.
32. *Social Contract,* 203.
33. Ibid.
34. *Social Contract,* 177.
35. Miller, 127.
36. Cicero, *The Republic,* Niall Rudd transl. (Oxford: Oxford University Press, 1998), 7.
37. *The Political Writings of Rousseau,* Vol. II, C. E. Vaughan ed. (New York: B. Franklin, 1971), 349.
38. *Political Writings of Rousseau,* Vol. II, 297.
39. Conor Cruise O'Brien, "Virtue and Terror," *New York Review of Books,* September 26, 1985, 28, 29.
40. *Intellectuals,* 25.
41. *The Federalist,* No. 1 (Hamilton).
42. *The Federalist,* No. 55 (Madison).
43. *Social Contract,* 203.
44. *Emile or On Education,* Allan Bloom transl. (New York: Basic Books, 1979), 308.
45. *Social Contract,* 268–277.
46. Georg Brandes, *Voltaire,* vol. 2 (New York: A. & C. Boni, 1930), 341.
47. Alexis de Tocqueville, *Selected Letters on Politics and Society,* James Toupin and Roger Boesche transl. (Berkeley: University of California Press, 1985), 5.
48. Quoted in J. H. Huizinga, *Rousseau: The Self-Made Saint* (New York: Grossman, 1976), 189.
49. Jacques Maritain, *Three Reformers: Luther, Descartes, Rousseau* (New York: Charles Scribner's Sons, 1929), 118.
50. *Reflections on the French Revolution* (New York: Doubleday Anchor, 1973), 187.
51. Edmund Burke, *A Letter to a Member of the National Assembly* (Oxford: Woodstock Books, 1990), 41.

CHAPTER 8

1. Quoted in Russell Kirk, *Edmund Burke: A Genius Reconsidered* (Wilmington: Intercollegiate Studies Institute, 1997), 14
2. "A Letter to a Noble Lord," in *Edmund Burke: On Empire, Liberty, and Reform, Speeches and Letters,* David Bromwich ed. (New Haven: Yale University Press, 2000), 484.
3. The best biographies of Burke are Conor Cruise O'Brien, *The Great Melody: A Thematic Biography of Edmund Burke* (Chicago: University of Chicago Press, 1992) and F. P. Lock's magisterial *Edmund Burke,* 2 vols. (Oxford: Oxford University Press, 1998 and 2006). I am indebted to O'Brien's biography for the details about Burke's life in Ireland.
4. O'Brien at 28 n.2.

5. O'Brien at 12–13.
6. O'Brien at 1.
7. See O'Brien at 590.
8. William Blackstone, *Commentaries on the Laws of England*, Vol. I, *31.
9. Paul Johnson, The Birth of the Modern (New York: Harper Collins, 1991), 187.
10. Quoted in O'Brien at xxxiv–xxxv.
11. James Boswell, *Life of Johnson* (Oxford: Oxford World's Classics, 1980), 1079.
12. Boswell at 696.
13. O'Brien at 41.
14. "First Letter on a Regicide Peace," in *Selected Works of Edmund Burke*, Vol. 3 (Indianapolis: Liberty Fund, 1999), 59, 151.
15. Boswell at 615–616.
16. Boswell at 333–334. The quoted lines of poetry referring to Burke were written by Oliver Goldsmith.
17. O'Brien at xxxv.
18. O'Brien at 50–51.
19. O'Brien at 63–64.
20. Burke to Shackleton in *Selected Letters of Edmund Burke*, Harvey C. Mansfield ed. (Chicago: University of Chicago Press, 1984), 50.
21. O'Brien at 44.
22. O'Brien, 191, 201.
23. Boswell at 696.
24. "Speech on Moving his Resolutions for Conciliation with the Colonies," in *Edmund Burke: On Empire, Liberty, and Reform, Speeches and Letters*, 66.
25. Burke, Letter to John Cruger, quoted in O'Brien at 136.
26. "Speech to the Electors of Bristol," in *Edmund Burke: On Empire, Liberty, and Reform, Speeches and Letters*, 51, 54–55.
27. Burke to Samuel Span, in *Selected Letters* at 405.
28. John Morley, Edmund Burke: A Historical Study (London: Macmillan, 1867), 9.
29. Harvey C. Mansfield, Jr., "Edmund Burke," in *History of Political Philosophy*, Strauss and Cropsey eds., 3rd ed. (Chicago: University of Chicago Press, 1987), 687.
30. O'Brien at 370.
31. "Letter to a Noble Lord," 483–484.
32. William Wordsworth, "The French Revolution as It Appeared to Enthusiasts at Its Commencement."
33. Letter to Charles-Jean-François Depont in *Selected Letters*, 262.
34. Harvey C. Mansfield, Jr., *Statesmanship and Party Government: A Study of Burke and Bolingbroke* (Chicago: University of Chicago Press, 1965).
35. Burke, *Reflections on the Revolution in France* (New York: Doubleday Anchor, 1973), 37.
36. Burke, *Reflections*, 91.
37. Burke, *Reflections*, 236–237.
38. Burke, *Reflections*, 21.
39. Burke, *Reflections*, 48.
40. Burke, *Reflections*, 33.

41. Burke, *Reflections*, 46.
42. Discussed in Francis Canavan, "Edmund Burke," in *History of Political Philosophy*, Strauss and Cropsey eds., 2nd ed. (Chicago: University of Chicago Press, 1973), 659, 662.
43. Burke, *Reflections*, 53, 121.
44. John Morley, "Edmund Burke" in *Encyclopaedia Britannica*, 11th ed., Vol. 4, at 824.
45. J. H. Plumb, "Edmund Burke and his Cult," in *In the Light of History* (Boston: Houghton Mifflin, 1973), 101.
46. Winston Churchill, "Consistency in Politics," in *Amid These Storms: Thoughts and Adventures* (New York: Scribners, 1932), 39, 40.
47. "American colonies, Ireland, France, and India
    Harried, and Burke's great melody against it."
    William Butler Yeats, "The Seven Sages," in *Collected Poems of W. B. Yeats* (New York: Macmillan, 1957), 237.
48. "Letter to a Noble Lord," 496.

CHAPTER 9

1. Hugh Brogan, *Alexis de Tocqueville: A Life* (New Haven: Yale, 2006), 279.
2. Joseph Epstein, *Alexis de Tocqueville: Democracy's Guide* (New York: Harper Collins/Atlas Books, 2006), 70.
3. André Jardin, *Tocqueville: A Biography*, Lydia Davis with Robert Hemenway transl. (Baltimore: Johns Hopkins, 1998), 34.
4. Jardin, 279.
5. Jardin, 73.
6. Brogan, 78.
7. Brogan, 79.
8. Montesquieu, *Oeuvres complètes*, tome 1 (Paris: Gallimard, 1973), 977.
9. Jardin, 81.
10. Brogan, 126.
11. Alexis de Tocqueville, *Recollections*, George Lawrence transl. (Garden City, New York: Doubleday Anchor, 1971), 82.
12. Donald R. Kelley, *Historians and the Law in Postrevolutionary France* (Princeton: Princeton University Press, 1984), 57.
13. Jardin, 89.
14. Jardin, 89.
15. Epstein, 48.
16. Jardin, 90.
17. Jardin, 200.
18. Jardin, 54.
19. Alexis de Tocqueville, *Selected Letters on Politics and Society*, James Toupin and Roger Boesche transl. (Berkeley: University of California Press, 1985), 5.
20. Brogan, 283.
21. Brogan, 333.
22. Jardin, 295–296.
23. Epstein, 79.

24. Seymour Drescher, quoted in Epstein, 78.
25. De Tocqueville, *Recollections*, 17.
26. Alexis de Tocqueville, "Preface" to the 1848 (12th) edition of *Democracy in America*, George Lawrence transl., J. P. Mayer ed. (Garden City, NY: Doubleday Anchor, 1969), xiii.
27. De Tocqueville, *Recollections*, 107.
28. De Tocqueville, *Recollections*, 6.
29. Brogan, 435.
30. Brogan, 443.
31. De Tocqueville, *Recollections*, 279.
32. De Tocqueville, *Recollections*, 250–251.
33. De Tocqueville, *Recollections*, 298.
34. Brogan, 494.
35. Quoted in Harvey C. Mansfield, Tocqueville: A Very Short Introduction (Oxford: Oxford University Press, 2010), 9.
36. De Tocqueville, *Democracy in America*, Harvey C. Mansfield and Delba Winthrop ed., (Chicago: University of Chicago Press, 2000), 483.
37. De Tocqueville, *Recollections*, 118.
38. Brogan, 466.
39. Karl Marx, "The Eighteenth of Brumaire and Louis Napoleon," in *The Marx-Engels Reader*, Richard C. Tucker ed. (New York: W. W. Norton, 1972), 436.
40. Jardin, 461.
41. Brogan, 530.
42. De Tocqueville, *Recollections*, 82.
43. Jardin, 303.
44. Jardin, 302.
45. Brogan, 47.
46. Jardin, 301.
47. De Tocqueville, *Recollections*, 103.
48. De Tocqueville, *Recollections*, 104.
49. Jardin, 305.
50. Brogan, 304.
51. De Tocqueville, *The Old Regime and the French Revolution*, Stuart Gilbert transl. (New York: Doubleday Anchor, 1955), 169.
52. Cf., "Constant revolutionising of production, uninterrupted disturbance of all social conditions, everlasting uncertainty and agitation distinguish the bourgeois epoch from all earlier ones. All fixed, fast-frozen relations, with their train of ancient and venerable prejudices and opinions, are swept away, all new-formed ones become antiquated before they can ossify. All that is solid melts into air, all that is holy is profaned, and man is at last compelled to face with sober senses his real conditions of life and his relations with his kind." Karl Marx and Friedrich Engels, The Communist Manifesto, in *The Marx-Engels Reader*, 331, 338.

CHAPTER 10

1. Max Weber, "Science as a Vocation," in *From Max Weber: Essays in Sociology*, Hans Gerth and C. Wright Mills eds. (London: Routledge, 1991), 129.

2. Weber, "Politics as a Vocation," Id. at 77.
3. Weber, "Science as a Vocation," 132.
4. Id.
5. Id. at 146.
6. Id. at 134.
7. Id.
8. Id.
9. Id. at 135–136.
10. Id.
11. Id.at 138.
12. Id. at 153.
13. Id. at 152.
14. Id.
15. Id. at 153.
16. Id. at 155–156.
17. Karl Jaspers, *On Max Weber*, John Dreijmanis ed., Robert J. Whelan transl. (New York: Paragon House, 1989), 188–189.
18. Gerth and Mills, *From Max Weber*, 23–24.
19. Marianne Weber, *Max Weber: A Biography*, Harry Zohn transl. (New York: Wiley & Sons, 1975), 185.
20. Id. at 114.
21. Id. at 162.
22. Id. at 166.
23. Id. at 162.
24. Id. at 165.
25. J. P. Mayer, *Max Weber and German Politics*, 2nd ed. (London: Routledge, 1998), 29.
26. Marianne Weber, at 224.
27. Id. at 223–224.
28. Id. at 306.
29. Jaspers at 114.
30. Max Weber, *The Protestant Ethic and the Spirit of Capitalism* (New York: Scribner's, 1958), 183.
31. Gerth and Mills, 47.
32. Raymond Aron, *Main Currents in Sociological Thought*, Vol. II, Richard Howard and Helen Weaver transl. (New York: Doubleday Anchor, 1970), 294.
33. Id. at 295.
34. Marianne Weber, 519.
35. Marianne Weber, 118–119, 585.
36. Id. at 399.
37. Id. at 552.
38. Id. at 552–553.
39. Jaspers, 60; Marianne Weber, 643.
40. Nicholas Capaldi, *John Stuart Mill: A Biography* (Cambridge: Cambridge University Press, 2004), 321.
41. Karl Loewenstein, *Max Weber's Political Ideas in the Perspective of Our Time*, Richard and Clara Winston transl. (Amherst: University of Massachusetts Press, 1966), 102.

42. "Science as a Vocation," 150.
43. Jaspers, 120.
44. J. P. Mayer, 105.
45. "Politics as a Vocation," 118.
46. Marianne Weber, 627.
47. Id. at 657.
48. Id. at 656.
49. Politics as a Vocation, 77.
50. Id. at 78.
51. Id. at 84.
52. Id. at 111.
53. Id. at 113.
54. Id. at 115.
55. Id. at 117.
56. Id. at 126–127.
57. Id. at 127.
58. Id. at 128.
59. Marianne Weber, 665.
60. Id. at 672.
61. Henry A. Kissinger, *A World Restored* (Gloucester, MA: Peter Smith, 1973), 1.
62. *Max Weber and Sociology Today*, Otto Stammer ed., Kathleen Morris transl. (New York: Harper & Row, 1971).
63. Raymond Aron, 303.
64. *Max Weber and Sociology Today*, 66. See also the critical view of Weber's politics in Wolfgang Mommsen, *Max Weber and German Politics 1890–1920*, Michael S. Steinberg transl. (Chicago: University of Chicago Press, 1984) (first published in Germany in 1959).
65. Loewenstein, 101.

CHAPTER 11

1. Alexis de Tocqueville, *Democracy in America*, Harvey C. Mansfield and Delba Winthrop eds. (Chicago: University of Chicago Press, 2000), 247.
2. Id. at 191.
3. Id. at 189.
4. Id. at 528.
5. Id. at 603.
6. Id. at 288.
7. Id. at 436.
8. Max Weber, "Politics as a Vocation," in *From Max Weber: Essays in Sociology*, Hans Gerth and C. Wright Mills eds. (London: Routledge, 1991), 111.
9. Id. at 108.
10. Alexis de Tocqueville, *Journey to America*, George Lawrence transl., J. P. Mayer ed. (Westport, CT: Greenwood Press, 1981), 208.
11. Mark De Wolfe Howe, *Justice Holmes: The Shaping Years 1841–1870* (Cambridge, MA: Harvard University Press, 1957), 282.

12. Mark De Wolfe Howe, *Justice Holmes: The Proving Years 1870–1882* (Cambridge, MA: Harvard University Press, 1963), 10.

13. Howe, *The Shaping Years*, 282.

14. Howe, *The Shaping Years*, 281.

15. Howe, *The Proving Years*, 135.

16. De Tocqueville, *Democracy in America*, 288.

17. *The Common Law* (Boston: Little, Brown, 1881), 1.

18. Ibid.

19. Ibid.

20. Howe, *The Proving Years*, 280–281.

21. Id., 282.

22. Id., 281.

23. Weber, "Politics as a Vocation," 96.

24. Quoted in *The Essential Holmes*, Richard A. Posner ed. (Chicago: University of Chicago Press, 1992), 115.

25. "The Profession of the Law," in *The Occasional Speeches of Justice Oliver Wendell Holmes*, Mark De Wolfe Howe ed. (Cambridge, MA: Harvard University Press, 1962), 28, 31.

26. Quoted in G. Edward White, *Oliver Wendell Holmes, Jr.* (Oxford: Oxford University Press, 2006), 71.

27. De Tocqueville, *Democracy in America*, 264.

28. James Q. Wilson, *American Government: Institutions and Policies*, 5th ed. (Lexington, MA: D.C. Heath, 1992), 398.

29. Quoted in *The Essential Holmes*, Richard A. Posner ed. (Chicago: University of Chicago Press, 1992), 115.

30. E.g., *Lochner v. New York*, 198 U.S. 45 (1905).

31. Quoted in Bernard Schwartz, *The Law in America* (New York: American Heritage Press, 1974), 191.

32. *Lochner v. New York*, 198 U.S. 45 (1905).

33. Id. at 75–76.

34. Holmes, "The Path of the Law," 110 *Harvard Law Review* 991, 994 (1997) (first published 1897).

35. Id. at 993.

36. "Natural Law," 32 *Harvard Law Review* 40 (1918).

37. "The Law," in *The Occasional Speeches of Justice Oliver Wendell Holmes*, Mark De Wolfe Howe ed. (Cambridge: Belknap Press, 1962), 21–22.

38. "The Path of the Law," 110 *Harvard Law Review* at 992.

39. Id. at 1005.

40. The story is told in Catherine Drinker Bowen, *Yankee from Olympus: Justice Holmes and His Family* (Boston: Little Brown, 1944), 414.

CHAPTER 12

1. I am grateful to Dr. Habib Malik for permission to quote from his father's unpublished papers and diaries.

2. See Mary Ann Glendon, "The Forgotten Crucible: The Latin American Influence on the Universal Human Rights Idea," 16 *Harvard Human Rights Journal* 27 (2003).

3. Letter from Charles Malik to Alfred North Whitehead, June 27, 1945 (Malik Papers, Library of Congress, Manuscript Division.)

4. Quoted in Doris Kearns Goodwin, *No Ordinary Time: Franklin and Eleanor Roosevelt: The Home Front in World War II* (New York: Simon & Schuster, 1994), 619.

5. For a detailed account of the framing of the Universal Declaration of Human Rights, see Mary Ann Glendon, *A World Made New: Eleanor Roosevelt and the Universal Declaration of Human Rights* (New York: Random House, 2001).

6. Eleanor Roosevelt, "The Promise of Human Rights," *Foreign Affairs* (April 1948), 470, 473.

7. American Anthropological Association, "Statement on Human Rights," 49 *American Anthropologist* 539 (1947).

8. *Human Rights: Comments and Interpretations* (London: Wingate, 1949), 259.

9. Id. at 9.

10. Id. at 10.

11. Id. at 35.

12. Ibid.

13. *The More Important Speeches and Interventions of Charles Malik, Taken from the Verbatim Records of the First Session of the Human Rights Commission*, 11–12 (Papers of Charles Habib Malik, Library of Congress, Manuscript Division).

14. Human Rights Commission, First Session, Summary Records (E/CN.4/SR.8, p.4).

15. Human Rights Commission, First Session, Summary Records (E/CN.4/SR.8, p. 4).

16. Verbatim Record, in *The More Important Speeches and Interventions of Charles Malik*, 35–37; Human Rights Commission, First Session, Summary Records (E/Cn.4/SR.9, p. 3).

17. Verbatim Record, in *The More Important Speeches and Interventions of Charles Malik*, 36–37; Human Rights Commission, First Session, Summary Records (E/CN.4/SR 14, pp. 3–4).

18. Verbatim Record, in *The More Important Speeches and Interventions of Charles Malik*, 37–38; Human Rights Commission, First Session, Summary Records (E/CN.4/SR 14, p. 4).

19. Verbatim Record, in *The More Important Speeches and Interventions of Charles Malik*, 38.

20. Id. at 44.

21. Id. at 38–39.

22. See generally, Glendon, *A World Made New*, at 115–117.

23. Human Rights Commission, First Session, Summary Records (E/CN.4/SR.12, p. 5).

24. Eleanor Roosevelt, *On My Own* (New York: Harper Brothers, 1958), 77.

25. Ibid.

26. *Peng Chun Chang 1892–1957: Biography and Collected Works*, Ruth H. C. and Sze-Chuh Cheng eds. (Privately printed, 1995).

27. John P. Humphrey, *Human Rights & the United Nations: A Great Adventure* (Dobbs Ferry, NY: Transnational Publishing, 1984), 17.

28. Aloysius Derso and Emery Kelen, *United Nations Sketchbook* (New York: Funk & Wagnall's, 1950), 9.

29. "Talk of the Town," (E. J. Kahn) *The New Yorker*, December 9, 1950, 32.

30. Howard Schomer, "In Homage to My Icons and Mentors," *Berkeley Outlook Club*, February 20, 1992, 19–20.

31. "International Bill of Rights to be Drafted," UN Weekly Bulletin, June 17, 1947, 639.

32. Memorandum of July 3, 1947, Meeting (Eleanor Roosevelt Papers, Box 4587, Roosevelt Library, Hyde Park, New York.

33. Human Rights Commission, Third Session (E/CN.4/SR.64, pp. 5–6).

34. Human Rights Commission, Third Session (E/CN.4/SR.72, pp. 7–8).

35. Charles Malik, "1948—The Drafting of the Universal Declaration of Human Rights," UN Bulletin of Human Rights (1986), 91.

36. Quoted in *Current Biography 1948*, Anna Rothe ed. (New York: H.W. Wilson, 1949), 411.

37. John P. Humphrey, *Human Rights and the United Nations: A Great Adventure* (Dobbs Ferry, NY: Transnational Publishing, 1984), 23–24.

38. John P. Humphrey, *On the Edge of Greatness: The Diaries of John Humphrey, First Director of the United Nations Division of Human Rights*, Vol. 1, A. J. Hobbins ed. (Montreal: McGill University Libraries, 1994), 24–25, 31.

39. Eleanor Roosevelt in Howard Langer, *Human Rights: A Documentary on the United Nations Universal Declaration of Human Rights*, featuring an interview with Mrs. Eleanor Roosevelt (Folkways Records 1958).

40. Charles Malik, "Introduction," O. Frederick Nolde, *Free and Equal: Human Rights in Ecumenical Perspective* (Geneva: World Council of Churches, 1968), 7–9.

41. Humphrey, *Human Rights*, 63.

42. Quoted in Joseph P. Lash, *Eleanor: The Years Alone* (New York: W. W. Norton, 1972), 79.

43. Charles Malik, December 9, 1948, Speech to the General Assembly, in *The Challenge of Human Rights: Charles Malik and the Universal Declaration*, Habib C. Malik ed. (Oxford: Centre for Lebanese Studies, 2000), 117.

44. Statement by Mrs. Franklin D. Roosevelt, Department of State Bulletin, December 99, 1948, 751–52.

45. "Mrs. Roosevelt, First Lady 12 Years, Often Called 'World's Most Admired Woman,'" *New York Times*, November 8, 1962, p. 1.

46. Joseph P. Lash, *Eleanor and Franklin* (New York: Signet Books, 1973), 616.

47. Thomas Kuhn, "The Essential Tension: Tradition and Innovation in Scientific Research," in The Essential Tension: Selected Studies in Scientific Tradition and Change (Chicago: University of Chicago Press, 1977), 225, 227–228.

EPILOGUE

1. Plato, Theaetetus, in Collected Dialogues of Plato, Edith Hamilton and Huntington Cairns eds., F.M. Cornford transl. (Princeton: Princeton University Press, 1971), 845, 878–879.

2. Id., 879.
3. Cicero, *On the Commonwealth and on the Laws*, James Zetzel transl. (Cambridge: Cambridge University Press, 1999), 61.
4. John Locke, *Posthumous Works of Mr. John Locke* (London: W. B. for A. and B. Churchill, 1706), 9–10.
5. Cicero, *De Oratore* (Cambridge, MA: Harvard University Press, 1942), Book III, ch. 33.
6. The Federalist Papers, Clinton Rossiter ed. (New York: New American Library, 1961), 344.
7. Alexis de Tocqueville, *Democracy in America*, Vol. I, Harvey C. Mansfield and Delba Winthrop eds. (Chicago: University of Chicago Press, 2000), 247.
8. "Politics as a Vocation," in *From Max Weber: Essays in Sociology*, Hans Gerth and C. Wright Mills eds. (London: Routledge, 1991), 108, 111.
9. Ibid.
10. Francis Fukuyama, *The End of History and the Last Man* (New York: Free Press, 1992), 160.
11. Id. at 153.

INDEX